Behavioural Sciences for Managers

Second Edition

**A G Cowling, M J K Stanworth,
R D Bennett, J Curran and P Lyons**

Edward Arnold
A division of Hodder & Stoughton

LONDON   NEW YORK   MELBOURNE   AUCKLAND

© 1988 A G Cowling, M J K Stanworth, R D Bennett, J Curran and P Lyons 1988

First published in Great Britain 1977
Reprinted 1980 (twice), 1982, 1985
Second edition 1988
Reprinted 1988

British Library Cataloguing in Publication Data

Behavioural sciences for managers.—2nd ed.
1. Management 2. Social sciences
I. Cowling, A. G. II. Boot, Richard
658.4   HD38

ISBN 0-7131-3658-8

Typeset in Linotron Times with Univers by Northern Phototypesetting Company, Bolton. Printed and bound in Great Britain for Edward Arnold, the educational, academic and medical publishing division of Hodder and Stoughton Limited, 41 Bedford Square, London WC1B 3DQ by Richard Clay Ltd, Bungay, Suffolk

Preface

The first edition of this book was published nine years ago. During this period it has given clear evidence of meeting a real need. Steady sales have indicated that it met its original target of providing a book on the behavioural sciences written in a style that combined readability with a rigorous approach to its subject matter. Envisaged as a book primarily for young graduate managers undertaking the Diploma in Management Studies, then as now the most popular management course in the country, it soon became popular with students on the new MBA programmes springing up around the country. It also found its way into reading lists of personnel management courses and final year undergraduate business studies programmes. The authors have also been delighted to receive appreciative comments from busy managers who appreciated its lack of jargon and avoidance of over-academic terminology.

This second edition aims to retain the virtues of the first and to provide a major revision reflecting recent developments in the subject. The mid-1970s were the heyday of a behavioural sciences movement that emphasised the importance of harmonious relationships at work. Today's manager inhabits a harder world where the quest for greater output, productivity and cost savings requires the pursuit of better motivation and group behaviour in a highly realistic manner. The first edition was in advance of most contemporary publications in considering the realities of power and conflict in the workplace and this is carried a stage further in this book. The 'coming of age' of organisational development means that training groups and change programmes are the beginning rather than the end of attempts to create more effective organisations.

As well as updating material and reflecting new trends in the behavioural sciences, a new chapter is included that focuses on the individual at work. Whilst the contents of both editions inevitably refer to individual aptitudes and attitudes, it was felt that a new chapter devoted to this topic would redress a balance that might seem to favour social systems and organisational forces at the expense of the individual. A distinctive feature of the first book was the inclusion of a chapter on the small firm, which proved to be a prophetic decision in its anticipation of the importance subsequently attached to the small firm in the regeneration of our economy. As before, this chapter concludes this book.

The small team of authors that prepared this second edition are drawn from leading business schools in the public sector of higher education in this country. All have extensive teaching experience on management programmes as well as practical experience in industry supplemented by research and consultancy assignments. This team acknowledges their debt to Richard Boot for his contribution to the first edition, and some of his ideas find their way into this second edition. Whilst each chapter has been drawn up by just one or two authors, care has been taken once again to relate the contents of one chapter to another in an integrated fashion. It is our hope that this new edition will communicate the excitement the authors feel about the importance and relevance of the behavioural sciences. The management of human resources deserves a professional and competent approach based on the latest findings from the behavioural sciences.

Preface to First Edition

This book has been written for students of management and practising managers interested in the application of the behavioural sciences to the field of work. The expansion of management education in recent years has led to a demand for publications which present practical guides for management based on an analysis of both empirical and theoretical considerations.

Accordingly, *Behavioural Sciences for Managers* has been written with a variety of audiences in mind. It should prove particularly useful to students taking Part I of the Diploma in Management Studies Course and the Applied Behavioural Science Course in Part II of the Institute of Personnel Management Membership examinations. It should also interest students taking an industrial or commercial course, with a behavioural science content, leading to a degree or professional qualification. We have also considered practising managers who find themselves unable to vacate their positions in industry for long enough to undertake a formal course of study but who are concerned with decision-making and who pursue an interest in the management literature. Amongst others, we have tried to keep the small firm owner–manager and his management team in mind.

The value of the behavioural sciences to the manager lies in the fact that their subject matter is concerned with one of the most important, if not the most important, aspect of his work – human resources. The practising manager may feel that there is more to be learned about the tasks of management by actually pursuing them than by reading about them. He is sometimes prompted to make this claim by a feeling that the theoreticians he criticises are intent on obscuring their ideas within fortresses of jargon.

In this book, we do not attempt to belie the importance of practical experience but hope to complement it. It has been written for managers and students of management who probably have no intention of becoming specialists in the behavioural sciences but who wish to become familiar with them. In addition to examining the practical implications of the behavioural sciences at work, we introduce readers to many of the concepts and terms used in behavioural science literature so that they may be understood when they are encountered again either in the work situation or in other published materials.

It is doubtful whether any single book can cope with so wide a range of topics in sufficient detail to satisfy fully the interests of a broad and diversified readership. The interested reader will, however, be able to extend his appreciation of topics of particular interest through the references given at the end of each chapter.

Contents

Biographical notes

Alan Cowling

Alan Cowling is currently Head of Management Courses at the Middlesex Polytechnic Business School, a constituent part of Middlesex Polytechnic. His early industrial experience was with Cadbury Brothers and in the Gas Industry, and he has subsequently lectured and acted as a consultant in the behavioural sciences and personnel management. He is co-author (with Chloe Mailer) of *Managing Human Resources*, Published by Edward Arnold in 1981.

John Stanworth

John Stanworth is Director of the Small Business Unit and Research Professor at the Faculty of Management Studies, Polytechnic of Central London. His early industrial experience was as a Metallurgist in engineering industry. However, in recent years he has specialised in the social sciences, publishing widely in both scholarly and popular outlets. His partnership with James Curran spans nearly twenty years.

Roger Bennett

Roger Bennett is currently Professor of Management Education and Training with ICMB, and was formerly Head of Postgraduate Studies and Research at the Oxford School of Business. He is a prolific writer on management and edits two journals. Roger Bennett is a publisher with MCB Ltd.

James Curran

James Curran is Reader in Industrial Sociology at Kingston Polytechnic. His main research interest is the small enterprise and he has carried out several major research projects on this topic since the early 1970s. He has also written extensively in book and article form on the small firm and related subjects.

Paul Lyons

Paul Lyons is Senior Lecturer in the Psychology Division at Hatfield Polytechnic, responsible for the MSc degree in Occupational Psychology. His organisational research and consultancy activities centre on training, assessment and counselling systems. He has worked in the docks industry for a number of years in the personnel management function, including several years as head of the staff development unit in the Manpower Directorate of the Port of London Authority.

1

Management and the relevance of the behavioural sciences

What is management? What do managers do? What makes managers effective? Why are the behavioural sciences relevant to managers? These questions are addressed in this opening chapter, in order to show that a knowledge and understanding of behavioural science, and the application of some of the key ideas about behaviour, can help improve both managerial and organisational performance. In answering these questions, we shall also answer others, such as: what is behavioural science? How is behavioural science knowledge generated? In what key areas can a knowledge of behavioural science contribute to managerial and organisational performance? By the end of this chapter you should be able to understand the relevance and application of the content of each following chapter.

But why bother? Isn't 'good' management simply a matter of knowing what you're supposed to do and getting on with it? Well, yes, it is – in part. Good managers, i.e. effective managers, know what is expected of them, what goals they are reaching and what targets have to be met. But it goes further than that. The difference between an average manager and a really good one lies in the *quality* of management. We know this to be true both from experience and research. Let's start with experience.

The boss of one national chain of furniture stores demonstrates the importance of quality in management. This man runs a chain of 130 stores from Plymouth to Aberdeen. Keeping tabs on what is going on and enthusing store managers is no easy task. How does he do it? Well, clearly he knows where he wants the business to go. More importantly, he sees management as a team effort. He believes that it is very important for the leader to be visible and approachable; a tall order when most of your subordinates are spread across the country. He makes sure he visits the stores, often at closing time, when he is least expected. He knows that the good store managers will take this in their stride. They are set high standards of presentation and housekeeping. More importantly, they know he will listen to their opinions on all aspects of business. He makes sure his attitudes to his employees and customers are fair and considerate. He gets commitment from his people. In short, he builds teamwork based on positive attitudes and gets high motivation in return.

We see the positive aspects of high quality management coming through in several studies which emphasise the importance of behaviour. A recent British study[1] looked at the factors contributing to the success of Britain's top companies. They found that being successful was very much a matter of management style, how managers go about doing the things they do – their attitudes, values and approach to the job. They also found that the company culture contributed to success. This refers to the relationships, values, philosophy and ways of doing things in the company as a whole. Among the specific factors in success were leadership, autonomy, control, innovation and integrity (almost a common code for the conduct of business). All of these factors define quality in one way or another. They are also qualitative in the sense that they are difficult to measure and are heavily concerned with the behavioural aspects of the business. As we shall see later in this chapter, most of the characteristics of the really effective manager are also qualitative and include things such as working well with a wide variety of people, a need to achieve results and experience of leadership.

So both experience and research tell us quite strongly that management is very much concerned with behaviour – the behaviour of the manager, colleagues and subordinates. This is how most of the experts define management.

What is management?

There are probably as many definitions of management as there are writers on the subject. We shall not spend time reviewing and debating these definitions. It is more helpful to consider the most commonly held view of management.

As long ago as 1949, Sir Charles Renold[2] stated that 'management is a process of getting things done through the agency of a community'. The 'community' might be the employees of a private company, the staff of a local authority, members of the armed services, or whatever. This definition is often expressed in simple terms; that management is about getting things done through people.[3] Other writers and experts have taken a slightly more detailed view of management. For example, Drucker[4] suggests that there are a number of 'jobs of management', namely:

1 producing economic results
2 managing a business by managing objectives
3 managing managers
4 managing workers and work.

He argues further that, without people, all the technical, economic and managerial paraphernalia would not produce a single product or service. Somewhere along the line, people are involved – even in the most highly automated factories.

The economic theme is shared by Scott and Rochester[5] who, after examining a variety of jobs, conclude that management is a process of 'getting things done *economically* through other people'. Such a definition would exclude, say, technicians and accountants but would include a chief accountant or chief technician responsible for people, budgets and results.

Management has also been considered to comprise of a number of principles and/or functions.[6] This refers to the distinction between *what* managers do and *how* they do it. The *what* consists of their major functions or activities, namely:

1 Planning – deciding what to do and how to achieve it
2 Organising – achieving the most appropriate form of activities and relationships for achieving desired results
3 Motivating – getting other people to give of their best
4 Controlling – measuring and monitoring work and taking corrective action when required.

The *how* has been set down in the form of a number of principles, such as the division of labour (breaking jobs down into relatively small, easily performed tasks), unity of command (having only one boss to report to), unity of direction (each section working towards a common goal), and span of control (managers having a limited number of subordinates). The length of this list of principles varies with the practitioner or author putting them forward – twelve is not uncommon. As we shall see in Chapter Eight, such 'universal principles' of good management do not apply equally to all situations! All of them depend on people behaving, communicating and working together in a way that makes for the economical achievement of organisational goals.

So what is management? If we consider the various views put forward, it is possible to define management as a process of achieving desired results through other people in a planned and economical fashion. But does this definition apply to supervisors? The answer to this will depend on the nature of the supervisor's work. In some organisations, the term 'supervisor' is applied to senior managers, equivalent to factory or workshop managers. In others, supervisors are really progress chasers and perform very few, if any, managerial tasks.

Thus, whilst management is concerned with the effective and efficient use of *all* resources, the linchpin is 'other people'. To get the most out of them, we need to understand them, just as we need to understand how money markets work, how technical equipment operates and so on.

What managers do

Arguments over what constitutes managerial behaviour – what managers really do – still take place. One significant change in the nature of the debate is that instead of reading prescriptions for what managers should do, we now have some evidence of what more and less effective managers do in real situations.

Some of the first evidence to appear emerged from Carlson's pioneering study in the late 1940s of nine senior Swedish directors.[7] Using the now well-known and frequently used diary method, he obtained daily records of their activities. His findings cover working time, communications and work content. The working days of these executives were usually fragmented. They had little uninterrupted time to sit, think and plan, and had little control over the design or pattern of each work day. Their communication patterns were dominated by time spent with visitors. In addition, office layout had some effect on whom they saw and how frequently. Perhaps not surprisingly, the work content for each executive varied from one to another.

This empirical work led to the development of a number of other studies, particularly in the UK, on larger numbers of managers. The major study was that carried out by Rosemary Stewart.[8] She analysed the diaries of the working days of 160 managers. From her analysis emerged five basic job profiles:

1 *The emissaries* who spent much time away from their company, dealing with outsiders. They worked long hours, but did not usually suffer from fragmented work. Sales managers and senior executives who act as public figures are examples.

2 *The writers* who spent a good deal of time in writing, reading, dictating and figure work, and whose working hours were shorter than others. They tended to be staff specialists.

3 *The discussers* these were the 'average managers', who spent a lot of time talking with other people (especially colleagues) and who were involved in a diverse range of activities. This category included many types of managers.

4 *The trouble shooters* who spent a good deal of time coping with crises. Their day was fragmented, but involved spending a lot of time with subordinates rather than peers. Production managers are part of this group.

5 *The committee men* these are managers who spend a lot of their time at committees. They had lots of contacts vertically and horizontally in the organisation, but few outside. They tended to exist mainly in the larger organisations.

In a later study[9] Stewart looked at the work patterns of several hundred managers, in terms of the demands that were placed upon them. The jobs fell into twelve definable types, based upon the contact patterns which the study revealed. There were four fundamental or 'common' types.

1 *Hub* where managing people took a lot of time; where there was contact with peers, seniors and juniors; where the jobholder was dependent upon the co-operation of other people in other departments; and where the contact time was normally well over 50%.

2 *Peer dependent* where peer contact was high (over 50%), taking as much or more time than contact with subordinates; where it was important to get co-operation from people not in the direct line of authority; and where conflicting demands were a usual part of the job.

3 *Man management* where peer contacts were low, and where there was little dependence on other people over whom the manager had no authority, except with external contacts.

4 *Solo* where contact time was under 50%; where sustained attention, low level of uncertainty, and few subordinates existed; and where the manager was responsible for a separate, fairly self-contained unit.

A major example of the study of managerial work in the USA is that by Mintzberg.[10] Based on hypotheses and evidence stemming from this study, ten working roles of the manager were formulated. These are as follows:

Interpersonal roles (derived from the manager's authority and status):

1 *Figurehead* representing the unit or organisation in a formal way
2 *Liaisor* interacting, and co-ordinating activities, with peers and colleagues
3 *Leader* developing, encouraging and supporting subordinates.

Informational roles (derived from interpersonal roles and the access to information they provide):

4 *Monitor* receiving and collecting information relevant to the manager's general task
5 *Dissemination* transmitting specific external information to subordinates and ensuring conveyance of internal information amongst subordinates
6 *Spokesman* transmitting information about the manager's unit and subordinates to the outside world.

Decisional roles (derived from the manager's authority and information):

7 *Entrepreneur* initiating relevant change in the unit
8 *Disturbance handler* dealing with tensions and threats imposed by external, uncontrolled change
9 *Resource allocator* determining where and how best to deploy the resources available
10 *Negotiator* dealing with situations requiring compromise on behalf of the manager's unit or organisation.

Many other studies have been carried out and a good number of them are described in one of the appendices to Mintzberg's own book. But what do these studies tell us about what managers actually do? In one sense they tell us so much that we cannot really make use of it. With so many different typologies and classifications, we are faced with a genuine possibility of being unable to develop sensible strategies for managerial action. In another sense, they tell us something very simple, and which has pointed out in a 'research based theory of managerial action'.[11] In this treatise, Sayles suggests that the logic of managerial work comprises two basic elements:

1 *Contingency responses* coping with potential or actual threats to the integrity of the work system and its regularities (i.e. keeping the system going).
2 *Uncertainty reduction* seeking to improve the system and adapt to changing circumstances.

He then analyses the kinds of behaviour necessary for effective leaders to operate in this way.

Studies of managerial work certainly emphasise the contingency aspect. The roles or types emerge from quite clearly differing points in the organisational system. Change the forces, contacts etc. operating on them, and the contingency response will change – or should do if the manager is to remain effective. Circumstances will change with time, and the uncertainty this can produce reinforces the contingent nature of managerial work. This is particularly true of behaviour in organisations and again points to the need for managers to understand influences on the behaviour of people at work.

The effective manager

A better awareness of the causes of behaviour can lead not only to a better understanding of the nature and role of managerial work but also to improved effectiveness. During the past ten years or so, a number of studies have looked at what makes managers effective. Yet again, behavioural factors figure highly in their findings. To demonstrate this, we shall look at a few of these studies. First, however, we must define 'effectiveness'.

As with most things managerial, views on the meaning of

effectiveness vary. They range from the highly philosophical[12] to the highly pragmatic.[13] Our position[14] is more in line with the pragmatic view, which happens to coincide with a dictionary definition. Such a definition is given in terms of results or consequences, bringing about effects in relation to a purpose, giving validity to particular activities. As the inimitable Drucker has said,'even the most efficient business cannot survive, let alone succeed, if it is efficient at doing the wrong things, that is, if it lacks effectiveness . . . efficiency is concerned with doing things right. Effectiveness is doing the right things'.[15]

In our view, this is on target. Effective managerial work brings about the desired results in terms of the purpose of the organisation and in terms of the task requirements of the manager's job. Naturally, the manager's personal ambitions and goals will influence and shape his perception and understanding of the task requirements. In addition, the goals pursued by the organisation will be an amalgam of a variety of competing pressures and interests: unions, consumers, top management, government policies, market conditions and so on. These we recognise, as we recognise the difficulty in stating what objectives, and whose objectives, the manager is pursuing. But at the end of the day, the manager is pursuing some objective, however ill-defined or little understood at the conscious level. Management is about achieving results through people. These results must be related to some goal or purpose – they are not anarchic – and effective managerial work must therefore be equally purposeful. In simple terms, effective managerial work gets the job done. A wide range of factors can influence effectiveness. It is well documented[16] that such influences fall into two categories: those that persist across jobs, situations and organisations; and those that are specific to a given set of circumstances.

Research shows that about a third of the characteristics that distinguish effective from ineffective managers are stable across job levels and firms: the rest reflect the special nature of the particular job being done. The characteristics of the effective manager appear to fall into the following main categories:

1 *Self-management* gets stuck into the work; thinks before acting or speaking; doesn't allow people to waste his time).
2 *Decision-making* individual (puts priorities on what needs to be done; takes action when needed; tolerates compromise).
3 *Decision-making* group (influences policies at early stage; gives best effort wherever policy comes from).
4 *Relations with peers and superiors* informs colleagues in other departments; is easy to track down out of the office; gives and seeks advice).
5 *Management of subordinates* (lets them know what he expects; delegates as appropriate; gives his people credit).

6   *Attitude to change*   (comes up with ideas for change; monitors effects of change; is ready to modify changed plans).
7   *Social skills*   (feels at ease with strangers; inspires people).
8   *Communications*   (passes on information when necessary; uses various, clear means of communication).
9   *Specialist skills*   (has good technical knowledge; absorbs and retains information; has an adequate knowledge of other people's specialisations).

Influences also vary with the level of work done. At the lower levels of responsibility, much of the effectiveness of an individual is determined in advance: targets, schedules, resources, timing and so on are pre-planned and often impose tight limits on flexibility. At higher levels, particularly in top management, individual action and organisational performance become indistinguishable. Personal assessments of the business environment influence the nature of organisational policies; and the form of its reward system, general management system, physical and social characteristics of the working environment, the design of each task, the nature and quality of immediate supervision, the technology, goals and resources – all have their effect on overall performance. For the individual manager, important determinants include previous relevant education and experience, values and views of work that govern choices, behaviour and aspirations. There are a number of prescriptions as to what makes for managerial effectiveness. Perhaps the most famous are those of Fayol.[17] He argued that if an enterprise is to be soundly constituted and to function effectively, there are five determining elements: planning, organising, commanding, co-ordinating and controlling. These are things that most managers do, but doing them does not in itself make the manager effective unless he achieves the right results within the constraints and opportunities of the culture and environment of the organisation. Techniques have been developed and training provided to help the manager to carry out these activities, but they cannot tell us why some managers are more effective than others.

In a similar way, Gardner[18] and Drucker[19] offer advice to managers on becoming more effective. For Gardner, the key elements of effectiveness are time, delegation, planning, decision-making and management controls; for Drucker, effectiveness can be learned, and managing time, establishing priorities, building on strengths and making 'good' decisions are the essentials. Both have thoughts in common, although Drucker has achieved considerably more impact with his words of wisdom than Gardner.

Many others have written and argued about the same question. For Reddin[20] managerial effectiveness is concerned with – or determined by – the relationship between behaviour, task and situation, and will increasingly be influenced by personal qualities of intellect and behavioural flexibility. The theory of leadership effectiveness developed by Fiedler[21] suggests a broader set of contingent relationships, based on the proposition that effectiveness in management is more than the possession of personal qualities or specialised skills and techniques. Cummings and Schwab[22] set out to demonstrate that, by focusing on determinants, organisational productivity and performance can be improved. However, they narrowed their perspective, arguing that performance was ultimately an individual phenomenon and therefore primarily a matter of personal ability and motivation. That led them to the major premise that improvement can best be attained by operating through appraisal systems on the behavioural determinants. The model of managerial behaviour proposed by Campbell *et al.*[23] portrays a network of relationships with personal, job and organisational dimensions. A similar standpoint is taken by Burgoyne[24] who stresses, inter alia, that a proper consideration of managerial effectiveness presupposes an adequate account of the organisational culture or context in which the judgements are made.

Research[25] on developing managerial effectiveness was based on the regularly occurring results of past research on the activities of managers. This resulted in a minimum of six major areas of activity:

1 general effectiveness
2 communication
3 delegation
4 job knowledge
5 relationships with subordinates
6 decision-making.

Four of these are clearly about behavioural relationships. The initial research produced more than 100 statements of behaviour covering these six categories. Further research reduced the number considerably by rejecting statements which managers saw as ambiguous or not properly descriptive of the category they represented. Examples of statements achieved are:

General effectiveness
Keeps an eye on the implementation of plans and solves blockages quickly (effective behaviour: +).
Makes inferior copies of other people's initiatives (ineffective behaviour: −).

Decision-making
Obtains all relevant information before making up his mind on something (+).
Constantly side-steps decisions (−)

Delegation
Allows subordinates to organise work in their own way as long as the desired results are achieved (+).
Interferes continually when work has been delegated (−).

Communication
Keeps in touch with others on the progress of various jobs and passes on other information necessary for day-to-day running (+).
Communicates only through written documents (−).

Job knowledge
Keeps up to date with changes in the technical knowledge of the subject area covered by the work (+).
Cannot take a firm grasp on what is happening in the organisation (−).

Relationships with subordinates
Handles and motivates with tact less work-inclined staff (+).
Is indifferent to the well-being of subordinates (−).

It is interesting to note that these statements were obtained from managers who were asked to describe an effective or ineffective manager they had known.

A recent piece of research carried out at Cranfield School of Management[26] was essentially concerned with identifying the factors to which top managers ascribe their success. The majority thought the following factors important:

1 an ability to work with a wide variety of people
2 a need to achieve results
3 early overall responsibility for important tasks
4 early experience of leadership
5 width of experience in many functions before the age of 35.

These findings have been verified in studies of the police in the UK[27] and managers in the public sector in Australia.[28]

Is effectiveness enough?

So far in this chapter we have laid stress on *what* managers do and *how* they can be effective at what they do. We have also shown that management is very much both a behavioural process and also concerned with the behaviour of others. To be effective requires attention to these behavioural aspects. But is this enough for the really good, successful manager? We believe, as do others, that managing can and should be enjoyable. The manager who gains little pleasure from what he does is not likely to remain happy for very long. There must be some fun in it!

This may not sound a very important point, yet we are serious about it. Many successful managers are serious about it, too. Take, for example, Robert Townsend. He was a successful manager – indeed, he was President and Chairman of Avis. Many have read and benefited from his book *Up The Organisation*, now updated as *Further Up The Organisation*.[29] Not only does he look at what we do wrong in managing companies but he also shows how to humanise business and above all, make it fun. That message has spanned the 16 years since he wrote the first version, and still holds true today.

Two other successful people – as managers, consultants and academics – are Scott and Söderberg. In 1985 they published their view of *The Art of Managing*,[30] in which they argue that managers need to seek a balance between four key areas, if they are to be successful, i.e. effective and happy. These four areas or fields, as they call them, are derived from examples, and are:

1 *Fun* the sheer pleasure of managing
2 *Results* the production of positive results
3 *Ability to achieve* reaching a position where one has the resources and the relationships necessary but not sufficient for success.
4 *Direction* ensuring that one's activities are heading in a profitable direction.

Their examples show that managers who achieve 2, 3 and 4 are not always as successful as they could be. When the enjoyment of managing ceases to exist, the urge to get home quickly begins to increase! That takes the edge off the other three. Successful managers regularly take stock of the balance between all four fields.

Enjoyment is an important part of life. At work, managers can not only make sure that they get enjoyment themselves but can also make it possible for others. This is partly a matter of personal style and values, but it is also concerned with the way we manage teams and groups, seek to motivate people, recognise differences between people and design jobs and organisation structures to facilitate effective work and enjoyment at doing work. As we shall see later, the behavioural sciences have much to offer in all these key areas.

The relevance of behavioural science

We have seen that the nature of management, the work managers do and the causes of their effectiveness are largely concerned with behaviour – their own and that of others in the organisation. This implies an understanding of how and why people behave in certain ways. A study of behavioural science is, we believe, of considerable importance in gaining such an understanding.

In this final section, we outline the nature of behavioural science and seek to demonstrate further its relevance to managers and what they do.

Management and behavioural science

So far in this chapter we have seen that management and the effectiveness of managers have a lot to do with people in organisations. It has been argued that managers require a knowledge and understanding of behaviour in order to improve their performance. This has been the theme of many books on management and performance.[31] But where does our knowledge of behaviour in organisations stem from? In a sense, we all have our own theories, experience and understanding of what makes people tick. But there is a body of systematically derived knowledge about behaviour, variously known as behavioural science, the behavioural sciences, or the social sciences. Whatever we call that body of knowledge is not too important: what is important is that it exists and can be used to good effect. In this book we shall refer to that body of knowledge as 'behavioural science'.

Behavioural science as a discipline or body of knowledge has developed because our knowledge of human behaviour stems from different sources. It has not been possible to retain the traditional distinctions between disciplines such as psychology, sociology and anthropology when attempting to solve problems of industry and other social institutions.[32] Disciplines concerned with human behaviour include psychology, social psychology, sociology and anthropology, and even economics and political science. Some of these, such as psychology, are basically concerned with the behaviour of the individual; others, such as sociology and anthropology, are more concerned with the behaviour of groups and societies.

Our concern in this book is with the contributions to our understanding of work and work organisations made by people in various disciplines, especially psychology, social psychology, sociology and management theory. By combining such contributions, we can get a better view of how people behave in organisations and how they can be more effectively managed.

Psychology helps us understand the make-up and behaviour of the individual. So, for example, we can learn from this discipline how individuals differ in their characteristics and attributes, levels of intelligence and so on, how an individual's attitudes are developed, transformed and sustained, how personality is shaped and how it influences behaviour, and how people are motivated through internal mechanisms. All of these and other aspects of individual psychology have great importance for recruiting, employing, managing, training and developing staff in any organisation.

From social psychology and certain aspects of sociology we begin to learn more about groups, about social settings and about wider social processes. Examples include the description and explanation of values, of change in society, why people behave in so called deviant ways, the effects of religion on behaviour, and the pattern of family life and its effect on behaviour generally. We see how groups are formed and developed in the work place and how, for example, they can exert considerable influence to resist change or new processes within the organisation. We also learn how leadership is exerted through groups both formally and informally and also how work can be designed to take into account the social and group needs of individuals at work. Sociologists and social psychologists have also taken a look at the wider organisational sphere. They have studied such aspects as organisation structure, wages systems, technology, formal and informal patterns of relationships within the organisation, communication, industrial relations, and management values and attitudes.

From anthropology, arguably one of the earliest of the behavioural sciences, we draw knowledge gained from the study of whole communities and societies, particularly of those sometimes referred to as 'primitive' societies. In particular we have been able to understand the complex interrelations within social groupings and social processes. Some anthropologists have studied whole industrial communities, for example in coal mining and fishing. This has been valuable in helping us to understand the relationship between work and life.

In summary then, behavioural science can contribute to our understanding of the individual at work, how the individual relates to other people at work and how groups and wider aspects of the organisation develop and can be managed effectively. This book explores many of the concepts relevant to managing people at work.[33]

But is behavioural science 'scientific'? It can be argued that a primary aim of a scientific discipline is to formulate general laws governing some aspect of nature. In this sense, behavioural science is a misnomer. There is little, if anything, in behavioural science that approximates to the laws of, say, the physical sciences. Another aspect of a science is that certain parts of the body of knowledge can be verified. Here again there are problems for the behavioural scientist. It is very difficult to repeat experiments under exactly the same conditions – as a physicist or engineer would be able to do. Human nature is too variable for this to be realistically attainable. So can behavioural science be called 'scientific' because of the methods of enquiry adopted? According to one writer[34] such enquiry takes the form of 'systematic exploration, description and explanation'. The aims of this enquiry are concerned with understanding, predicting and controlling behaviour at levels above those achieved by what we might call unaided common sense. The methods of the natural or physical sciences tend to emphasise the importance of experiment in achieving their aims. However, there are many problems in doing this when dealing with human behaviour. It is seldom possible to identify, let alone measure, some aspects of that which we are studying. Because of this, studies making extensive use of statistical analysis may often be seen to be suspect. If the behavioural scientist then reverts to looking at behaviour in a more qualitative form we go back to the problem of how far the research can be verified or repeated under exactly the same circumstances to test the results.

What methods *are* used in behavioural science? Here we describe very briefly some of the approaches used by behavioural scientists to generate knowledge of human behaviour.

Laboratory experiments attempt to reproduce the controlled conditions of the natural sciences. Such conditions allow the researcher to manipulate one variable at a time and so more easily establish a causal relationship between variables (i.e. to say that a change in A causes a change in B). In other words, it makes it easier to explain the phenomena being studied. Unfortunately such settings are artificial and therefore it is not possible to be certain of how applicable the findings are outside the laboratory.

Attempts to overcome some of this artificiality include the *experimental field study*, which is carried out in real organisational settings. Some variables are manipulated while others are kept constant. Since the experimenter is operating in a natural environment there is a greater chance that uncontrolled variables will influence the results.

Both these approaches are however limited in the extent to which their findings can be generalised to other situations. The *survey method* makes it possible to include a much wider range of situations in the study. It means, however, that the researcher cannot manipulate variables and study the effect on other variables. By statistical analysis he can establish that certain variables are related or associated with each other, but he cannot be certain that one causes another. Many of the studies referred to in this book are of this type.

The final method used fairly widely in the study of organisational behaviour is the *case study*. Here the researcher makes no attempt to manipulate variables but makes a study in depth, over a period of time, of a particular organisational setting. He then attempts to arrange his observations into some meaningful generalisations. The researcher has virtually no control, and the value of his study depends on his skill in interpretation and his freedom from bias. Potentially, however, such studies can be a rich source of understanding of a real situation and can be particularly useful for generating hypotheses that can subsequently be 'tested' in a more controlled manner.

With each of these designs a number of data collection techniques may be used. These vary with the extent to which the researcher is personally involved in the situation being studied. The more involved the researcher, the less extensive can be his field of study; but it will probably be more intensive because he will be able to record complexity in the data. The technique entailing most involvement is usually referred to as *participant observation*, in which the researcher actually becomes a part of the social situation which he is studying. At the opposite extreme, some studies employ secondary analysis of existing *documentary information*, such as company records and reports or government statistics. Between these two extremes are the techniques of *unstructured interviews, structured interviews, non-participant observation, psychological tests* and *self-completion questionnaires*.

None of the research designs or techniques mentioned is necessarily better or worse than any of the others. In fact they are probably best regarded as complementary to each other, the disadvantages of any one approach being reduced when used in combination with another. There is, however, plenty of room for improvement in the methodology of the behavioural sciences before they can attain the degree of objectivity and certainty claimed by some (but not all) of the methods of the natural sciences. On the other hand, the systematic methods of enquiry developed by behavioural scientists do enable a level of understanding of social phenomena above the levels achieved by unaided common sense. The value, then, of the behavioural sciences to the manager do not rest on whether or not the label 'science' is justified, but rather on the fact they do represent a genuine alternative to what Gellerman[35] refers to as 'the accumulated folklore, mythology and superstition that too often passes for traditional managerial wisdom'.

Conclusion — the way forward in this book

We have seen that good management is essentially a matter of quality, that quality has much to do with the behaviour at work of both manager and managed and that the behavioural sciences can help us better to understand the processes and aims of management. The remainder of this book explores some of the key issues in managing people at work.

We start in Chapter Two by looking at the meaning of work. Why do people make particular choices of work? How do they view their work? How does work connect with non-work activities? These are important issues, for on them depend the willingness of people to work and the ease with which they can be managed. In Chapter Three we look more closely at how individuals are different from and similar to each other. How do we vary in ability, intelligence, personality and so on? What affects on management can these differences and similarities have?

Two central concerns have to do with explaining why people work hard or not, and how they work with others. In Chapter Four we consider some theories of motivation and their application to the work situation, and in Chapters Five, Six and Seven we discuss the roles and relationships of people at work.

Behaviour at work and the effectiveness of managers are not influenced solely by individual and group factors. The way work is divided up and organised, the nature of power and authority within the organisation and how the organisation develops and responds to change are key features in the management of people. We look at these in Chapters Eight, Nine and Ten.

Finally, we focus on one important aspect of management in the near future. As has been experienced in the USA and is now being recognised in the UK and elsewhere, small firms are contributing to employment and economic success in a major way. Is the management of a small firm any different to running a large company? We explore the issues of small firm management in Chapter Eleven.

References

1   Goldsmith, W. and Clutterbuck, D., *The Winning Streak*, Weidenfeld and Nicolson, 1984.
2   Renold, C., 'The nature of management', *Occasional Paper No. 2*, BIM, 1949.
3   Armstrong, M., *How to be a Better Manager*, Kogan Page, 1983.
4   Drucker, P., *The Practice of Management*, Heinemann, 1955.
5   Scott, J. and Rochester, A., *What is a Manager?*, Sphere/BIM, 1984.
6   Sadler, P., 'Principles of management' in Lock, D. and Farrow, N., *Handbook of Management*, Gower, 1983.
7   Carlson, S., *Executive Behaviour*, Stronbergs, 1951.
8   Stewart, R., *Managers and their Jobs*, Pan/MacMillan, 1967.
9   Stewart, R., *Contrasts in Management*, McGraw-Hill, 1976.
10 Mintzberg, H., *The Nature of Managerial Work*, Harper and Row, 1973.
11 Sayles, L. R., *Leadership – What Effective Managers Really Do, and How They Do It*, McGraw-Hill, 1979.
12 Burgoyne, J. C., 'Managerial effectiveness revisited', discussion paper, University of Lancaster, 1976.
13 Reddin, W. J., *Managerial Effectiveness*, McGraw-Hill, 1970.
14 Brodie, M. B. and Bennett, R. B., 'Effective management and the auditing of performance', *Journal of General Management*, Spring, 1979.
15 Drucker, P., *Management Tasks, Responsibilities and Practices*, Harper and Row, 1974.
16 Stewart, A. and Stewart, V., *Tomorrow's Managers Today*, 2nd edn., IPM, 1981.
17 As illustrated in Brodie, M. B., *Fayol on Administration*, Lyon, Grant and Green, 1967.
18 Gardner, N. B., *Effective Executive Practices*, MacDonald, 1965.
19 Drucker, P., *The Effective Executive*, Heinemann, 1967.
20 Reddin, W. J. 'Managerial effectiveness in the 1980s', *Management by Objectives*, **3**, no. 3, 1974.

21 Fiedler, F. E., *A Theory of Leadership Effectiveness*, McGraw-Hill, 1967.
22 Cummings, L. L. and Schwab, D. P., *Performance in Organisations – Determinants and Appraisal*, Scott, Faresman and Co., 1973.
23 Campbell, J. *et al.*, *Managerial Behaviour, Performance and Effectiveness*, McGraw-Hill, 1970.
24 Burgoyne, *op. cit.*
25 Bennett, R. and Langford, V., 'Exploring managerial effectiveness' in Williams, A. (ed.), *Using Personnel Research*, Gower, 1982.
26 Margerison, C., 'Highway to Top Management', *Personnel Management*, August, 1979.
27 Kakabadse, A., 'The Police – A Management Development Survey', *Journal of European Industrial Training Monograph*, **8**, no. 5, 1984.
28 Hawkless, J. and Lansbury, R., 'Why managers succeed in the public sector – an Australian study', *International Journal of Manpower*, **5**, no. 3, 1984.
29 Townsend, R., *Further Up the Organisation*, Coronet, 1984 (1970).
30 Scott, W. and Söderberg, S., *The Art of Managing*, Gower, 1985.
31 See, for example, Bennett, R., *Managing Personnel and Performance – An Alternative Approach*, Business Books, 1981.
32 Drake, R. and Smith, P., *Behavioural Science in Industry*, McGraw-Hill, 1973 (Chapter One).
33 For more personalised approaches, see, for example, Hunt, J., *Managing People at Work*, McGraw-Hill, 1979, and Bennett, R., *op. cit.*
34 Sills, P. 'The behavioural sciences – their potential and limitations', *Personnel Review*, **4**, 1975, pp. 5–12.
35 Gellerman, S., *Behavioural Science in Management*, Penguin, 1974.

2

The meaning of work

'Work' is a seemingly down-to-earth word whose meaning we all know – or do we? To most people, 'work' means paid employment of some kind, but behavioural scientists have recently been probing the ambiguities of the term. For instance, one person's work may well be another person's leisure:[1] the snooker player on television may earn more in two weeks than most of those watching earn in a year, but for most snooker players the activity is not 'work'. Women often spend long hours at home caring for children, husbands and aged relatives, but women rarely receive a direct wage for such activities and so some would not define these as 'real' work. Yet if women undertake similar tasks for a local authority children's or old people's home for an income then it *is* 'work'.

Historically, notions of work have varied a great deal, as recent scholarship has demonstrated.[2] What is sometimes called 'waged work', that is, conventional employment in a firm or organisation in return for a wage or salary, is a relatively modern phenomenon in the sense of being the dominant form of work in society. For much of the eighteenth and nineteenth centuries, waged work was only one of a variety of ways in which ordinary men and women obtained the necessities and sometimes a few of the luxuries of life. People might spend their year in a variety of activities, inside and outside the household, which could be described as 'productive'.[3]

Our notions of the importance of waged work are partly based upon our experience of the very recent past. Full employment, in the sense of continuous paid employment for virtually all who wished to participate, has occurred for only very short periods over the last hundred years; most obviously in the 1950s and 1960s. For the majority of the remaining period many people experienced regular or irregular periods of being 'laid off'. Seasonal influences, bad weather, fluctuations in demand and downturns in the economic cycle were all common causes of underemployment.

Moreover, some observers argue that waged labour is already in decline or, at the very least, undergoing fundamental change.[4] One observer has pointed out that 30 per cent of the workforce consists of part-time employees and the self-employed.[5] This may be largely a result of necessity rather than choice, at least initially, but it does show a considerable erosion of what has been termed our 'over-dependence on wage labour'.[6] What is occurring, is, in effect, a re-expansion of alternative ways of getting by, of alternative economies in which 'work' or the mental and physical efforts to produce goods and services takes on different meanings to those of 'waged work' in the conventional economy.

The dominant economy in any industrial society – sometimes called the 'formal' or the 'white' economy – is the one in which waged labour takes place. All of us have some connection with it as consumers, even if we do not have a waged job. But there is also an 'informal' economy, that is, the production of goods and services where no cash changes hands. People maintain and decorate their homes, grow food and repair their own cars. Many of these activities could be done for cash by somebody and would then be part of the 'formal' economy or the 'black' economy, discussed below.

Although no precise figures exist for the value of goods and services produced in the informal economy, it has been expanding rapidly over the last twenty years. DIY, for example, has expanded enormously as a part of the *formal* economy to supply the raw materials used in the *informal* economy. Domestic labour, cooking, cleaning, washing and so on is also part of the informal economy; this 'women's work'[7] has not, despite popular belief, declined much in this century. Rather, as more appliances have become available to mechanise domestic tasks, standards of domestic management have risen.

The third economy, the black economy, has received enormous publicity in recent years. It involves the production of goods and services for cash, such activities being hidden from the state in order to avoid the payment of taxes or compliance with other laws. Again, there is wide agreement that this form of production has expanded greatly over the last decade or so but again there are no exact figures. Some would argue that it is worth as much as 15 per cent of the national income[8] but in 1985 the Inland Revenue made a more modest (but still large in absolute terms) estimate of six to eight per cent of the gross domestic product, say, £16 billion per year[9].

Equally, nobody really knows how many people work in the black economy. Most of these activities involve a single person or, at most, a handful of people operating as a single illegitimate enterprise (although some also occur within large formal economy enterprises).[10] Once such units grow too large they run the risk of detection or must become legitimate. Some industries such as building and construction offer plenty of opportunities for black economy enterprise and many who work in these industries, the so-called 'moonlighters', have in effect two jobs, one in the formal economy and one in the black economy. The total value of products and services produced in the informal and black economies has been estimated as equivalent to almost half of that of the formal economy.[11]

The reasons for the growth of alternative forms of work to conventional waged labour are numerous, but there are three main ones. First, the reduction of jobs in the formal economy. Since 1981, about one million jobs in Britain have disappeared. Second, economic restructuring has destroyed millions of jobs in some sectors of the economy, notably in manufacturing, and created millions of jobs (though not as many as were lost elsewhere) in the service industries. People cannot always easily change from one sector to another: a coal miner may find it difficult to become a hotel chef. Third, the supply of labour has been expanding. Between 1961 and 1981 it grew by 2.2 million and will continue to grow apace as the baby boom of the 1960s becomes available for employment over the next ten years[12]. The overall result is a high level of unemployment in Britain, with other industrial societies showing similar, if less pronounced, patterns.

The re-expansion of alternatives to waged labour in contemporary industrial societies means that an examination of the meaning of work has to take into account the more complex economic structure which has emerged over the last 20 years. It might be argued that these alternatives to conventional waged labour are probably only temporary and will decline as full employment returns. But the balance of opinion is opposed to this optimistic view. One expert observer bluntly answers the question, 'will there be full employment again?' with a succinct 'not in our lifetime'[13]. And any amateur statistician, looking at unemployment levels over the last 150 years, would have to conclude that 'full' employment (in the sense that it existed in the 1950s and 1960s) has been very much the exception rather than the rule in the past.

Work and the individual

'Work' is done by people: what does 'work' mean to them? Again, this question is more complex than it might seem. One aspect of the meaning of work for the individual is that 'by their occupations are they defined as people'. In other words, when people want to place other people, to put them into meaningful categories, the first question they ask is 'what does he/she do?' A person's occupation is held to say a great deal about them as a person. 'He is a systems analyst', 'she is a social worker' conjure up a whole range of expected attributes – ways of talking, thinking, behaving etc. – in the minds of those who ask the question.

Occupation is also a powerful determinant of social status – the prestige, positive or negative a person has in the eyes of others[14]. Occupations in the higher reaches of the occupational hierarchy confer all kinds of benefits besides the high earnings that usually go with high status. Doctors are listened to with respect on all kinds of issues which have nothing directly to do with medicine, and probably find it easier to get their cars serviced or work done on their houses, since association with them also confers status. Road sweepers, sewage workers and kitchen hands, on the other hand, may be less likely to mention their occupations outside work because the status of these jobs is low. Indeed, they will probably be more successful socially if they neglect to mention what they do[15].

It has been argued that not having an occupation – usually a waged occupation – diminishes the person in the eyes of others. 'Do you work or are you just a housewife?' As we shall see later in this chapter, the negative definition of a person without a paid occupation is clearly revealed in studies of the unemployed. Unemployed people often find themselves viewed by others as failures and deviants[16]. Not having a paid job – especially for a man but also, increasingly, for women – robs a person of a place in contemporary society's focal institutional framework, the formal economy. But it also robs them of a place in other forms of social and communal activities: the unemployed male withdraws from friendships with former workmates and associates, family relations come under strain (especially where a father feels he has failed his wife and children as a breadwinner) and, of course, leisure activities that cost money usually have to be abandoned.

But, in a stricter sense, for those who are in conventional paid employment, there is also 'meaning' in the form of ways of defining work. This form of meaning has attracted a great deal of research attention, though, as much of that research shows, it is an elusive phenomenon. Most attention has been given to male manual workers, yet sufficient research has been carried out on other occupations to produce some broad generalisations. What has emerged is that work meanings, in the sense of people's ways of viewing involvement in the formal economy, are not randomly distributed but correlated closely with the status and the income level of occupations.

Broadly, the results of much of the relevant research suggest that the meaning of work is more *intrinsic*, that is, concerned with non-material aspects, the higher the occupation is in the status/ income hierarchy. Professional employees value work as a way of life, as highly involving, challenging, stimulating and fulfilling. For instance, the work and non-work parts of their lives are not sharply demarcated, so that social and leisure activities overlap with paid employment. Conversely, the lower the occupation in the status/ income hierarchy, the more likely the individual is to define work in *extrinsic* terms. Here work is defined in material terms and often as a means to an end – an enjoyable life in the non-paid-employment parts of life[17].

In one of the best known studies of manual workers ever carried out in Britain, Goldthorpe et al.[18] argued that three contrasting ideal types of employee orientations might be analytically distinguished:

1   *Instrumental*   where the primary meaning of work is as a means to an end – a way of acquiring the wherewithal to support a way of life of which work itself is not a valued part. People with this orientation see their paid employment in calculative terms; effort and attachment to the occupation are balanced coolly against the rewards on offer. Emotional involvement in the job is low and 'work' is sharply separated from other segments of life. On the whole, manual workers are seen as the most likely group to have work orientations approximating to this type.
2   *Bureaucratic orientation*   where the meaning of work is in terms of a commitment to the organisation in return for a steady rise in the status/income hierarchy but material rewards are not primary – it is the intrinsic rewards and opportunities for personal involvement that are important. Other areas of social life are orchestrated to link with work life so that the separation of work from non-work is not sharp. On the whole, this orientation is strongest among non-manual workers.
3   *Solidaristic*   where work is defined as a group activity involving an immediate set of workmates or even all those participating in, say, a small enterprise. Economic rewards are only maximised where this does not threaten group solidarity: loyalty to workmates or the firm might mean accepting lower material rewards. But involvement in work is high and, again, there is no sharp separation between work and other spheres of social life[19].

Later researchers criticised these formulations as being oversimplified. For example, the *bureaucratic orientation* was clearly meant to refer to the white collar workers, particularly those in the middle and higher reaches of the occupational hierarchy, such as accountants and managers in large enterprises. But this has been seen, in the light of other research, to be rather over-inclined to accept the public image offered by such workers and to fail to account for the substantial variations in work meanings found in these occupations. The idea that professionals and managers are not especially materially minded, but people selflessly dedicated to their jobs and organisations, seems to go against both the salary and benefits patterns observed and the actual behaviour and attitudes displayed.

The rewards for holders of middle and senior management positions and for the established professions[20] measured in incomes and fringe benefits, have tended to be much greater than those lower down the occupational hierarchy and, indeed, in recent years have become much more so as a result of changes in taxation and the political acceptance of the need for greater financial incentives to improve managerial performance[21]. This evidence is hardly consistent with an alleged indifference to material rewards.

Studies of managers and professionals have also revealed considerable variation and complexity in their definitions of work. One particularly sensitive study[22] records the complexities and contradictions of managerial definitions of work as well as some of the sub-types of orientation. The latter ranged from the *lumpen management*, the backbone of the management hierarchy, the middle-aged in middle level jobs who will never go much further in their organisation, to the *ideas men* brought in from other companies, who owe allegiance to no one and no single department and whose task is to plot the future of products and the organisation.

Other observers have stressed a developing fragmentation of management in the sense that specialisation within management produces managers tied to particular functions. In Britain, this puts finance, sales and marketing at the top and production and design at the bottom[23]. Other countries display rather different hierarchies: for example, engineers and designers tend to have higher status in Germany and Japan. This affects the self-esteem and work meanings for those in these roles. Particular definitions of the meaning of management linked to specific functions may also clash with each other. Several studies have reported that interdepartmental conflict at managerial levels is a normal part of life in the business organisation[24]. This is not to say that such conflict is necessarily 'bad', since conflict can have positive advantages in helping resolve problems and improve performance within the enterprise. But if one definition of managerial work consistently outweighs others, the result may well be weaknesses in aspects of the firm's total performance[25].

The ideal type of the *solidaristic orientation* has been criticised for its romanticism. The notion of groups of workers who are 'one for all and all for one' and who will not allow material rewards or management to divide them, is usually seen as part of a golden age of the working class. Coal miners, dockers and ship-building workers are seen as exemplifying this orientation. However, as the 1984–1985 coal demonstrated, if this golden age ever existed, it is now much weakened. Research on the work orientations of ship-building workers[26], for example, also seems to show that, despite the traditions of the industry, their attitudes are not so very different to manual workers in many other industries. In short, they do not offer a particularly close approximation to the ideal type.

Equally, the idea that a solidaristic orientation may be the distinctive characteristic of the meaning of work for workers in the small firm is not borne out by research. Indeed, if anything, this literature shows that employees of small firms are often *less* attached to the enterprise than the alleged instrumentally orientated workers in large firms studied by the originators of the typology, since rates of labour turnover, for example, are often substantially higher in small firms.

The *instrumental orientation* was, at first sight, the best supported of the three ideal types; Goldthorpe *et al.* interviewed well over 200 manual workers in three large firms (including the Vauxhall car plant at Luton). But critics have argued that the isolating and emphasising of a *single* orientation represents an over-compression of the actual findings. In practice, the meaning of work may well be context-bound, that is, people may well hold or emphasise one set of meanings in relation to one aspect of their job but offer another set of meanings when other contexts come to the fore. Daniel[27], for example, argued that in relation to rewards, workers naturally stress money and the deprivations of the job which should be compensated financially. But in relation to the job itself, the stress will be on its intrinsic aspects, the quality of the job environment, tasks and relations with others.

A further criticism here is that the orientation or set of meanings attributed to respondents is over-rational, implying a clear, well-thought-out, consistent set of meanings elicited by the study's interviews. More recent research has suggested that manual workers, like other human beings, are often vague, inconsistent and even contradictory in their ideas about any particular segment of their lives. This criticism, in effect, extends that of Daniel mentioned above. Not only are work meanings *context-related* but people may also hold inconsistent or contradictory views over a range of contexts linked to the *same* broad activity. For much of the time they are unaware of these differences because they are rarely called upon to produce a fully articulated version of the meanings they hold in relation to participation in the formal economy.

A major reason for the fragmentary, vague and sometimes contradictory character of work meanings, it may be suggested, is that the work environment and life experiences in general often contain contradictions. In other words, if people live in a contradictory, inconsistent world, should we be surprised if their attitudes, meanings and views reflect this inconsistency and contradiction? Nichols and Armstrong[28], in a study of manual workers in a chemical plant in England, set themselves the task of explaining not only why people often hold confused and inconsistent views but also why these are translated into apparently equally confused and contradictory behaviour. Their explanation is complex but seeks to take into account not just the enterprise environment itself but the wider economy and the society of which it is a part.

Finally, critics of the orientations ¬pproach to work meanings have also questioned the implied stability built into the descriptions offered. Daniel[29], for example, has argued that meanings might have a cycle, with material rewards and antagonism towards management becoming central during the annual wage bargaining period while, at other times, intrinsic factors might be more central. Others[30] have argued that it is difficult to discern any set of lasting stable orientations and that factors such as the individual's position in the life cycle, what is happening in the industry in which the firm is located and the wider economy, may well produce a changing mix of work meanings over time. For instance, when a person marries, the need for resources to set up home and start a family may lead to work being interpreted in highly material terms but, at other times, more intrinsic expectations may come to the fore.

What emerges from this over-view of the development of behavioural scientists' analyses of work meanings is an apparent trend towards emphasising the greater complexity and changeability of such meanings. This is partly the result of an accumulation of studies and interpretations, but the main cause is a radical change in methodological approaches to the topic. Until the mid-1970s, most studies were survey or questionnaire based, asking respondents to tick boxes to indicate agreement or disagreement with particular statements. These research instruments were often administered en masse or respondents were put through a quick 'yes', 'no', 'don't know' session with an interviewer.[31]

The results were then sorted into categories, perhaps fed into a computer, and researchers simply totted up the totals to produce a list of work meanings. These procedures account to a great extent for the apparently rational, coherent clarity of the meanings attributed to respondents. In other words, the researchers were *looking* for a clear, rational and consistent view of work and the analytical procedures adopted were of a kind likely to *produce* just this kind of result: the neat tabulations and percentages ironed out the inconsistencies and vagueness of the respondents' own ideas.

Later researchers have relied increasingly on qualitative approaches to the study of work meanings. This *ethnographic* perspective[32] tries to capture not only what people say but how they say it, to include their incoherence, inconsistencies and changes of view from one context to another. The results are much more difficult to summarise but capture much more closely the thoughts and feelings of those studied[33]. The method also carefully traces the links between voiced opinions and actions: people do not always do what they say or say what they do or, put more technically, there is a strong likelihood of a discrepancy between accounts and action. It must be stressed that these observations do *not* apply only to manual workers. People at *all* levels of organisational life display similar predispositions, from the managing director or highly educated professional downwards.

Ethnographic approaches to occupational groups are still rather thinly spread and many key occupations remain unresearched. But what they have achieved so far is to force us to see employees and others in the organisation as *people* rather than simply as types of labour, the study of which is likely to result in fairly simple and straightforward recommendations for management strategies. It is now becoming evident that, despite the welter of research, we still have much to learn about the relationship between work and the individual, but this realisation is in itself a substantial step forward.

Work meanings and gender

The study of individuals and work by behavioural scientists has historically been the study of *men* at work, at least until recently. This curious omission seems to turn on widespread and pervasive assumptions about gender in relation to paid work which have only come under challenge in the last decade or so. These assumptions suggested that women participating in the formal economy were not 'real' workers but only marginal members. 'Men are the breadwinners, the real workers: women only work for pin money' and 'women are less interested in promotion or organisational life, they won't commit themselves'. Women, in other words, were seen as temporary visitors to the world of real work, the formal economy. Conversely, the 'real' world of the woman was seen as revolving around home and domestic commitments. As we noted earlier, work outside the formal economy, 'unwaged work', is often not considered real work. Never mind that caring for children might be seen by a fair-minded observer as not only extremely time-consuming but also very highly skilled. Moreover, male contributions to the formal economy often rely heavily but implicitly on the support provided by women in managing a home and providing a retreat from the demands of organisational life; without these contributions the formal economy could not function even if women themselves never participated directly[34].

But, of course, women do participate in the formal economy and always have done. Our view of the nineteenth century contains two opposing stereotypes of women's relations to the formal economy. The first is of middle and upper class women, married or single, whose lives were devoted to leisure, conspicuous consumption and status display. The second is of the girls and women who formed part of the factory army in industries such as textiles or who worked in the coal mines prior to the 1842 Act of Parliament forbidding their employment in this industry. The reality was rather more complex but the latter stereotype is closer to the truth.

Women who participated fully in the formal economy in the nineteenth century were mainly single and mainly in domestic service. The proportion of married women employed in the formal economy was relatively low and tended to decline as the century wore on. By 1911 less than ten per cent of married women were so employed.[35] Women factory workers did exist but recent scholarship has suggested that their numbers can be exaggerated: in fact, Pahl estimates that women are more likely to be 'factory workers in the mid-1980s than at any time in the past'.[36] The 1841 Census, for instance, records that less than one per cent of factory workers were women.[37]

However, this did not mean that married women were confined to the domestic economy. On the contrary, historical data shows that many married women were marginally and intermittently involved in the formal economy. Many did home work of some kind for shops and factories, again commonly in textiles and clothes making, while others took in washing or lodgers or did part-time cleaning. Some of the work was seasonal such as fruit picking, dressmaking and millinery. What comes across strongly in this data is the episodic character of women's involvement in the formal economy in the nineteenth century, whether they were single or married.

In this century changes have been dramatic, particularly the vast increase in married women's participation in the formal economy. From less than ten per cent of married women doing waged labour in 1911, in 1981 the proportion had risen to just under 50 per cent.[38] This has meant a similarly dramatic increase in the proportion of women in the formal economy labour force. In 1848, almost halfway through the century, women constituted just over one third of the paid labour force; by 1980 they made up 41.7 per cent.[39] In 1980, the *Women and Employment Survey* reported that 65 per cent of women were in the formal economy (though this included five per cent who were unemployed when surveyed).[40] Another major change is in the *kinds* of work women do in the formal economy. Domestic service has declined and non-manual work, particularly routine white collar work, has expanded enormously. Women have also become factory workers, particularly in the unskilled and semi-skilled jobs in the newer areas of manufacturing which emerged in the first half of the century.

Despite this great increase in participation in the formal economy, women still tend to be segregated into particular occupations. *Census* data shows that 70 per cent of women are in service and routine white collar work.[41] A large number of occupations contain over 75 per cent of women – typists, secretaries, shop assistants, nurses, primary and secondary school teachers are good examples – while others have relatively few women. Occupations with less than ten per cent of women, for example, include administrators and managers, engineers, accountants, barristers and solicitors.[42]

Women also tend to be part-time members of the formal economy and this trend has been increasing recently. Between 1971 and 1981 the proportion of women part-time employees increased from 33 to 42 per cent.[43] This type of work has, in any case, been increasing, that is, full-time jobs in the economy have been declining while part-time jobs have been expanding. Much of this change is due to the shift in the economy towards services, where such jobs are more common, and to the decline in primary and manufacturing industry.

The above is a necessary background to any serious consideration of the meaning of work for women and any comparison with male workers. In the past, such comparisons have been bedevilled by conceptual confusions linked to gender stereotypes. Feldberg and Nakano Glenn,[44] in an extremely perceptive analysis of these comparisons have argued that many previous studies operated with two different sets of assumptions when analysing men and women in the formal economy. In explaining male variations in work meanings the major causal factors are assumed to be the work task and environment, resulting in a *job model* of worker orientations. But when the work meanings of female employees are discussed, the major causal factor is all too often assumed to be the personal characteristics and domestic situation of the individual – a *gender model.*

For example, Blauner,[45] in a famous study of manual worker alienation, took textile workers as one of this groups of employees . He reported that women complained more about job conditions than men, with more saying they had to work too quickly or were tired at the end of the day. In explaining these differences Blauner resorted to a gender model when discussing the women, stressing that they had less physical stamina and more domestic commitments than men. The men's reactions were, on the other hand, interpreted in terms of a job model, that is, by reference to the conditions under which they worked. Feldberg and Nakano Glenn argue that this ignores the data which shows that the women's working conditions were more demanding because they did more machine-paced work and they were more closely supervised. Nor did Blauner apparently examine what proportion of the women were mothers and wives and what proportion had no domestic responsibilities[46].

The stereotypes of women working in the formal economy only for pin money are also undermined by empirical data. For example, one in every eight families in Britain is a single parent family and nine out of ten of these are headed by a woman[47]. *The Women and Employment Survey* noted earlier also reported that a high proportion of women work to provide basic necessities for themselves and their families. Other studies have produced similar findings[48]. In other words, economic and extrinsic factors are important for *some* women in defining the meaning of work (just as they are for *some* men) and for a much larger proportion than the popular stereotype would lead us to believe.

The stereotype that women are less committed than men to their roles in the formal economy and to their employer similarly looks weaker after scrutiny. First, the implied assumption that men display the opposite characteristics needs examining: the literature on the work meanings of males indicates that a high proportion have no such strong job commitments. Indeed, the *instrumental orientation* claimed by Goldthorpe *et al.* as increasingly typical of the British male manual worker at the end of the 1960s, was making exactly this point. Secondly, women are heavily segregated into particular kinds of work. Many of these are more boring, less well paid, and offer fewer career opportunities than the typical work role of the male employee. This, in itself, might account for differences in commitment to the job and organisation between male and female workers. Where comparisons have been made on a strict basis researchers have been struck by the similarities rather than the differences between men and women in the ways they define work.

Recent studies of women in the formal economy, particularly those using an ethnographic approach, in effect mix the gender and job models to provide a fuller account of what work means for women. (The same approach would also add to the fullness of the interpretation of men's involvement: the term 'gender' should not be employed in a sexist fashion if it is to be used effectively in studies of people in work settings.) As might be expected, they do not show a single set of meanings held by women in the formal economy. As is the case for men, meanings very in relation to type of work role, type of industry, position in the life cycle, personal circumstances, previous work experience and type of community.

Studies of women manual workers such as those of Pollert, Cavendish and others[49] bear out the above points very fully. But there are also studies of other kinds of work roles, routine white collar work, for example, where women are also heavily represented[50]. Again, what is distinctive about women's involvement and what is shared with men is carefully isolated, particularly in the more recent studies. Some women have higher level roles – managerial and professioval roles – but studies here are rare[51]. This may reflect the fact that relatively few women have reached this level. In 1980, one estimate[52] suggested that only two of the United Kingdom's top 100 companies had women directors and, though the position has undoubtedly improved since then, it would be wrong to assume any dramatic change.

When women do enter management, they tend to do so, more than proportionately, in 'female' areas such as personnel, retailing, catering and marketing. The assumption usually made, however, is that there will be a steady rise in the number of women in professional and senior managerial roles in the future. Two points tell against this assumption. First, women's participation in the formal economy tends to be bimodal: most women still tend to have two periods in paid work roles broken by a withdrawal at pregnancy and when caring for young children[53]. Second, although more women are now actively encouraged to seek a 'career', there appears to be little decline in the role demands associated with home and motherhood[54]. Both factors make it difficult for women to compete with men for higher paid, high status roles in the formal economy.

This section has examined gender and work meanings in some detail, concentrating on women. In the past, management texts have neglected women, so the rather lengthier treatment here redresses the balance somewhat. It is, in any event, justified, given the increasing participation of women at all levels in the formal economy and the differences which exist between them and men in their patterns of economic involvement. The notion that women are a marginal work force or a 'reserve army of labour' for the formal economy is simply wrong as a characterisation: women are permanently a part of the formal economy even if *some* women move in and out of waged work in relation to factors such as personal circumstances or changes in the level and kind of formal economic activity in Britain.

The meaning of non-work – unemployment

In the 1950s and 1960s Britain had virtually full employment in the sense that almost anybody who wanted a job in the formal economy could get one. The meaning of work was, it may be surmised, strongly affected by such conditions. In the 1970s and 1980s very different conditions hold: in January 1971, just over 580,000 – 2.5 per cent of the work force – were officially unemployed in the UK but by January 1985 this figure had risen to just over three million or 12.7 per cent[55], and may again be expected to affect the meaning of work, especially for those who suffer frequent or prolonged periods of involuntary unemployment.

Unemployment is not randomly distributed. Certain kinds of people are much more likely to experience unemployment than others. In the age spectrum, for example, those in the youngest age groups (those under 25) are most likely to suffer unemployment. In January 1982, those aged under 20 had an officially recorded unemployment level of just under 23 per cent while the average for all ages was 13.2 per cent[56]. Interestingly, women have a lower level of registered unemployment than men, though women, like men in recent years, have generally suffered an increasing likelihood of being unemployed[57]. Ethnicity is also a factor, particularly for women and young ethnic minority members. The relative difference has also tended to increase as the overall level of unemployment has grown[58]. Similarly, there are large regional differences, the South East having a rather lower level than the average for the UK while other regions, such as Northern Ireland, Scotland, Wales and the North of England, consistently showing higher than average levels.

The impact of unemployment on the individual is now well-documented, though the inconsistencies and contradictions noted earlier in relation to work meanings emerge once again. On the one hand, there are myriad reports of the shock and psychological pain of being made redundant, particularly when it is unexpected. On the other hand, there are also plentiful reports of the newly unemployed feeling liberated or on holiday. In the long term, however, pessimism tends to set in, accompanied by a deterioration in self-confidence and relations with others in and outside the family, and a loss of hope of finding another job[59].

Again, as with the meanings of work, we must be careful not to over-simplify or over-generalise. Not all the unemployed react in the same way and neither do they all follow any particular sequence of feelings as the period of unemployment lengthens. For instance, whereas for married males unemployment is reported as undermining not only the self but relations with wives and children as well as friends, some of the evidence on the young unemployed suggests that friendships with other young people (mainly but not exclusively unemployed like themselves) remain strong and family relations may be maintained if parents are sympathetic and supportive[60]. Many commentators, including Lord Scarman, have made a link between youth unemployment and inner city disorders, implying that if apathy is present it may also explode into protest given suitable conditions.

Reactions to unemployment may also be related to gender and ethnicity. Although specific studies of unemployed women are scarce the indications are that, as might be expected, situational rather than gender differences may explain why women show different attitudes and behaviour in relation to unemployment as compared to men[61]. Ethnicity is often closely connected with youth and inner city unemployment but has its own special aspect, discrimination. The evidence suggests that part of the higher levels of unemployment among ethnic minorities may be attributed to overt and covert discrimination by employers[62].

Fineman has argued persuasively[63] that one way of exploring work meanings is to explore the opposite role; non-work or unemployment. People do not always find it easy to put into words what they feel about any area of their lives, however central it may be. This may be due partly to a lack of ability or desire to put their feelings into words, but another reason may be a lack of awareness. Behavioural scientists have frequently noted that we all live in a world of 'taken-for-granted' or latent meanings, which we rarely make explicit because we rarely have any reason to do so. But occasionally we experience a radical break with ordinary experiences and this may make us see the disrupted aspect of life afresh. Unemployment is just such a disruption, especially if it follows a long period of stable employment.

In his study of newly unemployed managers and professionals, employees who are normally seen as highly involved in their work, Fineman reported that about a third expressed high levels of alienation; only about a fifth talked in terms of losing a highly valued and positive centre to their lives. Many of those who expressed dissatisfaction confessed that while at work they had suppressed their negative feelings or had been only dimly aware of them. Of course, it might be argued that some negative feelings were to be expected from people who had just been publicly humiliated by being told they were no longer wanted by their employers. Nevertheless, the study again supports the idea that work meanings are often complex and contradictory.

Work meanings: the decline of the work ethic?

As noted earlier, many commemtators believe that high levels of unemployment will persist into the foreseeable future, which raises the question of whether this trend will be linked with a permanent decline in commitment to work in industrial society. There is evidence that prolonged periods out of work lead to apathy and resignation. The search for a job becomes perfunctory or is abandoned. However, because somebody no longer believes they *can* find a job does not mean they do not still *want* a job[64]. Given the importance of participation in the formal economy for the individual's status as well as for achieving an acceptable living standard, we might expect that if job opportunities increase people will want them. Despite claims to the contrary, welfare payments for the long term unemployed are not generous in comparison with average earnings[65].

Rose, in a recent, carefully argued examination of research on the work ethic[66], concludes that not only is there a large element of exaggeration in accounts of the strength of the work ethic in the past, there is no firm empirical foundation for claims of a current collapse of the work ethic. There might have been something like a revolt against work in the 1960s – a period when participation in the formal economy was easy – but this seems to have disappeared with the onset of a harsher economic climate. Rather, Rose argues, there has been a reconstruction of work values (at different rates and in different ways in different occupations), the continuation of which is probably a permanent process of cultural change in relation to the experience of 'work' in all its forms. For instance, talk of a decline in the work ethic clearly ignores the growing participation of women in the formal economy, particularly women from the middle and upper classes who in the past shunned any association with work. A life devoted conspicuously to leisure is no longer acceptable. Now middle class women need a 'career' or an 'interesting' job if they are to be seen by many of their peers as interesting people.

Success in Britain in the 1980s is still primarily defined in terms of employment and employment rewards: the trappings of the 'good life' for many have become and are becoming more, not less, dependent on rewards to be gained only from participation in the formal economy. The quantity and quality of material possessions deemed necessary for an acceptable living standard, the increasing commercialisation of leisure (the phrase 'free' time is hardly appropriate any more) the tendency to owning your own home and setting up in an independent household earlier in life, all increase the pressure on the individual to participate in the formal economy.

These commitments to paid employment can be accompanied by a change in people's views of the proper relationship between themselves and the organisation. Automatic acceptance of authority may well have declined (and its existence in the past is easily overstated) and more jobs may offer opportunities for discretion as the white collar and service sectors of the economy expand. Among the middle class there may be an increase in the number of married partners both having a career, so that male commitment to the organisation also has to take into account the other partner's job commitments and needs, but does this necessarily signify a decline in the commitment to work?

In other words, while it is entirely plausible to argue that work meanings in industrial society are changing, perhaps at a faster rate and in more ways than in many periods of the past, this is not the same as saying that commitment to work is collapsing or even declining in any marked fashion. Some writers argue, in fact, that these processes should not be left to themselves but that public policy should push towards a closer accommodation with the options for participation in the emerging economy of the future[67]. We should accept that the full employment of the 1950s and 1960s will never return and think in terms of a shorter working week and life – perhaps from the typical 100,000 hour working life of the past towards a 50,000 hour one. Only in this way can we cope with unemployment and allow people a wider range of ways of relating to 'work' in all its possible forms in the informal and formal economies.

Change, socially engineered through public policy, is politically out of fashion in the 1980s, so it is much more likely that changes in the meaning of work will occur in an haphazard fashion. For the 15–20 per cent of the adult population who are unemployed for shorter or longer periods, the meaning of work will probably continue for a long time to be the painful denial of the good life as defined by the majority. For the bulk of the adult population there will be a continuing evolution of work meanings arising out of the interactions between personal circumstances and ambitions and the demands of the dominant formal economy.

References

1   The notion of 'leisure' is also elusive. We need not examine this here, but those who want to explore this further should see Parker, S. R., *The Sociology of Leisure,* Allen and Unwin, 1976, which provides an introduction.

2   See Anthony, P. D., *The Ideology of Work*, Heinemann, 1983, (2nd edn); Pahl, R. E., *Divisions of Labour,* Blackwell, 1984, especially Part One, and Kumar, K., 'The social culture of work: work, employment and unemployment as ways of life', in Thompson K., (ed.), *Work, Employment and Unemployment, Perspectives on Work and Society,* Open University Press, 1984.

3   Pahl, *op. cit.* pp. 49–56. Of course, some employees did have stable, regular employment, which was much prized, but the technological change connected with current structural unemployment in Britain is far from new: many workers in the last century and earlier this century were familiar with the job-destroying effects of new technology. Electricity and the internal combustion engine, for instance, destroyed as well as created a great number of jobs.

4   See, for example, Rose, R., *Re-working the Work Ethic,* Batsford, 1985, Handy, C., *The Future of Work,* Blackwell, 1984, Pahl, *ibid.,* Chapters Five and Kumar, *op. cit.*

5   Handy, *ibid.* p. 39.

6   Pahl, *op. cit.,* pp. 56–57.

7   'Women's work', however, was not always necessarily done by women in the past as Pahl, *ibid.* (pp. 57–62) shows. There is certainly much current debate on the gender distribution of domestic tasks, even if, again, the evidence on the actual division between men and women is rather thin.

8   Feige, E. L. and McGee, R. T., 'Tax revenue losses and the unobserved economy in the UK', *Journal of Economic Affairs,* 2, no. 3, 1982.

9   Inland Revenue spokesperson talking on the *In Business* programme on Radio 4, October 30th, 1985.

10 Henry, S., *The Hidden Economy,* Martin Robertson, 1978.

11 Handy, *op. cit.,* p. 19.

12 All figures in this paragraph are from Handy, *ibid.,* pp. 16–17.

13 Handy, *ibid.,* p. 37.

14 The German Soliologist Max Weber was among the first to analyse the complexities of the relations between occupation and status, which are much more complex than this paragraph indicates. See the excerts from his work in Giddens, A. and Held D., *Classes, Power and Conflict, Classical and Contemporary Debates,* Macmillan, 1982, especially pp. 60–73.

15 For a good example of the negative status effects of a particular

occupation, see Roles, J. and Garbin, A. P., 'Stripping for a living: an occupational study of the night club stripper', in Bryant, C. D., *Deviant Behaviour, Occupational and Organisational Bases,* Rand McNally, 1974.

16 See Kelvin, P. and Jarrett, J. E., *Unemployment, the Social Psychological Effects,* Cambridge University Press, 1985, Chapter Six, for a careful review of much of the supporting literature on this point.

17 The established literature on work meanings produced in the period 1955–75 offers numerous examples of studies supporting these generalisations. For a list and critical review, see Fineman, S., 'Work meanings, non-work and the taken-for-granted', *Journal of Management Studies,* 20, no. 4, 1983, especially pp. 144–46.

18 Goldthorpe, J., Lockwood, D., Bechhoffer, F. and Platt, J., *The Affluent Worker: Industrial Attitudes and Behaviour,* Cambridge University Press, 1968.

19 *Ibid.,* pp. 38–41.

20 The phrase 'the established professions' is a vague one, and certainly some occupations with a claim to the title 'profession' have not shared in the general upward shift in middle and higher level rewards, most notably teaching.

21 The results are shown in recent statistics: '. . . in 1978 the lowest paid tenth of Britain's male workers received 67 per cent of average earnings but in 1985 the proportion was only 61 per cent. Yet the proportion received by the highest paid tenth grew from 158 per cent to 171.5 per cent.' *New Society,* January 17th, 1986, p. 105.

22 Fletcher, C., 'The end of management' in Child, J. (ed.), *Man and Organisation,* Allen and Unwin, 1973. See also the more recent Wilkinson, B. and Smith, S., 'From old school hunches to departmental lunches', *Sociological Review,* 32, no. 1, 1984.

23 Lawrence, P., *Management in Action,* Routledge and Kegan Paul, 1984, especially Chapter 3.

24 The 'classic' study here is Dalton, M., *Men Who Manage,* Wiley, 1959. Lawrence, *ibid.,* discusses more recent research on this issue.

25 It has been argued, for example, that management in business organisations in Britain consistently underplays the importance of people while over-emphasising finance, with the result that motivational levels are lower than in business organisations in other industrial societies such as Japan and the USA.

26 Brown, R. K. and Brannen, P., 'Social relations and social perspectives amongst shipbuilding workers', *Sociology,* 4, 1970, pp. 71–84 and 191–211. For a more theoretical version of this criticism see Critcher, C., 'Sociology, cultural studies and the post war working class', in Clarke, J. *et al.,* (eds.), *Working Class Culture, Studies in History and Theory,* Hutchinson, 1979.

27 Daniel, W. W., 'Understanding employee behaviour in its context', in Child, J. (ed.) *op cit.;* 'Industrial behaviour and orientation to work: a critique', *Journal of Management Studies,* 6, October 1969, pp. 366–375.

28 Nichols, T. and Armstrong, P., *Workers Divided, a Study in Shopfloor Politics,* Fontana, 1976.

29 Daniel, W. W., *op. cit.,* 1973.

30 See, e.g., Curran, J. and Stanworth, J., 'Self-selection and the small firm

worker – a critique and an alternative view', *Sociology*, **13**, no. 3, 1979; and 'A new look at job satisfaction', *Human Relations*, **34**, no. 5, 1981.

31   Not all survey-based studies were as crude as this and some researchers produced sensitive and thoughtful interpretations of their findings. The study by Goldthorpe *et al*, *op. cit.*, for example, has been criticised extensively (as noted earlier), but deserves considerable credit for the stimulating and intelligent interpretation provided by the researchers, which was subsequently enormously influential on later research.

32   For a fuller account of this perspective, see Silverman, D., *Qualitative Methodology and Sociology*, Gower, 1985, Part Three, Chapters Five to Seven.

33   Among the studies already cited that show this perspective at work are: Fineman, *op. cit.*; Fletcher, *op. cit.*; Wilkinson and Smith, *op. cit.*; Dalton, *op. cit.*; and Nichols and Armstrong, *op. cit.* The modern 'classic' of this approach is relation to work meanings is Willis, P., *Learning to Labour, How Working Class Kids Get Working Class Jobs*, Saxon House, 1977. Another highly accomplished exponent of this approach is the American, Studs Terkel. See, in particular, Terkel, S., *Working People Talk About What They Do All Day and How They Feel About What They Do*, Revised edn., Wildwood House, 1975 and Penguin Books, 1985.

34   For analyses of domestic work roles see Oakley, A., *The Sociology of Housework*, M. Robertson, 1974; and *From Here to Maternity: Becoming a Mother*, Penguin Books, 1979.

35   Scott, J. W. and Tilly, L. A., 'Women's work and the family in nine-teenth-century Europe', *Comparative Studies in Society and History*, **71**, no. 1, 1975, cited in Pahl, *op. cit.*

36   Pahl, *op. cit.*, p. 64.

37   Pahl, *op. cit.*, p. 64.

38   Department of Employment 'A changing labour force: constants and variables', *Employment Gazette*, **91**, February, 1983.

39   Dex, S., *The Sexual Division of Work, Conceptual Revolution in the Social Sciences*, Wheatsheaf Books, 1985, p. 3.

40   Martin, J. and Roberts, C., *Women and Employment: A Lifetime Perspective*, HMSO, 1984.

41   Analysis of the 1971 Census data by Joseph, G., *Women at Work, the British Experience*, Philip Allan, 1983. The picture is unlikely to have changed significantly in the intervening years.

42   Hakim, C., *Occupational Segregation*, Research Paper No. 9, Department of Employment, 1979, pp. 32–34.

43   Dex, *op. cit.*, p. 5.

44   Feldberg, R. and Nakano Glenn, E., 'Male and female: job versus gender models in the sociology of work', *Social Problems*, **26**, no. 5, 1979.

45   Blauner, R., *Alienation and Freedom*, University of Chicago Press, 1964.

46   Feldberg and Nakano Glenn, *op. cit.*, pp. 528–29.

47   Ellis Cashmore, E., *Having to: the World of One Parent Families*, Allen and Unwin, 1985.

48   Brown, R. K., Curran, M. M. and Cousins, J. M., *Changing Attitudes to Work*, Research Paper No. 40, Department of Employment, 1983, summarises many of the relevant studies.

49   Pollert, A., *Girls, Wives, Factory Lives*, Macmillan, 1981; Cavendish, R.,

Women on the Line, Routledge and Kegan Paul, 1982; Coyle, A., *Redundant Women,* The Women's Press, 1984; Wajcman, J., *Women in Control,* Open University Press, 1983. The last two offer different viewpoints on women and the meaning of work, since one is concerned with redundancy and the other with a women's producer co-operative.

50 See, e.g., Crompton, R. and Jones, G., *White Collar Proletariat, Deskilling and Gender in Clerical Work,* Macmillan, 1984; and McNally, F., *Women for Hire: A Study of the Female Office Worker,* Macmillan, 1979.

51 But see Marshall, J., *Women Managers: Travellers in a Male World,* Wiley, 1984; and Cooper, C. and Davidson, M., *High Pressure, Working Lives of Women Managers,* Fontana, 1982.

52 McRae, H., 'Why British women deserve a seat on the board', *The Guardian,* August 8th, 1980.

53 Dex, *op. cit.,* p. 4. He points out, however, that the distribution is changing to a tiered one, with more women returning to the formal economy between pregnancies; although this does not substantially alter the main point that such withdrawals do not help women in their competition with men for higher level jobs.

54 Pahl, *op. cit.,* Chapter Ten, provides a very careful empirical analysis of the division of labour between partners and broadly confirms the idea that any assertion that there has been a very marked redistribution of domestic tasks so that men now do a great deal more in the home than they did, say, 30 or 40 years ago, should be treated with scepticism.

55 Department of Employment, 'Unemployment adjusted for discontinuities and seasonality', *Employment Gazette,* **93,** no. 7, 1985.

56 *Employment Gazette,* **92,** no. 1, January 1983, Table 2.15. Note that January is a favourable month for this comparison in the sense that had the July figures been used, for example, the youth unemployment level would have been substantially higher because of the summer school leavers who would have just joined the statistics. By January some of these have found work. The more recent figures would differ because of the Youth Training Scheme temporarily taking young people off the labour market and changes in the way the statistics are compiled.

57 Hughes, J. J. and Perlman, R., *The Economics of Unemployment, A Comparative Analysis of Britain and the United States,* Wheatsheaf Books, 1984, pp. 182–84. However, there are considerable reservations to be made about the official statistics for women's unemployment. See, e.g., Dex, *op. cit.,* pp. 61–63.

58 Hughes and Perlman, *ibid.,* pp. 184–86.

59 For reviews of the literature on the psychological impact of unemployment, see Jahoda, M., *Employment and Unemployment, A Social Psychological Analysis,* Cambridge University Press, 1985.

60 Kelvin and Jarrett, *ibid.,* pp. 54–55.

61 Dex, *op. cit.,* pp. 52–58, thoughtfully interprets a range of studies of female unemployment.

62 Smith, D. J., *Unemployment and Racial Minorities,* Policy Studies Institute, 1981, and Commission for Racial Equality, *Annual Report 1982–1983,* 1983.

63 Fineman, *op. cit.*

64   Economist Intelligence Unit, *Coping with Unemployment: the Effects on the Unemployed Themselves,* 1982.

65   De la Cour, M., 'MSC report on the long term unemployed', *Unemployment Unit Bulletin,* no. 8, 1983.

66   Rose, *op. cit.*

67   Handy, *op. cit.*

3
The individual at work

Human resource management is an important part of every manager's role. It involves selecting the best employees, training and developing them, and making sure that their equipment and work environment enables them to do their work well. The wise manager becomes adept at 'sizing people up', realising the many aspects of temperament and ability in which individuals vary, and being able to match these individual differences to job requirements. Behavioural science offers many insights into the assessment of individual differences and human abilities, and also points to the kinds of problem arising from faulty work design[1]. In Section A we will look at human attributes, such as personality and mental abilities, and their measurement; in Section B we will analyse aspects of work design that cause avoidable stress, errors and accidents.

A: Individual differences

We are unique as individuals, but also share many features by which we can be compared with others. Our unique but comparable ways of thinking, feeling and acting are summed up in what we call our personality. In a recent survey on managerial selection, the IPM[2] concluded that managers in the UK are selected primarily on personality. The typical checklist of managerial qualities used in selection is:

Energetic
Ambitious
Intelligent
Creative
Business-oriented
Selfconfident
Good communicator
Analytical
Decisive
Persuasive
Forceful

This sort of checklist seems straightforward, but it can be difficult to put into practice. Some of the ingredients, such as communication, are skills or aptitudes easily recognised in action. Others, such as intelligence, are more elusive and harder to define. Although we feel we know what personality is, it is hard to define and measure, unlike height or weight or technical knowledge. Paradoxically, our personality is both stable and also a dynamic process, an interaction between our own tendencies and the surroundings in which we live. This interaction has patterns; our habitual ways of behaving, which are observable, and our relatively stable qualities which others come to know and expect of us.

The Johari Window[3] offers four views of our personality. These are: the self we share with others, the self others see but which may not be obvious to us, the private self which others do not see and the self hidden both from others and ourselves. This model is used in exercises to help people better understand themselves and their social interactions, and borrows from Freud's view of the importance of the unconscious mind. If there are important mental processes which subconsciously influence our actions, then there are important aspects of our own personality of which we may be unaware.

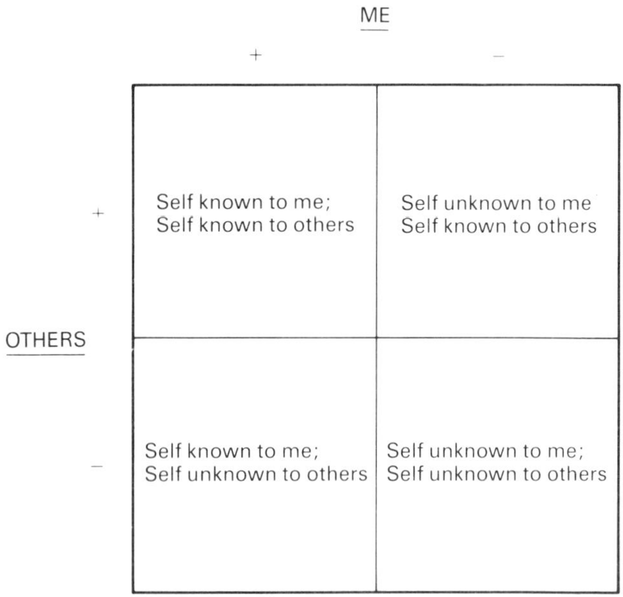

ME

	+	−
+	Self known to me; Self known to others	Self unknown to me Self known to others
OTHERS		
−	Self known to me; Self unknown to others	Self unknown to me; Self unknown to others

Fig. 3.1 Adaptation of the Johari Window

Personality measurement: need for achievement

Because of the complexities already hinted at, personality measurement is difficult, but it is not impossible. For example, unconscious aspects of personality may be revealed by projective tests. McClelland (see Chapter Four) used this technique in assessing need for achievement (nAch), a significant aspect of managerial motivation. McClelland asked his subjects to make up explanatory stories about pictures of everyday life, then scored their nAch by the number of achievement themes which emerged i.e. the need for achievement which they had projected into their stories. This use of the Thematic Apperception Test (TAT)[4] for managerial assessment has obvious drawbacks. It is time-consuming, imprecise and lacks relevance (face validity) for the clients.

More acceptable measures of managerial personality have used work-based materials. Fineman[5] approached nAch measurement in this way. Having criticised existing questionnaires for lack of managerial content and standardisation, Fineman developed a questionnaire using a range of managers in different work settings and on management courses in the UK. By focusing the questionnaire items on their preferred type of boss and preferred type of work conditions, he generated a well-constructed and practical test that 'makes sense' to the user.

Introversion, extraversion and neuroticism

Fineman's Work Preference Questionnaire examines just one personality feature, but many others attempt a comprehensive account. By studying large groups one can identify particular types of people, and then develop questionnaires which distinguish the individuals belonging to these major types. Eysenck[6] developed personality inventories indicating the extent to which individuals vary in the major dimensions of introversion-extraversion, neuroticism (emotionality), and tough-mindedness. These can be applied to the context of work, and indeed we tend to use the introvert–extravert dimension a lot in forming casual impressions and judgements about the people with whom we work. Using Eysenck's inventories, Jessup[7] found a correlation in RAF pilot trainees between the interaction of neuroticism (N) and introversion–extraversion (E), and their success in training. Highest failure rates were observed for those with high N and low E, and lowest for those with low N and low E. Other studies show that successful pilots in practice have relatively high E scores and low N scores,[8] leading to the conclusion that the personality type successful in training may differ somewhat from the type successful in action. This highlights the point that describing and measuring personality is feasible, but links between personality and job success are not straightforward.

Cattell's 16PF

For most selection purposes, a detailed personality profile is more useful than broad identification of personality type. The Cattell 16PF (Sixteen Personality Factor) questionnaire[9] is a well-established inventory of this sort. Derived from factor analysis of individual scores on a multitude of test items covering all aspects of personality, this inventory gives us a means of comparing ourselves with others on sixteen relatively independent personality factors. These factors are identified statistically by clustering those scores that suggest underlying dimensions, and are coded alphabetically (Cattell also invented names for them). They include factors which singly and in association give similar dimensions to those used by Eysenck, e.g. being shy, easily upset, anxious and tense on a 16PF profile can be seen to mirror a high EPI score on neuroticism.

The 16PF factors can be summarised by these descriptions:

A   Reserved : Outgoing
B   Less Intelligent : More Intelligent
C   Affected by Feelings : Emotionally Stable
E   Humble : Assertive
F   Sober : Happy-go-lucky
G   Expedient : Conscientious
H   Shy : Venturesome
I   Tough-minded : Tender-minded
L   Trusting : Suspicious
M   Practical : Imaginative
N   Straightforward : Shrewd
O   Self-assured : Apprehensive
Q1   Conservative : Experimenting
Q2   Group-dependent : Self-sufficient
Q3   Self-conflict : Self-control
Q4   Relaxed : Tense

It is relatively easy to match 16PF profiles to sets of occupations, e.g. artist, accountant, pilot, and use them as norms for occupational fit. But difficulties may arise in identifying the ideal personality profile associated with success in some occupations or jobs. A particular kind of occupation may tolerate quite a range of personalities, or may contain very varied job demands. In these cases, personality assessment is a weak predictor of success or failure, except for extreme personality types. The sophistication of some personality tests is often not matched by sophisticated job analysis, and their use may be based on traditional images of the ideal personality for the job, e.g. negotiators as aggressive, salesmen as highly extravert, social workers as mild and sensitive.

Work related inventories

One solution is to have very job-specific personality measures, such as the PASAT test for salesmen[10]. The other is to make general inventories more work-related, such as the OPQ (Occupational Personality Questionnaires)[11]. Based on studies in a large number of work organisations in the UK, this is a battery of tests which can be used to measure work-related personality either on a large number of relevant dimensions, or on selected key dimensions. The OPQ focuses on three major personality features: relationships with people, thinking style and feelings and emotions. Each of these is assessed under subheadings, giving thirty elements in the fullest version. As with the Eysenck and Cattell inventories, familiar dimensions emerge – anxious/relaxed, outgoing/reserved, tough/sensitive – but the material is framed in the language of work, and is designed for use in selection, training and counselling. It is directed at a range of jobs: managerial, supervisory, professional, technical, administrative and sales.

Comparison of individuals on standard personality measures is called the nomothetic approach. It demands that the tests are reliable – that repeated assessment of the same individual on the same or an equivalent test gives very much the same result – and that the tests are valid – are measuring the intended feature, which in turn is linked to the criterion of, for example, job success. Such tests are useless without norms derived from suitable standardisation samples: we should be able to compare one person's results on a test with the results typical of a relevant group.

Repertory grid

A contrasting approach to personality, the idiographic approach, emphasises the unique development of each individual. This approach is useful in counselling, training and developing the individual at work, and gives insights into more dynamic aspects of personality such as changing moods, expectations and morale. One technique of measurement in this field is the Repertory Grid, based upon the personal construct model of personality (Kelly 1955). This model stresses the unique experiences of each individual, which they have learned to interprete and evaluate with their own set of constructs or dimensions. Some constructs will be basic and clear cut, others more complex and hierarchical, and they are organised into a very individual way of seeing the world. As one acquires new experiences, one's personal construct system may change to incorporate them, just as one modifies a scientific theory in the light of new evidence[12].

The Repertory Grid technique of mapping the individual's personal constructs was first developed in clinical work. By asking the person to think of sets of significant individuals or events in his or her life, and to contrast and compare them, one can find the constructs which are being used. The technique extends to mapping employee motivations, and to monitoring the progress of individuals in management development programmes. It is even used in simple form to find the features which attract consumers to particular brands of product; qualitative market researchers use the repertory grid approach to get customers to say how various brands appear similar or different to them, and such information may be very useful in advertising. When used for personality exploration the procedure can be very complex, but has been speeded up dramatically by computer-based analysis. Although idiographic in conception, the repertory grid may be used nomothetically by turning the most common elements into a standard questionnaire.

Mental and physical abilities

Although some personality measurements include intelligence, individual differences in mental ability are usually assessed separately. Early psychologists speculated whether quickness of mind might be associated with quickness of hand or eye, but could not find a consistent relationship. Subsequent research resulted in much the same models as those used to describe personality. People's personalities can be classified into broad types, but in looking at the individual in detail we speak of a number of traits. Similarly, we can classify people broadly on the basis of intelligence, but more often refer to various mental abilities to describe the individual better. Just as we can draw up a personality profile, using various dimensions, we can draw up a profile of intellectual abilities. One method of measuring general intelligence is intelligence quotient (IQ). This is a comparison of one person's scores on a number of mental tasks with the norms, i.e. with the distribution of other people's scores, the average being 100. Technically, intelligence tests offer us a reliable way of comparing an individual's intellectual functioning and of predicting future intellectual performance. They can also cause problems and errors if used in isolation, since the score tells us nothing about motivation levels or prior lack of development opportunities. Thus a high scorer may not fulfil our hopes because of lack of drive, and a low scorer with, for example, poor language attainment, may surprise us later by 'catching up'. Many tests have been developed to measure and compare more specific mental abilities. These range from childhood tests used in education, where attainment and potential are monitored in relation to age, to high-level tests of adult aptitude for business professions. The primary mental abilities suggested by researchers such as Thurstone[13] are:

spatial
perceptual speed
numerical
verbal comprehension
verbal fluency
memory
reasoning

Tests can be used to measure aptitude for developing physical as well as mental skills, by simulating some of the physical aspects of the work. Among such work-sample tests are the Valpar Corporation assembly and sorting tests, which are related to an elaborate system of American job analysis codes, and which use test rigs. The Valpar Simulated Assembly test involves standing at a machine with a horizontal rotating disc into which the subject inserts pegs on to which coloured counters are to be placed in the correct order. The machine counts, disassembles and returns the components to the original trays for the subject to reassemble. This test simulates conveyor assembly jobs in which material moves towards and away from workers on the production line. Similar tests measure aptitude for bench assembly jobs; for work requiring physical manipulation and colour, letter and number sorting; the ability to use screwdrivers, pliers and spanners, the work often being blocked from vision; inspection and measurement tasks; and so on. The Purdue Pegboard[14] is an example of a simple but effective test of manual dexterity and aptitude for light assembly work, and can be carried in a briefcase. Work sample tests tend to be very good predictors of trainability and subsequent job success, and those in widespread use have clearly established norms for men and women in specific jobs.

Trainability testing

The Trainability Testing approach developed in the Industrial Training Research Unit[15] adopts a more advanced test strategy. Typical elements of the intended training are given in a short instruction session, and candidates are then tested in a practical way on the skills and knowledge gained. Standards (norms) will already have been set by studies of previous trainees, and so an early indication will be obtained of strongest and weakest candidates for training. Where standard tests are unavailable or unacceptable, employers can develop trainability tests for their own employees. An advantage of trainability testing is that the candidates demonstrate to themselves whether they have the necessary aptitude or not.

Technical test battery

One drawback of work sample tests is the time taken to administer them; pencil-and-paper tests are preferable for screening large groups. By focusing on the mental skills involved in particular jobs, one can design tests which retain psychological fidelity if not physical similarity to the job. The Technical Test Battery (TTB)[16] is a series of tests measuring primary mental abilities in a job-related way. The eight TTB tests are intended for those with a normal school background and who are aiming for scientific, craft or engineering occupations. Verbal, numerical, spatial, mechanical and diagrammatic reasoning and comprehension tests are used singly or in combination to find the candidates' suitability for developing the skills involved in engineering, printing, publishing, textiles, agriculture and so on. The tests are also relevant to the mental skills in jobs like computing and technical sales and, by offering two levels of testing, are suitable for a wide range of ability.

Graduate and managerial assessment

The Graduate and Managerial Assessment battery (GMA)[17] is a recently developed high level measure aimed at the top tenth of the population in terms of mental ability. It can be used for recruitment, selection and assessment of graduates, assessment of managerial and promotion potential e.g. for 'fast track' executives, and recruitment of high-potential school-leavers who have not opted for higher education. It taps three aspects of mental ability. The numerical test (GMA–N) tests problem-solving ability using number, and is particularly appropriate for those aiming for finance-related occupations. It is not a test of arithmetical competence, in contrast to the computational-intensive emphasis of some other numeracy tests; the electronic calculator has relieved the executive of mechanical arithmetic skills. Instead, the GMA–N tests problem-solving strategies. The verbal test (GMA–V) assesses verbal comprehension and thinking skills, in line with the need for managers to be able objectively to assess the content and logic of verbal reports, without being distracted by personal prejudices and beliefs. The abstract reasoning test (GMA–A) is aimed at the flexibility of thinking which characterises high-level occupations . . . the ability to switch between different levels of analysis, perceive relevant material and patterns in irrelevant detail, and use inductive reasoning. The candidate is presented in this test with the task of finding similarities and differences in sets of diagrams.

Although this task might appear to be far from the real work of an executive, the mental operations are similar.

Assessment centres

The work sample approach has been adopted for executive work as well as for jobs in which psychomotor (operative-type) skills predominate. In the assessment centre approach[18], both personality and aptitude measures are used, but traditional pencil-and-paper tests and interviews are supplemented by situational tests such as group discussions. In this way the assessor or observer can make first-hand judgements about the candidate's personality, motivation and social skills. This method has developed from the War Office Selection Boards used to improve the choice of officers with practical leadership potential. The assessment centre may simulate managerial tasks in various ways, for example directing a team, analysing a complex problem (perhaps presented on film), or working through the diverse problems presented in a simulated executive in tray. Initially used only for employee selection, assessment centres are now frequently used for the development and career planning of promising staff. Information gleaned by trained observers over a period of one to three days in the assessment centre is not purely for personnel management decisions. It is shared with the employee, who has volunteered to attend, and becomes not just an assessment episode but a learning opportunity and a motivating experience.

Vocational guidance

So far, this chapter has described how we can use questionnaires and tests to gain knowledge about the personality and work aptitudes of an individual. G. Kelly's personal construct theory, which gave rise to the repertory grid, was an attempt to give a balancing emphasis to the individual's own search for self-knowledge and better life decisions. The use of insights gained at assessment centres by individuals at work is mirrored by the use of tests and interviews for individual vocational guidance before a job choice is made, or when an individual has to change career. All these tests may not only be administered to, but also discussed with individuals in career guidance centres or rehabilitation centres. The Vocational Guidance Association is a voluntary, independent body carrying out such work in the UK. It offers a service to people of all ages who need guidance on work suitability, and also promotes vocational guidance through liaison with education authorities, employers, and others. Clients are given advice and interpretation of their results on various aptitude, personality and interest questionnaires selected as suitable for their age, experience and qualifications.

There are several major theories about career choice (see Chapter Seven). Some emphasise personality and self-image, others the importance of social factors such as parental influence and restricted opportunities. The simplest job interest inventories invite the respondent to compare and rank job titles in order of preference. Others ask the respondent to compare and rank the activities that occur within jobs. Both these approaches may wrongly assume that the respondent has a clear image of what various jobs entail. The opportunity to seek detailed information about job content, and then rank one's choice, has recently been provided by computerisation of occupational guidance material. This may be seen as rather impersonal, and the computer cannot react to the signs of doubt, interest and so on which the enquirer may display. A combination of the factual and interpersonal is provided by the Job Knowledge Index approach. The client completes a questionnaire on the occupation in which he or she is interested, revealing any misconceptions held about the job content, qualifications required, advancement prospects and so on. The counsellor can then correct any misconceptions and discuss particular motives and opportunities. All in all, vocational guidance tends not only to improve the individual's morale, but also to result in demonstrably better career fit[19]. In other words, it optimises 'satisfaction and satisfactoriness'[20].

In a hundred or so years of psychological testing (psychometrics) a great deal of technical and statistical expertise has been built up in the assessment of individuals. It is not possible to simply dismiss this work lightly because one does not 'believe in tests' since suitable tests, suitably applied, can substantially improve an employer's success in selecting, training and developing staff, and so save money. Schmidt and Hunter[21] gave these examples of actual and potential gains from aptitude tests for selection:

$18 million p.a. Philadelphia Police Department
$37 million p.a. for programmers in US Civil Service
$16 billion p.a. total US Civil Service

However, caution has to be exercised in the choice of selection methods. Tests should be scientifically sound, administratively convenient and organisationally acceptable[22], but, sadly, what is convenient and even acceptable may not be scientifically sound. Some would place handwriting analysis in this category, although the difficulty is partly one of over-interpretation. It is plausible, for instance, to judge that speed of writing indicates speed of thought. To judge moral character on the basis of shape of handwriting, as some enthusiasts claim to be able to do, seems highly risky and even indefensible.

Biodata

The most commonsense source of valid data for selection decision comes from the personal history of the job applicant as shown on application forms and references. By concentrating on the factual evidence of educational attainment, work experience, leisure activities and career achievements, and correlating them with similar data from personnel files, strong predictions can be made[23] In the US the method has been highly developed, so that biodata information can be scored against detailed criteria, and application forms have been extended by some employers to become, in effect, personality questionnaires, but there is unease about such a development in the UK. An informal way of gathering biodata at interview has been in use for many decades in the UK in the form of the Seven Point Plan (described in Chapter Five), but the new biodata approach is far more detailed, and developed to the level of aptitude testing. Despite careful selection, training and development, employees may produce disappointing results if put into an ineffective work system. We will now turn our attention to the design of the work system itself, or ergonomics.

B: Designing work for people

When work systems fail, the weaknesses of the human operator are often blamed, in terms of poor motivation, lack of training or lack of ability. Often, however, these failures could have been anticipated if attention had been paid at the system design stage to the limited capacities of the human operator. Ergonomic analysis operates at different levels. The simplest is that of 'man as machine'. Physically, the operator is a system of levers, pivots and pulleys, capable of limited energy output. At the next level, a person is an information-processing machine with optimal levels of arousal, limited information stores and processing capacities, and limited programmability (trainability). At a third and more complex level, the operator is self-directed, selective, and affected by states of satisfaction or dissatisfaction in the work done. At a fourth level of complexity the operator interacts with other individuals, and communications, conflict and collaboration are crucial social dimensions of the work system. Physical measurements suffice at the first level, but at higher levels of ergonomic analysis, sophisticated behavioural measures are needed to record attitudes and preferences, and analyse mental processes such as risk-taking, decision-making and skill development. Unfortunately, ergonomic aspects at all levels are often considered only when things have gone wrong.

Physical effort

The work we do should be within our physical capacity. Equipment should be designed to suit the physical dimensions of the user population, and in practice all but those at the extremes are catered for (i.e. to the 95th percentile). Nowadays the range has had to be extended where equal opportunity for male and female operatives has been introduced. Work should also be within the typical operative's range of speed, strength and accuracy. Fatigue has been closely studied since absenteeism and work-reject rates of munitions workers during the First World War led to the founding of the Industrial Fatigue Research Board. Paradoxically, shorter working hours generated more productivity, a lesson that was relearned in aircraft production in the Second World War. Hours of work are looked at in detail later in this chapter.

Physical effort can be measured physiologically by muscle effort, heart rate, calorie consumption and even standard sweat rate. In job evaluation, it is often judged by general agreement on the amount of effort required. Typically, pay will be allocated in these proportions: skill 36%, responsibility 25%, mental effort 15%, physical effort 15% and working conditions 9%. Fleishman[24] reports experiments requiring subjects to estimate the physical effort involved in a range of work and leisure activities (both as participants and non-participants), where accurate physiological measures of the effort involved were available. The results showed that people, particularly specialists such as personnel officers, can judge physical effort with a high level of accuracy and reliability.

Great physical effort or stamina is not demanded of most British workers, but such demands may occur through thoughtlessness. Tasks involving lifting, climbing, sustained physical effort or fine adjustment skills may be well within the capacity of young, healthy workers, but test older or infirm workers to the limit. Some tasks can be done as well, if not better, by a seated operator, but by custom are done standing. This task can then be thought to be beyond the ability of a handicapped person.

New technology: old problems

The problems of VDU operators demonstrate how we forget the physical demands of high-technology equipment. Haider[25] investigated an American police command-control centre equipped with TV displays, by getting the users (dispatchers/reporters), after practice, to carry out simulated periods of work, with a representative selection of police incidents to supervise. The physiological effects of using various elements – keyboards, lightpen, touch screen – were monitored by measuring activity times, eye movements (electro-oculogram), activity of arm and trunk muscles (electromyogram), and heart rate (electrocardiogram). The conclusion was that the workstations involved intolerable physical strains, and pointed to the need for anthropometric and physiological work system design. An analysis of further details of visual information retrieval showed that human abilities had not been considered in the design process.

In this case, only physiological measures were made. Springer[26], comparing VDU workstations, gathered data not only on performance rates, but also on users' reactions and attitudes. The workstations generating better performance and satisfaction were those offering comfort and opportunities for adjusting the seating, and the height, angle and distance of the VDU. One example of ergonomic research using a wide range of measures is Peacock's investigation of American police officers' reactions to changing from an eight-hour, twelve-day work cycle to a twelve-hour eight-day cycle. The researchers used urine analysis (catecholamine excretion), body temperature and sleep patterns, choice reaction-time tests, flicker-fusion level (the tired worker perceives colour bands or flickering light fusing into a steady state more readily than when not tired), memory and alertness tests, and attitudes to the change. It is unusual to use such a wide range of measures, because they are so intrusive and time-consuming.

The electronic office

The development of the electronic office is an example of very rapid and fundamental technological change in which both physiological and psychological aspects have been neglected. Some advertising suggests that equipment such as word processors can be installed overnight, will reduce effort and costs, and make work more enjoyable. The opposite sometimes occurs. Increased keyboard operation has coincided with an increase in complaints of painful wrist conditions (tenosynovitis and carpal tunnel syndrome), repetitive strain injuries which typically occur where key-depressions of more than ten thousand per hour are common. Other widespread complaints associated with VDU (visual display unit) operation are backache, eyestrain and headaches, and fears as to whether the work will lead to cancer, epilepsy, cataracts and birth defects[28].

Available evidence shows that the probability of major health risk is negligible or non-existent. Practical measures to alleviate the discomforts and strains are straightforward, and some are the responsibility of equipment designers. Eyestrain and headaches can be due to reflection or glare from screens or flicker, illegibility and poor contrast of text characters. Operators who already have eyesight defects are, of course, more prone to these problems. Other aches and pains may be due to unsuitable seating, posture and work layout, and duration of work (since even sedentary work involves tiring static muscular effort). Physical solutions are recommended by various bodies such as the National Computing Centre, the Heath and Safety Executive and the TUC[29], and include eyesight checks, adjustment facilities for equipment and work patterns with limits on work duration (e.g. a maximum of four hours VDU work in any one day, with a maximum of forty minutes continuous screen work in any hour). Equipment designers have guidelines on text aspects: character size, spacing, letter confusability, luminance levels, contrast; keyboard dimensions; key shapes, spacings, travel, layout and error signals. Most complaints have come from VDU operators doing the most routine data-capture work.

Mental effort

Mental effort is difficult to measure as it is complicated by the mental abilities and skill level of the individual, as well as the intrinsic interest of the work itself. People in many jobs build up a mystique about the level of mental effort involved, but closer analysis can sometimes bring their tasks within the reach of the inexperienced worker. Studies of inspection tasks[30] show that by giving the newcomer a set of examples of graded items against which to inspect (requiring relative rather than absolute judgements) he or she can perform as well as the experienced inspector making absolute judgements.

The information-processing model of human ability has been of great assistance in ergonomics, supplemented by basic psychological research on how memory works (information encoding, storage and retrieval), on how sensory information is perceived and processed, and on the mental processes of decision-making and skill development. A classic from this early body of work is Miller's article 'The magical number seven, plus or minus two: some limits on our capacity for processing information'[31]. Such work has led ultimately to better design of instrumentation, warning systems and so on, in the search for error-free work systems. This search is problem-driven, particularly in the armed forces, where early concerns with pilot error have been updated to concerns with operator error in electronic surveillance and weapons guidance systems. During the Second World War, advances in the technology of armaments dramatically highlighted the limited cognitive abilities of the human operator. Speed of reaction times and the complex decision-making demanded by high-speed aircraft created heavy demands on pilots, leading to modification of instrumentation to suit the human operator. The sustained vigilance required of radar operators also showed the limitations of the human operator on low-complexity tasks. Signals may be missed, non-existent signals perceived and the significance of signals may be misinterpreted. At that time, the emphasis began to change from motor skills to information systems design to help the human operator. Sometimes operators fail to register vital warnings. A few years ago a helicoper crashed into the sea in fog near the Scilly Isles, causing loss of life. It had simply flown too low, despite a warning light indicating loss of altitude. It is thought that the crew were staring ahead into the fog, looking for coastal landmarks, and failed to see the warning light below their line of vision on the instrument panel. Auditory altimeter warnings are now fitted, but auditory warnings may also have unintended effects.

Some aircraft crashes are said to have been due to pilots 'freezing' when loud warning sirens sounded, and pilots have sometimes concentrated on eliminating the warning signals rather than tackling the emergency. The Applied Psychology Unit at Cambridge[32] researched this problem, and identified the ideal ratio of warning signal loudness to background noise to alert without panic; the ideal onset level of signal to avoid 'startle' response; the ideal use of different pitch and rhythm of signals to allow a number to be effective at the same time. Instead of sounding continuously, the redesigned signals are repeated at intervals with increasing urgency if unattended. These are two examples of collaboration between the Civil Aviation Authority and behavioural science researchers which has led to improved design.

In the USA, in 1976, Seminara reported that 'nuclear power plants were designed with little or no formal attention to human factors engineering'. Despite dramatic disasters like Three Mile Island (1979) and Chernobyl (1986), ergonomic redesign or 'retrofit' may be resisted 'once metal has been bent', i.e. when the manufacture stage has been passed. In 1983, four years after the Three Mile Island occurrence, Seminara found problems of design in instrumentation of power station control rooms. Operators had had to stick up motley collections of handwritten notes and labels to make sense of poorly designed display and control systems. Functional elements of displays were identical in size, shape and colour, and distributed in sterile, symmetrical patterns, making it difficult to distinguish separate elements or related subsystems[33]. Cordes[34] (1983) reports that there were almost no ergonomics specialists on the staff of the Nuclear Regulatory Commission, the firms designing and building nuclear plants, or the organizations running them, at the time of the Three Mile Island accident. Since then about thirty psychologists have been recruited by the NRC, and a series of new regulations and guidelines issued on aspects such as control room design, operator training and emergency operating procedures.

Retrofits are often compromises and may involve retraining problems, but Seminara points to the major improvements that can be achieved by 'cosmetic' means, for example by adding taped borders to define panel subsystems and using colour codes, particularly useful if based on a psychological analysis of tasks. Of course, early ergonomists had clearly spelled out the guidelines for good instrumentation design, but problems often lie in the way a whole system operates. The difficulties of ensuring organisational efficiency are examined in later chapters.

High tech and superstition

Much research into human ability in high-technology focuses on mental skills and strategies. A researcher monitoring the installation of American police computers tells a story of an installation engineer called to mend a 'terminal that won't work' who found the terminal riddled with bullets from the gun of a frustrated user. Designers have achieved a great deal of success in making equipment 'user friendly' but attitudinal problems remain. Norman[35] suggests that the mental models we form of the machines we use may be incomplete, inadequate, confused and unscientific, i.e. superstitious. From making studies of people using computers, calculators, digital watches and video equipment and getting them to 'think aloud', Norman concludes that we rely heavily on 'seems to work but I don't know why' behaviours, regardless of machine capability.

'Clear' and 'Enter' buttons are pressed more frequently than necessary ('I feel safer', 'It doesn't hurt', 'Just to be sure', 'I've got used to doing it that way'), partial results are written down when they could be stored in machine memory, separate calculations are done laboriously when constants could be used, and so on. The difficulty is partly an instructional one. The designers' mental model is different from the manufacturer's, which is different from that of the trainer or that explained in the instructional booklet (or, worse still, by another user!). Early errors make us cautious, and anxieties about one machine become generalised to all machines, even to the extent of attributing malicious personalities to machines! Better preparation for user limitations at the design and instruction stage is the answer.

The problem of stress

The physical nature of fatigue is well understood in medical terms, but its psychological features are less easy to measure. In the 1920s[36], Wyatt noticed that the production rate of factory workers declined with reports of fatigue as the morning shift progressed, but then showed a marked upturn as breaktime approached. In the Cambridge cockpit studies[37], pilots under extreme conditions of fatigue and irritation continued functioning but with increased psychological cost.

Errors increased as peripheral signals were missed, but the human operator can mask physical fatigue by putting in more effort. In the Falklands war, RAF aircrews often exceeded the accepted levels of continuous flying hours, with the aid of drugs to maintain alertness and drugs to induce sleep[38]. Unfortunately, the ability of the human operator to adapt to bad conditions and poor equipment at work has reduced the effort that otherwise would have to be put into creating better work systems.

A major aim of ergonomics is to make work tolerable[39]. We should design work so that the person can carry it out for the duration of a career without damage to health or functions. Social concern and health and safety legislation has prompted research into errors and accidents at work. At the medical level, occupational diseases such as boilermaker's deafness (noise-induced hearing loss), miner's lung (pneumoconiosis), white finger disease (vibration-induced circulatory disease) and many other work-related diseases and injuries are well-chronicled.

The mental well-being of employees is harder to define and protect. Noise becomes irritating before it becomes deafening; partial deafness may be accompanied by neuroses; bad working conditions may reduce morale and adversely affect health over a long period. The effects of more subtle psychological pressures at work are often summed up as 'work stress'. Stress can arise from boredom as well as from over-demanding work. Strictly speaking, stress refers to the burden placed upon the individual, and strain rises within the individual when unable fully to meet the stress imposed. The effects of stress are partly physiological, such as fatigue, tremor, sweating, palpitations, headaches and stomach upsets. The psychological effects include insomnia, anxiety, irritation and errors, with compensatory behaviour such as heavier drinking, smoking and self-blame.

Stress is linked to diseases such as ulcers and coronary heart disease, and to increased mortality. Friedman and Rosenman[40] studied a group of executives whose personalities could be classified into Type A and Type B, the As being energetic, competitive, restless and impatient, and the Bs being more relaxed and less driven to achieve. The As showed far higher mortality rates than the Bs for their age and social class. Separately rated by psychiatrists and medical people, the forty- to fifty-year-old A types showed nearly seven times the incidence of coronary heart disease and related symptoms over several years of research. This effect is not restricted to business occupations; it has been reported even in religious communities.

The factors contributing to work stress include the temperament and constitution of the individual. Contributury work features include bad working conditions, boredom, pressure of deadlines, prolonged working hours, poor communications, uncertainty and change, unsympathetic bosses, difficult subordinates, competition and social isolation (Cooper)[41]. Caplan (1975) reported that Type A personalities are less likely to want or be able to modify their health-threatening behaviours by giving up smoking, reducing their workload, and so on. This will limit the effectiveness of self-help programmes, but Fletcher (1981) emphasised the beneficial role of social supports in the work setting[42]. Counselling is covered in Chapter Five.

Stress strikes not only executives and businessmen at the top of the organisational ladder, but seems to be even more prevalent at lower levels. Fletcher has drawn attention to national mortality rates from stress-related disease in lower income groups under the title 'the myth of executive stress', and has also highlighted intriguing correlations in these macabre statistics suggesting transmitted risk to spouses. Lest one imagine that the way to avoid stress is to be unemployed, Warr (1984) and other researchers report the potentially psychologically damaging effects of redundancy and unemployment. Job loss has been likened to bereavement, with the same stages of shock, shattered self-image and readjustment to lowered expectations to be gone through. Paradoxically, lowered self-image and expectations resulting from unemployment means lower rather than higher motivation to retrain, move home and so on[44].

Social acceptability of work conditions: hours of work

Ultimately, work design is governed by acceptibility. This is not the same as tolerability. Acceptability of work conditions emerges from social standards, and in Britain conditions of work have improved substantially over the past century. Advance in education and in employment legislation have helped. The behavioural sciences can help in an educational sense. An example of changing acceptability is length and pattern of working hours.

For a mixture of cultural, climatic and physiological reasons, the eight-hour working day and five-day working week is widespread in Britain. The working week has shortened in recent decades, particularly in lower-paid jobs as differentials have narrowed. The average basic weekly hours for manual workers covered by national agreements and wages councils fell to 39.2 in 1983 (Employment Gazette April 1984) and most office workers have a working week of 35 to 37.5 hours. Some occupations such as nursing, police work and food manufacture have always demanded night-work and shiftwork, but new technologies demanding continuous operation spread the practice of shiftwork in the postwar years. Approximately one-fifth of the British workforce are now reckoned to be used to patterns of work other than normal daywork.

There are many types of shiftwork arrangement, the most common

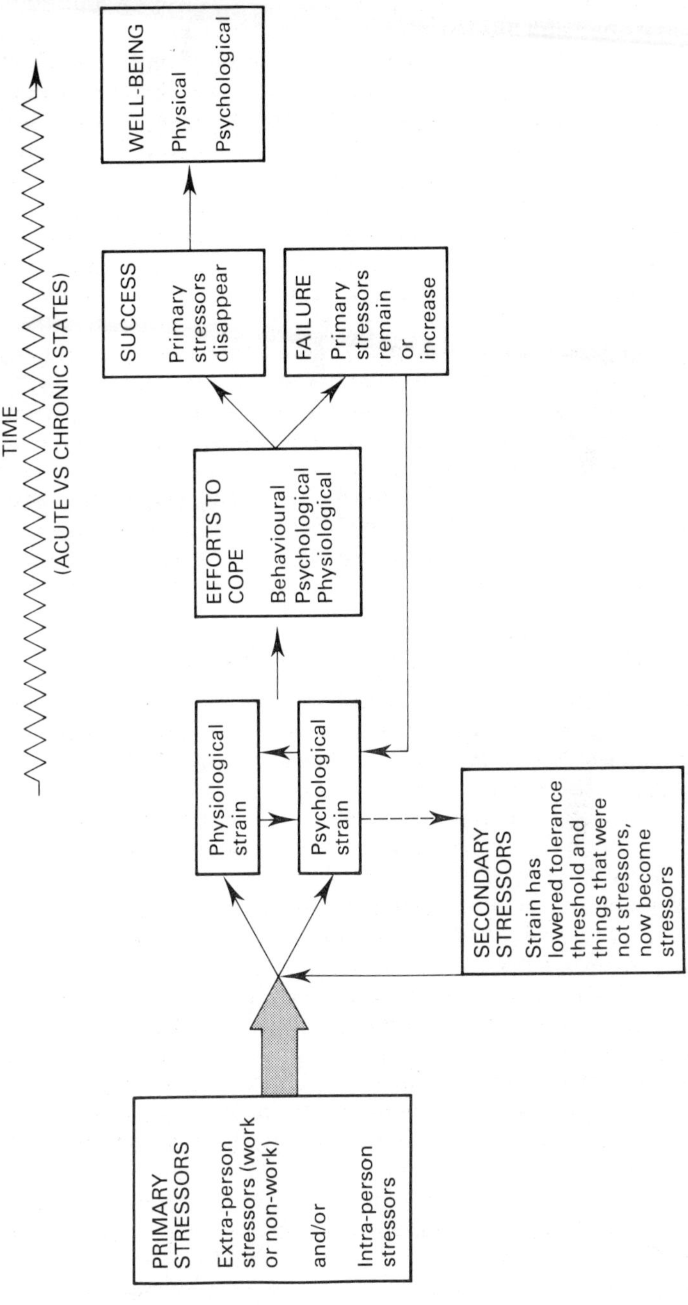

Fig. 3.2 A theoretical framework of stress and strain (courtesy of Fletcher, B. C. and Payne, R. S. 1980)[42]

being two-shift (early morning to early afternoon, and early afternoon to late evening) and three-shift (late evening to early morning in addition). Shifts may be continuous or discontinuous (no work at weekends), and workers may be on permanent shifts e.g. permanent nightworkers, or on alternating or rotating shifts.

Behavioural science research points to better ways of allocating and organising shiftwork. Physiologically, shiftwork disturbs the worker's circadian rhythm (the normal cycle of sleep and wakefulness in the twenty-four-hour cycle). The circadian rhythm adapts to change but a complete phase shift may take several days. In the meantime the worker tends to feel below par and to operate below par, like a traveller suffering from jet-lag. The most favourable shiftwork pattern will therefore be either permanent or one which alternates or rotates infrequently. Performance at work seems to be affected most adversely by shiftwork change when the work is repetitive and arduous, and where the incentives are low. Tendency to errors and accidents is noticeable at the low point of normal circadian rhythm (typically in the early morning hours when the body temperature cycle is at its lowest point).

The problems of shiftwork

Negative reports on shiftwork satisfaction and efficiency began to emerge in the 1950s. Mott reported adverse social, psychological and physical effects from a US study, including sleep-related problems, fatigue, poor appetite and gastric upsets. Some difficulties had external causes, for example disrupted sleep because of daytime noises at home, gastric upsets caused by mealtime changes or poor nightwork food facilities.[45] However, some individuals seem to have trouble adjusting to altered sleep patterns, and 'morning types' may adjust badly to late shifts (Breithaupt 1978)[46]. In more recent work in the US, Smith & Colligan still found adverse effects, particularly amongst shiftworkers on rotating and night shifts[47].

Akerstedt (1981) looked at duration and quality of sleep for workers on three-shift, two-shift and daywork[48]. Afternoon shiftworkers slept best, with morning shift next, and night shift worst. Afternoon shiftworkers had least complaints, dayworkers were next, morning shift next and night shiftworkers had most complaints. It seemed that increased age and shiftwork experience meant reduced duration and quality of sleep, although one might have expected the opposite. This effect was more pronounced for night shiftworkers. This investigation found no particular links between sleep sufficiency, and personality or marital, family or housing conditions.

The health aspect was pursued by Frese (1984) in a West German study of psychological and psychosomatic complaints of former shiftworkers. Those who had left shiftwork because of health complaints were less skilled, had stayed longer in shiftwork, were less often unemployed, and had been told to leave by their doctors. Frese hypothesised that shiftwork is potentially harmful for particular people; a vulnerability-stress theory. It could be that these less-skilled low-turnover employees had stayed too long in shiftwork, mainly for financial reasons. They appeared to have suffered cumulative chronic stress, and the study indicated that the effects persist[49].

Shiftwork absenteeism and social needs

Nicholson (1978) looked at the relationship between absenteeism and type of shift, time during shift cycle, and days of the week on which absences occurred. Weekend absences were higher, and Thurday (payday) absences lower. Absences were higher in the day shift and lower in the afternoon (swing) shift; and highest in the last two days of the cycle. The causes could be social, since the most socially advantageous times were taken off, with rest days 'infecting' the nearest shift days[50]. Canadian studies by Frost (1979) revealed that shiftworkers with a higher compatibility between work hours and non-work (leisure) hours scored higher on work need fulfilment and overall mental health, than shiftworkers with a low compatibility of work and leisure hours[51].

Attractions of shiftwork

On the positive side, Taylor (1967) reported lower sickness amongst shiftworkers, and generally both workers and managers seem to be in favour of shiftwork[52]. In the British steel industry, Wedderburn (1975) found that a substantial number of employees were in favour of shiftwork, with 18% of the sample strongly in favour, 29% in favour, 23% against and 8% strongly against[53]. The least-liked pattern was a three-shift rapidly rotating system. Particularly on a nightshift, the pay is usually greater for less hours, there is less supervision, more security, and often a sense of group identity and solidarity or even elitism[54]. In fact, the cohesion of nightshift groups can sometimes be seen as a threat by management. Attempts to identify a particular nightshift personality-type have not produced significant results, but some nightshifts attract predominantly older and more senior workers, and in some areas may be made up completely of ethnic minorities.

Flexible working hours

Flexible working hours (flexitime) is an innovation which overcomes some of the problems of traditional shiftwork and daywork. The organisation obtains more hours of productive work and the individual can choose the hours of work that suit him or her best, provided that the stipulated total hours are worked. Typically there is a prescribed core-time when all must work, and then there are varying amounts of freedom for the individual to arrange the remaining hours in a way which best suits his or her lifestyle. Ronen (1981) suggested that this is a fundamental move toward worker autonomy, which should result in higher motivation and job satisfaction[55]. Subsequent research does not demonstrate major changes in these aspects, but on balance employees have been happier, and employers have made major savings as a result.

Conclusion

In this chapter we have examined the theoretical and practical ways in which the manager may survey the individual differences of employees and prospective employees, their personalities, aptitudes, skills and interests, and how behavioural science has brought at least some methodical assistance to aid the manager in this complex task. In Chapter Five we will look at the range of interpersonal skills that a manager can develop for day-to-day communication and counselling, interviewing and bargaining.

We have also looked at some of the shortcomings in how work is designed. Much remains to be done, and every manager can improve matters to some extent by checking how work layout, timetabling and equipment suit both task and worker. Team discussions can be useful in identifying inefficiencies and unnecessary stress, and the Quality Circle method is described in Chapter Ten. Equipment design is, of course, beyond the manager's control but he can still influence this at the stage of purchase. Meister (1982) wrote that engineering designers and managers are relatively indifferent to behavioural problems and inclined to ignore human engineering inputs. He also suggested that ergonomists should do more to develop fully adequate techniques for assessing behavioural questions during system development, a plea for more and better behavioural science[56].

References

1   Furnham, A. and Schaffer, R., 'Person-environment fit, job-satisfaction and mental health', *Journal of Occupational Psychology,* **57**, no. 4, 1984, pp. 295–308.
2   Selecting managers: how British industry recruits, *IPM Information Report No. 34,* Technical Press.
3   Luft, J. and Ingham, H., 'The Johari Window: a graphic model for

interpersonal relations', Univ. Calif. Western Training Lab., 1955.

4 Murray, H. A. (1938) 'Thematic apperception test (TAT)', see Zubin, J. *et al., An Experimental Approach to Projective Techniques,* John Wiley & Sons, 1966.
Grant, D. L. *et al.,* 'Contributions of projective techniques to assessment of managerial potential', *Journal of Applied Psychology,* **51**, 1967, pp. 226–232.

5 Fineman, S., 'The work preference questionnaire: a measure of managerial nAch', *Journal of Occupational Psychology,* **48**, 1975, pp. 11–32; and 'The achievement motive construct and its measurement', *British Journal of Psychology,* **68**, 1977, pp. 1–22.

6 Eysenck, H. J. and Eysenck, S. B., *The Eysenck Personality Questionnaire,* University of London Press, 1975.

7 Jessup, G. and Jessup, H., 'Validity of the EPI in pilot selection', *Occupational Psychology,* **45**, no. 2, 1971, pp. 111–123.

8 Bartram, D. and Dale, H. C. A., 'The EPI as a selection test for military pilots', *Journal of Occupational Psychology,* **55**, no. 4, 1982, pp. 287–96.

9 Cattell, R. B., Eber, H. W. and Tatsuoka, M. M., *Handbook for the Sixteen Personality Factor Questionnaire (16PF),* NFER Publishing, 1970.

10 Poppleton, S., Allen, E. and Garland, D., *The Poppleton Allen Sales Aptitude Test Technical Manual,* High Wycombe: The Test Agency, 1984.
Poppleton, S. and Lubbock, 'Marketing life assurance: causes of success and failure in life assurance salesmen', *European Journal of Marketing,* **11**, no. 6, 1977, pp. 418–31.

11 Saville and Holdsworth Ltd, *Manual of the Occupational Personality Questionnaire (OPQ),* Windsor House, Esher Green, Surrey, 1984.

12 Bannister, D. and Mair, J. M. M., *The Evaluation of Personal Constructs,* Academic Press, 1968.

13 Thurstone, L. L., *Primary Mental Abilities,* Psychometric Laboratory, University of Chicago, Report No. 50, 1948.

14 Purdue Pegboard, Purdue Research Foundation, Science Research Associates, Chicago, Illinois.

15 Downs, S., *Testing Trainability,* NFER-Nelson, 1984; Warren, A. and Downs, S., *SL2,* Industrial Training Research Unit, Cambridge, 1977.

16 See Saville and Holdsworth Ltd, *op. cit.*

17 GMA (Graduate and Managerial Assessment): Blinkhorn, S. F. (1985) Psychometric Research Unit, Hatfield Polytechnic: NFER-NELSON.

18 Bray, D. W., Campbell, R. J. and Grant, D. C., *Formative Years in Business: a long-term AT&T study of managerial lives,* John Wiley & Sons, 1974.

19 Super, D. E. and Bohn, M. J., *Occupational Psychology,* Tavistock, 1971; and Watts, A. G., Super, D. E. and Kidd, J. M., (1981) *Career Development in Britain,* CRAC, Hobsons Press, 1981.

20 Rodger, A., 'Personnel selection and vocational guidance', in Welford *et al.* (eds.) *Society: Psychological Problems and Methods of Study,* Routledge & Kegan Paul, 1968.

21 Schmidt, F. L. and Hunter, J. E., 'Employment testing: old theories and new research findings', *American Psychologist,* **36**, no. 10, 1981, pp. 1128–37, 'The economic impact of job selection methods on size,

productivity and payroll costs of the federal work force: an empirically based demonstration', Personnel Psychology, **39**, no. 1, 1986, pp. 1–30; and Boyle, S., 'It pays to be selective', *Guidance and Assessment Review*, November, 1984, pp. 2–3.

22   Rodger, A., *op. cit.*

23   Drakeley, R. J., 'The ABC of biodata', *Guidance & Assessment Review*, 1985.

24   Fleishman *et al.*, 'Measurement of effort', Ergonomics, **27**, no. 9, 1984, pp. 947–54, Hogan, J. C. and Fleishman, E. A., 'An index of the physical effort required in human task performance', *Journal of Applied Psychology*, **64**, no. 2, 1979, pp. 197–204; and Hogan, Fleishman *et al.*, (1980) 'Reliability and validity of methods of evaluating physical effort', *Journal of Applied Psychology,* **65**, no. 6, 1980, pp. 672–9.

25   Haider *et al.*, (1982) 'Ergonomic investigation of police command-control centre equipped with TV displays', *Applied Ergonomics,* **13**, no. 3, 1982, pp. 163–70.

26   Springer, T. J., 'VDT workstations: a comparative evaluation of alternatives', *Applied Ergonomics,* **13**, no. 3, 1982, pp. 211–12.

27   Peacock *et al.*, 'Police officers' responses to eight and twelve hour shift schedules', *Ergonomics,* **26**, no. 5, 1983, pp. 479–93.

28   'VDUs and health hazards', Institute of Personnel Management Digest, November 1984.

29   Damodaran L., Simpson A. and Wilson, P., Designing systems for people. NCC/Loughborough, 1980.
      'Visual display units', Health and Safety Executive, 1983 and 'Health and Safety Bulletin no. 2', Trades Union Congress, 1984.

30   Landy, F. J. and Trumbo, D. A., *Psychology of Work Behaviour,* The Dorsey Press, 1980.

31   Miller, G. A., 'The magical number seven, plus or minus two: some limits on our capacity for processing information', *Psychological Review,* **63**, 1956, pp. 81–97.

32   Patterson, R. D., 'Auditory Warning Systems for High-Work-Load Environments', in Brown, I. D. *et al.* (eds.), *Ergonomics International 85,* Taylor & Francis (1985).

33   Seminara, J. L. and Smith, D. L., (1983) 'Remedial human factors engineering', *Applied Ergonomics,* **14**, no. 4, 1983, pp. 253–64.

34   Cordes, C., 'Human Factors and Nuclear Safety: Grudging Respect for a Growing Field', *American Psychological Association Monitor,* **14**, no. 5, 1983.

35   Norman, D. A., in Gentner, D., Stevens, A. (eds.), *Mental Models,* L. Erlbaum Associates. 1982.

36   Wyatt, S. *et al.*, 'The effects of monotony in work', *Industrial Fatigue Research Board Report,* No. 56, 1929.

37   Bartlett, F. C. (1943) in Legge, D., *Skills: Selected Readings,* Penguin Modern Psychology Series, 1970; and Dearnaley, E. J. and Warr, P. B. (eds.), *Aircrew Stress in Wartime Operations,* Academic Press, 1979.

38   Nicholson, A. N., 'Long periods of work and disturbed sleep', *Ergonomics,* **27**, no. 6, 1984, pp. 629–30.

39   Rohmert, W. in Sell, R. G. and Shipley, P. (eds.), (1979) *Satisfactions in Work Design: ergonomics and other approaches,* Taylor & Francis, 1979.

40 Rosenman, R. H., Friedman, M. and Strauss, R., 'Coronary heart disease in the Western collaborative group study', *Journal of the American Medical Association,* **195**, 1966, pp. 86–92. Quinlan (1969) re stress/CHD in monasteries, quoted in Cooper, C. L. and Payne, R. L. (eds.), *Stress at Work,* Wiley, 1978.

41 Cooper, C. L. in Warr, P. (ed.), *Psychology at Work,* Penguin, 1978.

42 Fletcher, B. C. and Payne, R. L., 'Stress at work: a review and theoretical framework', *Personnel Review,* **9**, nos. 1 and 2, 1980.

43 Fletcher, Ben, 'Marital Relationships as a Cause of Death: an Analysis of Occupational Mortality and the Hidden Consequences of Marriage – Some UK Data', *Human Relations,* **36**, no. 2, pp. 123–34, 1983.

44 Warr, P. B., 'Work, jobs and unemployment', *Bulletin of the British Psychological Society,* **36**, 1983.

45 Mott, P. E., Mann, F. C., McLaughlin, Q. and Warwick, D. P., *'Shift Work,* Ann Arbor, University of Michigan Press, 1965.

46 Breithaupt, H. *et al.,* 'Tolerance to shift of sleep, as related to the individual's circadian phase position', *Ergonomics,* **21**, no. 10, 1978, pp. 767–74.

47 Smith, M. J. and Colligan, M. J., 'Health and safety consequences of shift work in the food processing industry', *Ergonomics,* **25**, no. 2, 1982, pp. 133–44.

48 Akerstedt, T. and Torsvall, L., 'Shift-dependent wellbeing and individual differences', *Ergonomics,* **24**, no. 4, 1981, pp. 265–73.

49 Frese, M. and Okonek, K., 'Reasons to leave shiftwork and psychological and psychosomatic complaints of former shiftworkers', *Journal of Applied Psychology,* **69**, no. 3, 1984, pp. 509–514.

50 Nicholson, N., Jackson, P. and Howes, G., 'Shiftwork and absence', *Journal of Occupational Psychology,* **51**, no. 2, 1978, pp. 127–37.

51 Frost and Jamal, (1979) 'Shiftwork, attitudes and reported behaviour: associations with . . . work and leisure', *Journal of Applied Psychology,* **64**, no. 1, 1979, pp. 77–81.

52 Taylor, 'Shift and day work', *British Journal of Industrial Medicine,* **24**, 1967, pp. 93–102.

53 Wedderburn, *Ergonomics,* **21**, no. 10, 1978, p. 827.

54 De la Mare, G. and Walker, J., 'Factors influencing choice of shift rotation', *Occupational Psychology,* **42**, no. 1, 1968, pp. 1–21.

55 Ronen, S., *Flexible Working Hours: an innovation in the quality of working life,* McGraw Hill, 1981.

56 Meister, D., 'The role of human factors in system development', *Applied Ergonomics,* **13**, no. 2, 1982, pp. 219–23 and no. 3, pp. 119–24.

4

Motivation at work

In the previous two chapters we have looked at some of the aspects of individuals that both link them to the work situation and differentiate them from each other. The nature of individual behaviour has fascinated scholars for centuries, and we still see that fascination in the ideas and theories of contemporary behavioural scientists. One major focus of this fascination is motivation. It is this subject to which we now turn our attention.

But why bother? Surely we all know what motivates people? It is money, or power, or self-satisfaction, or . . .! The list can become a pretty long one. Try asking some of your colleagues what motivates people – they will produce more than a handful of ideas. Then ask them what motivates manual workers, or unemployed clerks, or women, as compared with what motivates themselves. You will find some surprising differences – and some surprising similarities.

So yes, we all know what motivates people – anything or everything. Clearly, this is not very helpful to managers, or anyone else, puzzling over the question, 'how can I improve the performance of the people in my team?', or to teachers who are wondering, 'why is Jane so bright, yet doesn't seem to want to do any homework?', or the worried parent asking, 'what can I do to keep my son from getting into trouble with the local police through the gang he's joined?' These are all questions about motivation, in one sense or another. They are all asking the basic question, 'why do people behave in particular ways?'

Motivation at work is an important area of concern for managers and for all those involved with seeking to improve the productive involvement of people in organisations. As one employee commented in an interview with a researcher, 'My manager seems to think that all I care about is money. Sure, money is important, but I wish he'd realise that's not the only reason I, or many of my colleagues, come to work. If only he could see the way I work at home, with no financial incentive at all. He'd then soon realise what makes me tick[1].' This worker was quite clearly saying that motivation at work is not much different from motivation at home, although certain factors (for example the presence or absence of financial incentives) may differ. While the work situation is our area of concern in this book, we must not forget that work and non-work situations are not always completely dissimilar or unrelated.

The meaning of motivation

We have thus far assumed a common understanding of the term 'motivation'. This is not necessarily the case. Often, the reason people have different views as to what 'makes people tick' is that they attach different meanings to the phrase. Before going further into any study of motivation we need to establish a common definition or meaning of the term.

A typical dictionary definition of motivation[2] is derived from the word 'motivate', described as 'to supply a motive to, be the motive of; cause (person) to act in a particular way; stimulate interest of (person in studying etc.); hence motivation'. A 'motive' is concerned with 'tending to initiate movement' or 'concerned with movements' or 'what induces a person to act'. This is essentially the way in which management and behavioural scientists define the term. For example, Harries and Woodgate[3] define motivation as

'processes or factors causing people to act in certain ways . . . consists of the identification of need, the establishment of a goal which will satisfy that need and determination of the required action'.

Such a definition assumes the nature of the 'motive' to be a 'need'. As we shall see later, not all theories of motivation are based on 'needs'.

The mainstream psychologists see motivation in similar terms. Thus Krech et al.[4] describe motivation in terms of the direction and persistence of action. It is about why individuals adopt particular courses of action in preference to others and why, over a long period of time and in the face of difficulties, they continue with that action. Vroom[5] has described it as 'the process of governing choices made by persons or lower organisms among alternative forms of voluntary activities'. The use of the word 'voluntary' is important, as we shall see in a while.

In a recent review of theories of motivation, Mitchell[6] suggests four common characteristics that are involved in the definition of motivation. These are:

1 that motivation is typified as an individual phenomenon, to allow for individual differences and uniqueness;
2 that motivation is described, usually, as intentional, i.e. under a person's control;
3 that motivation is multifaceted, with the two most important facets

being what gets people activated (arousal) and the force to engage in desired behaviour (direction or choice), and

4   that the purpose of motivational theories is to predict behaviour i.e. it is concerned not with behaviour or performance themselves but with action and with the forces that influence choice of action.

Derived from these common characteristics, Mitchell proposes the following definition of motivation: 'the degree to which an individual wants and chooses to engage in certain specified behaviour'. This would seem to sum up most of the important aspects of motivation. It also reinforces the notion of 'voluntary' action, thus distinguishing 'motivated' behaviour from a range of involuntary behaviour such as reflexes (for example the knee-jerk or the eye-blink). Although one well-known psychologist[7] has been attributed with the phrase 'show me someone who isn't motivated and I'll be looking at a corpse', it is generally accepted that some behaviours are not caused by motivational forces: these include sleep-walking, talking in one's sleep or even the crazy, circular running of the headless chicken!

Two examples further illustrate this distinction. The first concerns driving a car. To get into the car you have to be motivated (unless kidnapped) – you have to need to go somewhere. This is the intent. When driving the car, however, a number of actions and behaviours are automatic or 'second nature'. You don't have to think about depressing the clutch pedal – you do it instinctively. If you daily take a similar route to work, and on occasion have to go somewhere different, you may well find yourself, simply out of habit, taking the same turnings as you would if going to work. The second concerns many types of sport. Let us take squash as an example. You have to be highly motivated to play the game in freezing cold weather or when feeling a bit 'down' or lethargic, yet on the court many of your reactions will be purely instinctive or reflexive. In many cases, then, voluntary (motivated) behaviour is supported by a range of involuntary behaviours.

In this chapter we shall be looking not at the seemingly automatic actions of the filing clerk, typist, or machine minder as they perform certain aspects of their work, but more at such aspects as why one filing clerk goes to great lengths to develop a well-organised system, why a typist is prepared to sign her boss's letters, and why a machine minder decides to 'go slow'. It is the 'intentional' that is the focus of motivation. We must, however, recognise at least one problem when studying motivation – we can't actually see it! It is not directly observable but is inferred from various actions in order to explain behaviour.

A basic model of motivation

Although a number of different approaches to or conceptions of motivation have been put forward, there is one underlying concept. This is concerned with 'equilibrium'. It is most easily demonstrated and understood by reference to the physiological aspects of the individual. In 1932, Cannon[8] coined the word 'homeostasis' to refer to the physiological mechanisms set into action to restore the internal state of an organism (e.g. blood sugar level, body temperature etc.) to its normal and optimal condition of functioning whenever such a condition has been disturbed. A simple example of this process would be the automatic response of perspiration when the human body temperature moves above its equilibrium state of 98.4°F. Extended to behavioural responses to internal disequilibrium the idea of homeostasis leads us to what is basically a deficiency or survival model of motivation. Thus behaviour can be explained in the following way. We all have a number of basic physiological needs (e.g. for food) which, if not met, give rise to specific drives (e.g. hunger). These drives give rise to activity (e.g. the search for food) aimed at attaining some incentive, goal, object or state (e.g. food) which can satisfy the original need. Such a deficiency model, however, is not adequate to explain research evidence[9] suggesting that some activities, for example play, exploration, curiosity and manipulation, have an incentive value of their own. But if we accept a broader definition of 'need' than the strict physiological one, we have the components of a basic motivational model upon which to build our understanding of motivation at work.

Such a model would be too basic to be of any real value to us. In addition to the state of 'disequilibrium' (or need) and the goal through which equilibrium (or satisfaction) may be sought, there has to be a mechanism – behaviour or activity – for moving the individual toward the goal and some further mechanism that tells the body when the need has been satisfied (when equilibrium has been restored) and to switch off the activity. Many engineers and scientists (and others) will recognise this as a feedback control mechanism, a simple example of which is the thermostatically controlled central heating system. Our basic model of motivation[10] can thus be depicted as in Figure 4.1.

Before describing some of the theories of motivation, it must be stressed that human motivation is much more complicated than the model suggests. We must take account, at least, of the following points.

1 The same goal may be reached by a number of different activities.
2 A single action or behaviour may lead to the attainment of a number of different goals.
3 The attainment of a single goal could satisfy a number of different needs or states of disequilibrium.
4 Not all people will seek to satisfy the same needs/states of disequilibrium to the same extent, if at all.

5   The nature of the behaviour or action may not always be of interest to or value to the manager.

Bearing these points in mind, let us now look at some of the major conceptions of motivation.

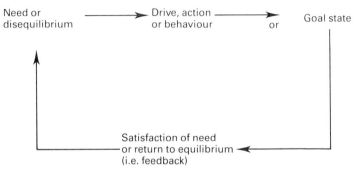

Fig. 4.1   Basic model of motivation

Approaches to motivation

Human needs

The very essence of the model is the assumption that people have 'felt needs' or experience some state of disequilibrium. Several approaches to motivation are based on this assumption (an assumption which not only makes good sense but has also been put to the test[11]. Any attempt to draw up a list of human needs must of necessity be tentative and as yet is unlikely to be universally accepted. One influential list compiled by Murray *et al*,[12] itemises forty such needs, divided into twelve 'viscerogenic' (physiological) needs and twenty-eight 'psychogenic' (psychological) needs. But in the area of organisational behaviour, one classification of human needs and related theory of motivation has probably been more influential than any other. This is the theory presented by Maslow[13], which will now be examined more closely.

Maslow's hierarchy of needs

In Maslow's terms the human being should be seen as a 'perpetually wanting animal'. Basing his research primarily on clinical observations, he maintained that nearly all individuals are motivated by the desire to satisfy certain specific needs, which can be classified into five major groups. These groups are as follows.

1   *Physiological needs*   the basic needs of the individual, such as

food, water, air and sleep, which are essential for survival. He would also include other physiological needs which appear to be basic but which do not have an obvious function in survival, such as sex and sensory stimulation (touching, smelling etc);

2 *Safety needs* the needs for a generally ordered existence in a relatively stable, threat-free environment;

3 *Love needs* the needs for affectionate relations with other people, a sense of belonging and acceptance as a member of a group;

4 *Esteem needs* a need or desire for a stable, firmly based, (usually) high evaluation of ourselves, for self-respect or self-esteem. There is a basic desire for independence and confidence in the face of the world. These needs also include the esteem of other people, which represents a desire for prestige, importance and attention, and

5 *The need for self-actualisation* The need for self-fulfilment, to become everything that one is capable of becoming, to realise one's full potential for doing or creating.

A second, fundamental aspect of Maslow's theory is that there is a set order of priority in which these needs become important to us. In other words they should be thought of as constituting a hierarchy with physiological needs at the bottom, followed by safety needs, then esteem needs and, at the top, self-actualization. The significance of the hierarchy is that the behaviour of any person is dominated by the lowest group of needs remaining unsatisfied. Only once a level of needs has been largely satisfied will the activities of the individual be directed towards satisfying the next level up. In other words, a person whose love needs remain unsatisfied will not be activated by the desire for self-actualisation. Once needs have been satisfied they cease to play an activating role. As Maslow puts it, 'a satisfied need is not a motivator'[14]. In later formulations of the theory[15] he suggests that the last point is not true of the highest level. In self-actualisation needs, increased satisfaction leads to increased need strength.

As has been indicated, this theory, originally formulated in a clinical setting, has been highly influential on the work of subsequent students of organisational behaviour. Surprisingly, however, there has been relatively little empirical research to test the relevance of the theory in organisation settings. This may, in part, be due to the relatively imprecise nature of the original hypotheses, which make it difficult to make sufficiently detailed predictions of behaviour for them to be operational. Lawler and Suttle[16], however, reviewing the research that has been done by themselves and others, suggest that these 'studies offer little support for the view that the needs of managers in organisations are arranged in a multilevel hierarchy'. But this does not necessarily mean that we must reject all of Maslow's ideas, for, as others have said, he

> is important because he directs attention to the point that many motives may direct behaviour, and that people may engage in activities simply because they believe they are valuable and not because of other extrinsic motives[17].

In addition, the ideas do provide a useful framework for studying the development of what might loosely be termed managerial approaches to motivation.

Alderfer's modified hierarchy

One of the few empirical tests of need theory was carried out by Alderfer[18]. His work led him to propose only three levels of needs: existence, relatedness and growth (his ERG theory).

These groups are described as follows.

1 *Existence needs*　those concerned with sustaining human existence and survival. They cover the physiological and safety needs of a material nature.
2 *Relatedness needs*　those concerned with relationships with the social environment. They cover love or belonging, affiliation, and meaningful interpersonal relationships of a safety or esteem nature.
3 *Growth needs*　those concerned with the development of potential. They cover self-esteem and self-actualisation.

ERG theory is similar to the hierarchy of needs, though it consists of only three levels. In addition, Alderfer's theory differs in the way people move through the hierarchy. In Maslow's version, if a particular need level is satisfied, it is the next higher order need that requires satisfying. Further satisfaction of the lower level will have little or no effect. Alderfer, however, suggests that extra reward at the lower levels can compensate for a lack of satisfaction at higher levels. More pay might, therefore, make up for a lack of job satisfaction!

As Cooper and Makin[19] point out,

> 'although these theories (i.e. of Maslow and of Alderfer) are not, despite their initial appeal, generally accepted as a view of how everyone is motivated, they do highlight a general feature about what people will find rewarding'.

Needs (and associated rewards) are arranged hierarchically, with some being important to some people and not to others. There can be no one, best approach, therefore, to motivating people at work.

Cognitive dissonance

Another way of looking at the initiating element (i.e. needs/disequili-brium) of Figure 4.1 is to consider the individual to be in a state of tension. The motivational process is thus concerned with the reduction of that tension. The theory that can be used to explain tension reduc-tion is 'cognitive dissonance'. This is based on the work of Festinger[20]. Although not purporting to be a theory of motivation, it is a useful way of thinking about alternative explanations for 'drive creation', and can be described quite briefly.

Basically, it states that when two pieces of information (cognitive inputs) in the mind or mental processes are out of line (dissonant), the person experiences psychological discomfort. That person is then motivated to reduce the discomfort. For example, if Fred doesn't like Bill, but has to work with him, dissonance occurs. Fred might be motivated to lessen the discomfort by pretending it doesn't exist, leaving the job, or attempting to make friends with Bill. However, if Fred feels that it is irrelevant that he should like Bill, dissonance will not occur, and the motivation to reduce it does not arise. (It should be noted that cognitive dissonance also plays an important part in attitude change.) This is an extremely simplified account, but it serves to make the point that cognitive elements may be an important part of moti-vation. We shall return to this point later.

Work-based approaches

The approaches described above are general theories of motivation. They can be applied to many aspects of life. A number of approaches developed in the last three or four decades are more specific to the work situation and are therefore of relevance to the issues faced by managers. We shall consider some of these, but first a brief summary of the assumptions made by various schools of thought about the nature of people in the workplace.

In the early part of this century, the prevailing view of the worker was that of economic man for whom any higher order needs were irrelevant. The thirties and forties saw the development of what became known as the Human Relations school of thought, which explained man's behaviour at work primarily in terms of his social needs. The theories which emerged in the sixties and which still underlie much of today's management practice placed much more emphasis on the importance of higher order needs in understanding man's motivation at work. The name most frequently associated with the early 'carrot and stick' or economic approach is that of F. W. Taylor, the 'father' of scientific management[21]. According to him:

What the workmen want from their employers more than anything else is high wages and what employers want from their workmen is low labour cost.

This view of man has been labelled by McGregor[22] as 'Theory X' and is, he maintained, based on the following assumptions:

1 'The average human being has an inherent dislike of work and will avoid it if he can.'
2 'Because of this human characteristic of dislike of work, most people must be coerced, controlled, directed, threatened with punishment to get them to put forth adequate effort toward the achievement of organisational objectives.'
3 'The average human being prefers to be directed, wishes to avoid responsibility, has relatively little ambition, wants security above all.'

The implications of this approach for management practice are: close supervision of subordinates; breaking tasks down to the simplest, most easily learned, repetitive operations; and the establishment and enforcement of detailed work routines and procedures. Such strategies, together with proper physical working conditions (it was claimed) would minimise worker inefficiency. They were, however, far from problem-free, and the underlying theory of motivation proved quite inadequate for explaining all work behaviour.

The subsequent development of theories to compensate for the inadequacies of this traditional model owes much to the 'Hawthorne Studies' carried out over a twelve-year period from 1927 at the Hawthorne Works of the Western Electric Company, Chicago, initiated by Elton Mayo, and described in detail by Roethlisberger and Dickson[23]. Ironically, the studies and resulting theories developed initially from attempts to examine the effect of various aspects of the physical working conditions upon production. The surprising finding – that output seemed to improve almost regardless of what variations were made to working conditions – led to a search for explanations outside the man-machine relationship. There emerged a set of assumptions based on the view of man primarily as a social animal, gaining his basic sense of identity through relationships with others. It was assumed that, as a result of industrialisation and rationalisation, work itself held no meaning, and meaning was therefore sought in relationships on the job. Peer group pressure was seen as more influential than incentives or management controls. Such assumptions led to greater concern for morale at work, the employment of group rather than individual incentive schemes, the development of company newspapers as means of keeping employees 'informed', and the emergence of strategies aimed at making the workplace a source of social satisfaction. But, as

Steers and Porter[24] point out:

   The basic ingredient that typically was not changed was the nature of the required tasks on the job.

Such a view of motivation, however, was still rather simplistic and proved just as inadequate for explaining the variety of behaviour at work as that which it replaced. In the 1960s, another group of theorists came to the fore, who, while sharing the Human Relations school's rejection of the traditional, scientific management ideas about motivation, claimed that that school's paternalistic orientation not only indicated a far from complete understanding of the nature of man but was no less manipulative than its predecessor's.

Schein[25] refers to this new group's theories as the Self-Actualising Man approach, which gives an indication of their basic orientation. For them the manager's task is to make full use of the human potential of his subordinates by providing opportunities for them to achieve self-fulfilment in their work. Followers of this approach are McGregor[26], Argyris[27], Likert[28], and Herzberg[29], all of whom have, either implicitly or explicitly, extended the ideas of Maslow into management practice.

We have seen that McGregor criticised the traditional management practice that he labelled Theory X. His preference was for the integration of individual and organizational goals based on assumptions he labelled Theory Y.

1 There is no inherent dislike of work itself (although established practice may be seen as distasteful and therefore to be avoided).
2 Man will exercise self-direction and self-control in the service of objectives to which he is committed.
3 The degree of commitment is a function of the rewards seen to result from meeting these objectives. In this context the most significant rewards are the satisfaction of higher order needs. Such rewards are intrinsic to work, not externally mediated.
4 If the conditions are right the individual will not only accept but seek responsibility.
5 A high proportion of the population is capable of imagination, ingenuity and creativity in solving organisational problems.
6 Industrialisation has meant that such capacities are underutilised.

Such assumptions imply that, if employees appear lazy, indifferent, or unco-operative, the causes lie in management's methods of organisation and control. This does not represent, however, a plea for 'soft' management and a slackening of discipline. McGregor maintained that:

   The essential task of management is to arrange organisational conditions and methods of operation so that people can achieve their own goals best by directing their own efforts toward organisational objectives.

Put differently, if he can get high performance targets and get his subordinates to accept them as their own, he is not likely to have to worry much about discipline.

Thus we can see that three major assumptions have underlain various work-based or managerial approaches to motivation: the employee as an 'economic' animal; the employee as a 'social' animal and the employee as a 'psychological' or 'self-actualised' animal. It will be noticed that each is contained in or explained by the hierarchy of needs approach. Which is true? As Schein[30] points out, people are much more complex than this, and motivation theory must take account of this complexity. Let us now look at some approaches that take a more complex view of the individual in the work place.

Motivation – hygiene theory

If Maslow's hierarchy of needs is one of the best known approaches to motivation, then Herzberg's motivation-hygiene (or dual-factor theory, or two-factor theory, as it has been variously called) is surely another. Herzberg's theory and supporting research evidence from a survey of two hundred Pittsburgh engineers and accountants was first published in 1959[31]. Since that time the theory and the research have been the source of continuing attention and controversy among managers and academics alike.

The ideas stem from the finding that, when men were asked to remember times when they felt exceptionally good about their jobs, they seemed to be referring to quite different events and activities from those they described when asked to remember times when they felt exceptionally bad about their jobs. In other words, job factors were allowed to emerge from descriptions of actual job situations rather than being based on responses to checklists or sets of statements prepared ahead of time by the researchers. The factors that emerged as major determinants of job satisfaction (and which were relatively unimportant in connection with dissatisfaction) were:

achievement
advancement
recognition
responsibility
work itself.

Dissatisfaction, on the other hand, seemed to be associated with:

company policy and administration
supervision

salary
interpersonal relations
working conditions.

These factors seemed rarely to be involved in job satisfaction.

From these findings it was concluded that satisfaction and dissatisfaction, rather than being opposites, represented two quite independent dimensions of man's nature. One dimension is primarily concerned with avoiding unpleasantness, the other is concerned with seeking personal growth. Satisfaction, then, according to Herzberg, will be sought in aspects of job content (achievement, advancement etc.) that provide opportunity for growth. These he called the *motivators*. Their absence will not cause dissatisfaction but merely lack of positive satisfaction. Avoidance of dissatisfaction, however, will be sought in aspects of the job context (company policies, working conditions etc.). Using a medical analogy, he called these *hygiene* factors. Their presence does not lead to positive satisfaction but simply to no dissatisfaction. Hence, Herzberg maintains that, while it is important to get the hygiene factors right, if the manager wants to motivate his employees, he should focus his attention on the job itself and attempt to manipulate the motivator factors. Such an approach implies a programme of 'job enrichment', which will be discussed more fully in the section on job design.

Herzberg's ideas have had a considerable impact on practising managers, perhaps partly because they offer relatively uncomplicated prescriptions and partly because of his own colourful way of presenting them, but they have been criticised on a number of grounds by fellow behavioural scientists. Criticisms have been made of the research methods used[32], the findings of further research[33] and the research conclusions.

Among the points raised are that the method tends to lead respondents to give socially desirable answers rather than really telling the truth, that the unstructured nature of the interviews can allow the researchers to put in their own bias when coding the responses, that no measure of job satisfaction was used, and that no precise definition of job satisfaction was given. Indeed King[34] has claimed that much of the controversy surrounding Herzberg's ideas stems from the fact that there has never really been an explicit statement of the theory itself and as a result it is possible to identify five quite distinct versions of the theory stated or implied by the researchers claiming to examine it. This obviously makes direct comparison of the subsequent studies claiming either to support or refute Herzberg's original findings very difficult. Such studies have been carried out in a number of different countries, using subjects from a much wider range of occupations and backgrounds than in the original research. The results continue to be conflicting but an interesting fact does emerge. This is that research supporting the theory tends to use very similar methods to those used in the original study, whereas research which refutes it has tended to use different methods. Such a pattern seems to lend weight to the 'social desirability' criticism.

As to the conclusions, it has been questioned, for example, whether there is sufficient evidence to suggest that motivators form a group distinctive from hygiene factors[35]. Re-analysis of the data presented by Herzberg suggests that, although many of the intrinsic aspects of jobs are more frequently identified as satisfiers, achievement and recognition are very frequently identified as dissatisfiers. There is also criticism about the implicit assumption made of the direct relationship between job satisfaction, motivation and performance.

Despite all these criticisms and the reservations about the value of the two-factor theory to which they must inevitably give rise, it must not be overlooked that Herzberg has made a considerable contribution to the study of motivation at work, not least in terms of the discussion and research that his ideas have stimulated. In addition, he has succeeded in convincing many managers that intrinsic aspects of job design can potentially have as much influence on work behaviour as contextual factors such as money and fringe benefits.

The approaches to motivation at work that we have examined so far, despite conflicting with each other and offering the manager differing prescriptions, have had one underlying theme in common. That is the assumption that it is possible to formulate principles of motivation and hence recommend procedures that will be applicable to any individual in whatever organisational setting. The fault lies not so much in the wrongness of the various approaches but in their simplicity and the failure to acknowledge that what is appropriate in one situation will not necessarily be appropriate in others. This is a point which will recur in this book, particularly when we come to deal with leadership or management style and organisational form or structure. In the context of motivation, what is required is an approach which allows for the complexity and variability of man and the complexity and variability of the social, organisational and work settings in which he finds himself. One approach that does explicitly recognise individual differences and personal variability and the impact of class is Achievement motivation theory.

Achievement motivation

Probably the name most frequently associated with this theory is that of McClelland[30]. His work was initially much influenced by that of Murray, who has already been mentioned in this chapter. Unlike Murray, however, his concern has not been with the examination of an entire set of needs but with three needs in particular: the need for achievement (often referred to as n-Ach), the need for power (n-Pow), and the need for affiliation (n-Aff). More precisely still, much of the attention was focused upon the first of these, defined as 'behaviour towards competition with a standard of excellence'.

McClelland maintains that there are two basic groups of people: those who are challenged by opportunity and are willing to work hard to achieve a goal and those who do not really care all that much. In other words, there are those with an urge to achieve and those without. His studies have attempted to probe this dichotomy to determine whether n-Ach is accidental, hereditary, or the result of environmental influences. In addition he has been concerned to find out whether it represents a single isolated motive or a combination of motives such as the desire to accumulate wealth, power and fame. He has also investigated the possibility of a technique whereby people with low n-Ach can be trained to develop a greater will to achieve.

His research has convinced him that this is a definite human motive, distinguishable from others, which can be tested for and found in any group. The strength of this motive, however, will vary considerably from one individual to another. This variability, he maintains, is not a function of heredity but of differing cultural backgrounds, childhood training, parental attitudes, education and the like.

The evidence accumulated suggests that people with high levels of need for achievement have a number of identifiable characteristics in common.

1 They prefer situations in which they can take personal responsibility for carrying out a task or solving a problem. If this were not so they could get little personal sense of accomplishment from success. It also seems that the satisfaction comes not from public recognition of accomplishment but from having initiated the successful action. But the high n-Ach individual is not a gambler and does not look forward to situations where the outcome depends not on his own abilities and efforts but on chance or other factors beyond his control.

2 The individual with high n-Ach has the tendency to set moderate achievement goals and to take calculated risks in reaching them. By adopting this strategy he has the greatest probability of getting the achievement satisfaction he wants. If he were to take an easy problem he would succeed but get little satisfaction from the success. In other words, he will not work harder under all probabilities of winning but only when there is some challenge involved, i.e. some chance of losing. On the other hand, he will not select an exceptionally difficult task since, being unlikely to succeed, he will be unlikely to gain any satisfaction. This obviously has implications

for target setting as a management activity. It also means that such individuals tend to have a high need for variety in their work and to innovate, because repetition tends to increase the probability of success to the point where the task becomes easy and no longer challenging.

3   The third major characteristic of these people is that they want concrete feedback on how well they are doing. Without this feedback they are unable to derive satisfaction from their own activities.

Such characteristics are similar to the traditional 'entrepreneurial spirit'. This was particularly significant for McClelland and his associates, who were concerned with the problem of how to accelerate economic growth in underdeveloped countries. They maintained that such economic growth is to a large extent a function of the level of entrepreneurial activity. Courses were developed and run for Indian and Black businessmen in Washington DC, which were intended to help them understand their own motives, enhance their self-esteem and strengthen their need for achievement. The follow-up studies indicate that such courses were successful in that the participants subsequently significantly increased their business activity.

These factors seem to be particularly relevant to the man who runs his own business and therefore has the independence to act; but what of the manager in the large organisation? In a more recent work[37], McClelland suggests the picture may be quite different:

> For one thing, because they focus on personal improvement, on doing things better by themselves, achievement-motivated people want to do things themselves. For another, they want concrete short-term feedback on their performance so that they can tell how well they are doing. Yet a manager, particularly one of or in a large complex organisation, cannot perform all the tasks necessary for success by himself or herself. He must manage others so that they will do things for the organisation. Also, feedback on his subordinates' performance may be a lot vaguer and more delayed than it would be if he were doing everything himself.

This can give some insight into the problems frequently associated with the highly successful salesman (of whom the high n-Ach characteristics are typical) who because of his performance is promoted to a managerial position to which he is unsuited.

These recent researchers also suggest that need for affiliation is even less appropriate for the effective manager. The general conclusions are that he should possess a high need for power (a need to influence people), and this need for power ought to be greater than his need for being liked by people. This rather alarming finding is, however, qualified by an additional measure – the degree of inhibition. The effective manager scores high on inhibition as well as power, which indicates that the power motivation is not directed towards personal aggrandisement but towards the institution for which he works, and that it is exercised on behalf of other people. This has been termed the 'socialised face of power'.

Expectancy theory

The basic model presented in fig 1 suggests that motivation is a process. The theories we have considered so far have been mainly concerned with the content of motivation; human needs, for example, or satisfaction gained at the workplace. We have yet not considered how the various components of the model interact with each other and with other workplace factors. We shall now consider some approaches to motivation which seek to describe and explain these interactions. One increasingly popular attempt at looking at the process of motivation is known as 'expectancy theory'.

The development of this theory owes much to the early 'cognitive' approaches to motivation[38]. These approaches view individuals as thinking, reasoning beings who have beliefs and expectations about future events in their lives. This includes expectations about the outcomes of their own behaviour and preferences for particular possible outcomes.

Several variants have been put forward and, before we consider the main elements of expectancy theory in general, we shall look at two other approaches:- 'path-goal' theory and 'equity' theory. 'Path-goal' theory[39] has been used to study differing levels of productivity within organisations. The approach is based on the following assumptions. Individual productivity is, among other things, a function of one's motivation to produce at a given level. In turn, such motivation depends upon the particular needs of the individual, as reflected in the goals towards which he is moving, and his perception of the relative usefulness of productivity behaviour as an instrument or path to the attainment of these goals. The path will be chosen if his need(s) is sufficiently high, or his goal(s) is relatively salient and if no other more effective and economical paths are available to him. But even if the individual is motivated to produce at a high level it is not certain that he will become a high producer. This would be the case only if there were no restraining forces, if no barriers blocked the desired path. Limiting conditions may hinder the translation of motivation to produce to actual productive behaviour of a given level.

'Equity' theory is based on the way individuals make comparisons about effort and rewards. It suggests that our level of motivation can be affected by the comparisons we make between the effort we put into a job and the rewards we get, and our perceptions of the efforts and rewards of others. If the effort we put into work is perceived to be too great in comparison with the rewards, our motivation may be reduced (unless there is a possibility that future rewards may be increased). If others doing similar work are perceived to be getting greater rewards for the same effort, we may judge that also as being 'inequitable' and respond accordingly. Whilst the judgement of equity (or parity) may often be made over money, other rewards will be considered. For example, the salesman who works hard and is paid well, but does not get much of the limelight, might respond in the same way as the skilled worker who receives less pay than an unskilled worker. These judgements are often important factors in pay and collective bargaining.

We can see, then, that our expectations about how much effort to put into a job, the likely rewards, the goals that will achieve such rewards, how we will achieve those goals, and the fairness or equity of the rewards, are important ingredients of motivation. They are, to a large extent, drawn together in current formulations of expectancy theory. We shall now look at a general formulation.

Expectancy valence theory

This is probably one of the most influential theories of motivation at present, at least among academic researchers. According to Cooper and Makin[40] this is because it recognises 'that an individual's behaviour is to a considerable degree influenced by that individual's expectations of what will happen in the future'. Furthermore, current approaches provide a framework into which many other theories can be fitted. The theory itself owes much to the work of a number of people[41] but here we shall describe a model that incorporates the elements of several major approaches[42]. This model or framework is shown diagrammatically in Fig 4.2. In describing it we shall work round each numbered box in turn.

Box 1 corresponds roughly to what might be termed 'force'. It is compounded from valence (the strength of an individual's preference for a particular outcome from his own effort or activity), and expectancy (the belief concerning the likelihood that a particular act will be followed by a particular outcome).

Valence is the attractiveness of possible outcomes to individuals. A given potential reward is differently desired by different individuals. The reward value of the outcome stems from their ability to satisfy one or more needs.

In this model, expectancy is divided into: the overall probability that rewards depend on effort is a product of the probability that rewards depend on performance (Box 1B); and the probability that performance depends on effort (Box 1A). For example, an individual may believe that a particular reward, say promotion, in no way depends on

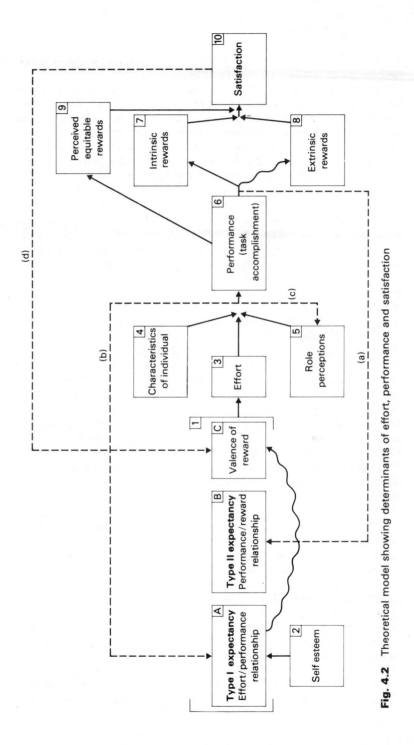

Fig. 4.2 Theoretical model showing determinants of effort, performance and satisfaction

his performance but is determined solely on grounds of seniority. In such a case he would have a Type II expectancy of zero. On the other hand he may perceive promotion as directly related to performance but his expectancy that rewards depend upon effort may still be low, because he feels that no amount of additional effort on his part will improve his performance, either because of situational factors beyond his control, or because he does not think he has the abilities to perform the job well enough to deserve the reward. He would have a Type I expectancy of zero. This is determined in part by the individual's self-esteem (Box 2). In addition, following achievement motivation theory, it might be suggested that for some people there will be a relationship between Type I expectancy and the valence of the outcome or reward (indicated by the wavy line). In other words, a high n-Ach person, as we have seen, will be more attracted to tasks in which he has some chance of failing. In the context of this model the implication is that the likelihood of achievement satisfaction is greater where the perceived relationship between effort and task accomplishment is less than perfect.

Effort (Box 3) is produced by the combined effects of expectancies 1 and 2 and the valence of the reward. Effort is distinguished from effective performance or task accomplishment (Box 6). Essentially, effort is how hard the individual is trying, how much energy he is expending in a given situation. But the amount of effort an individual puts into a task does not necessarily correlate with how successfully that task is carried out. In some senses, then, effort is the key factor, in that the strength of motivation should show up more clearly in the amount of effort expended than in the performance results attained. This can be so for a number of reasons.

Individual characteristics and role perceptions represent factors that can limit or enhance how effectively effort is translated into performance. The personal characteristics of the individual (Box 4) can set limits on his ability to perform effectively. In addition to effort, intelligence, skill and personality can all influence an individual's performance. There can often be variations or differences in role perceptions (Box 5). An individual has beliefs and expectations about the kind of activities and behaviour he should engage in to perform his task effectively. If, however, these perceptions do not correspond to those held by his boss, he could be expending a lot of effort without doing the task properly (at least in the eyes of his boss). Just as personal characteristics may limit an individual's capacity for translating effort into effective performance, so accurate role perceptions will limit the amount of effort needed for effective performance. This point will be explored in more detail in Chapter Seven.

It can be seen, then, that performance is by no means directly related to effort. Furthermore, this model does shed some light on the controversial relationship between performance and satisfaction. This model also allows us to examine the effect that rewards and perceptions of equity can have in moderating that relationship and also suggests the direction of causality.

Intrinsic rewards (Box 7) are rewards such as a feeling of accomplishing something worthwhile, a sense of achievement and the feeling of making full use of and developing one's skills and abilities. They are seen as fairly certain outcomes of performance because they are internally mediated; they are the rewards one gives to oneself (cf. Maslow's higher order needs and Herzberg's motivators). Hence the straight-line relationship with performance.

Extrinsic rewards (Box 8) are those controlled by the organisation, such as pay, promotion, status, security etc. The connection with these rewards is indicated on the diagram by a wavy line because it is likely to be relatively weak or at least indirect, with the exception perhaps of simpler incentive payment systems.

Satisfaction (Box 10) will not result from the receipt of rewards alone. It will be determined by the gap between the rewards actually received and the perceived equitable rewards (Box 9). By perceived equitable rewards we mean the level or amount of reward that an individual feels he should have or that is fair for a given level of performance. It can also refer to the rewards an individual feels should be associated with certain positions within the organisation. The line on the diagram connecting performance and perceived equitable rewards (Box 6 and Box 9) is an acknowledgement of the influence that an individual's own rating of how well he has done his job will have on what he will regard as fair reward. So satisfaction is only in part determined by the level of rewards actually received. High performance will lead to high levels of satisfaction only if it decreases the gap between what is received and what is seen as fair. Furthermore, a low performer, if his expected rewards are also low, might be equally or even more satisfied than a given high performer. The theory, then, suggests that satisfaction is primarily a dependant variable, not a causal one.

Another advantage of this model is that it regards motivation as a dynamic process. In other words, it incorporates learning from observed and actual experience in similar situations in the past. The way in which this learning may feed back and influence various aspects of the model is indicated on the diagram by the broken lines. Thus the way in which an organisation rewards (or does not reward) an individual for his performance will affect his perceptions of the connection between effort and performance (feedback (a)). Similarly, the process (or otherwise) with which effort is translated into performance will affect the individual's perceptions of the effort – performance connection. (Feedback (b).) It may also affect the subsequent accuracy of his role perceptions (feedback (c)). It is also suggested that when an individual feels satisfied after having received rewards, this will have an affect on the future valences of those rewards. (Feedback (d).)

How valid is this approach to motivation? Does it really portray what motivation is about, at least in the workplace? Several studies[43] have been carried out to test this. The evidence from these studies implies that expectancy theory has much to offer but that there is still a great need for conceptual and methodological refinement, not least in determining the impact upon work-behaviour of variables other than individual expectancies and reward valences. Even at this stage of development, however, the theory does have a number of practical implications. For example, attempts to measure and/or enhance satisfaction at work are likely to have little direct effect on performance (although they may still be very influential on absenteeism and turnover). In addition, there is a need to consider the appropriateness of rewards; what is seen to be rewarding by one individual may not be by another. In other words, individualised rewards systems should be considered, perhaps 'cafeteria-style'. Attempts must also be made to establish clear lines between effort, performance and rewards in the eyes of the individual. Finally, greater attention needs to be paid to the non-motivational factors that can affect performance, including adequacy of facilities and procedures, individual abilities, differing role perceptions and role conflicts (see Chapter Seven), group pressures on the individual (see Chapter Six), organisational climate and so on.

Although development and refinement of, and controversy about, motivation theory still continues[44], we have a sufficient grasp of the process to be able to look seriously at its application in the workplace.

Application of motivation theory

At the beginning of this chapter we sought to define the term 'motivation'. We saw that it is concerned with voluntary, intended actions or behaviour. If the theories we have subsequently reviewed are to be of any use to managers, or others, they must help to provide the conditions under which voluntary action and desired organisational behaviour will be (roughly) level. There are many areas where the theories can be applied. We shall consider one of these – job design – in some detail, because it is of central interest to the individual worker (via intrinsic satisfaction) and to the manager (via improved performance). We are not making the assumption that higher satisfaction leads to higher performance. We take the view that both satisfaction and performance are outcomes of working or behaving, and that each is linked to the other, but in a small way[45]. We do take the view, however, that increased job satisfaction ought to be a managerial goal, if only to reduce absenteeism, labour turnover and mistakes or poor quality. We shall also look at money and its motivational significance, because this is an important source of extrinsic reward, and shall also touch upon training and leadership. But first, let us put motivation in the context of the main factors that influence performance at work. There are several of these as shown in Figure 4.3. These are described as follows.

1 *Motivation to work* this requires little description. Suffice to say that it represents the effort, valency and expectation dimensions of the expectancy model.
2 *Relevant work* this refers to the actual work undertaken and its relevance to the individual and the organisation. In other words, it is something that is required and can actually be performed.
3 *Supports for work* these refer to all those supports required to make work possible, such as appropriate machinery, materials, desks, telephones and the like.
4 *Capacity to work* this includes the skill, experience and ability of the individual as well as attitudes towards and perceptions of the work (embraces the individual characteristics and role perceptions of the expectancy model).
5 *Organisation of work* this refers to work and organisation structure, work flows and relationships, task groupings and all those aspects of organisation that are designed to make work possible, effective and efficient.
6 *Management of work* this refers to those aspects of the manager's role not covered elsewhere in the framework and includes

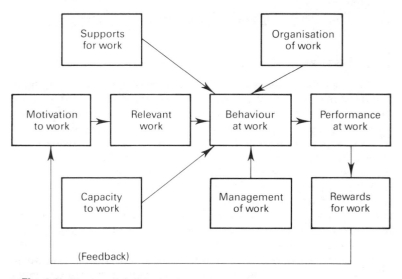

Fig. 4.3 The context of motivation at the workplace

leadership/management style.

7 *Behaviour at work*   this refers to all those activities in which the individual engages in the workplace and that lead, usually, to performance.

8 *Performance at work*   this refers to the quantity and quality of output or work activity actually achieved.

9 *Rewards for work*   these include both intrinsic and extrinsic rewards.

Clearly, many facets of organisation have been excluded (e.g. technology) for simplity's sake. A more elaborate framework has been developed by Bennett[46], from which Figure 4.3 has been adapted.

This framework has several implications for management practice and the application of motivation theory. It can be seen that motivation is a central concept and requires attention, and that, because other factors are involved, attention must not be placed solely on motivation. Highly motivated employees will find it difficult to perform well if, for example, they are given the wrong kind of work, or if the proper supports are not available, or if they do not have the necessary skill or ability. When thinking, therefore, of the application of motivation theory to the workplace, we must always be mindful of the other factors that influence performance and of the consequences of striking the wrong balance. A highly motivated employee who becomes frustrated through inadequate facilities, management or organisation can become dissatisfied, a low performer – or just another employee lost to a competitor.

With these points in mind, let us now turn to some of the applications of motivation theory.

Job design

Job design is concerned with the specification of the contents, methods and relationships of jobs. The aim is to satisfy technological and organisational requirements as well as the social and personal requirements of the person doing the job. It is concerned primarily with two aspects, job content and job relationships. Early managerial approaches to job content concentrated on attempts to achieve greater technical efficiency through simplifying jobs (task specialisation or division of labour). Recent approaches have been more concerned with improving the nature of the job content to allow for greater reward. The emphasis in work relationships is moving from technical to more social–psychological considerations, as will be seen in Chapter Eight. Again, what can be achieved through job design (greater efficiency and effectiveness, improved extrinsic rewards, greater job satisfaction) is a matter of balance. Given the centrality of the job in the workplace, and the importance of motivation in the 'performance equation', we should explore the contribution of one to the other and describe briefly some approaches to job design.

We can learn from motivation theory some important lessons about behaviour at work. One is that people may want to satisfy different needs through performing work (cf. Maslow), another is that some factors may have a bigger impact on motivation than others (cf. Herzberg) and a third is that perceptions or comparisons may be as important as 'objective reality' (cf. expectancy theory). It would be a tall order indeed to design any job to take account of all these lessons, but we can at least make an attempt to take some of them on board in our managerial thinking. Some approaches to job design achieve this to varying extents. There are essentially four approaches that are based on a recognition of the contribution of motivation theory.

Job rotation

This is not really a new approach to job design but it is often used as a way of alleviating borebom in fairly mundane jobs where technological and/or economic constraints make it very difficult to do much else. As implied, it simply involves moving people from one job to another. It does not involve a change in what is done in the job to any great extent. Simple examples would be clerks moving from the filing section to, say, the mailing section, for several weeks. It would not include the type of job rotation involved in management development exercises. Job rotation may give some added interest, or the expectation of greater interest, meeting new people etc., but in essence, one boring job is not much different from another. It may, therefore, have limited motivational effect. In fact, it can demotivate if, for example, bonus payments are interrupted or friendship patterns are fragmented. It is most often used in conjunction with another approach, such as group working.

Job enlargement

This involves extending the range of physical and skill requirements of a job. It adds to or enlarges the job already being done. Thus, the filing clerk cited above might do filing, mailing and some other element of the work. This increases the time span of the job, adds to the skills required and reduces repetitiveness. It may also require further training. The individual is thus developing skill and experience as well as receiving more variety. This certainly allows for the possibility of further needs being satisfied, but the range is still narrow. It does not go as far as Herzberg would have us, nor, unlike the next two approaches, does it take much account of expectancy theory.

Job enrichment

This involves enriching the job by putting back many of the skills and responsibilities 'designed out' by job design approaches based on 'economic man' assumptions. It involves not only increasing the physical or motor aspects of work but also the cognitive and affective aspects by allowing more responsibility, wider discretion and decision-making, more control over the immediate environment and greater involvement in the planning and scheduling of work. It has received a good deal of attention since the early 1970s, with the work of Herzberg acting as a catalyst. Indeed, Herzberg himself[47] suggested seven guiding principles for job enrichment, or vertical job expansion (as opposed to job enlargement, which is horizontal expansion).

1   Remove some controls while retaining accountability.
2   Increase the accountability of individuals for their own work.
3   Give a person a complete natural unit of work.
4   Grant additional authority to an employee in his activity – job freedom.
5   Make periodic reports directly available to the worker himself rather than to the supervisor.
6   Introduce new and more difficult tasks not previously handled.
7   Assign individuals specific or specialised tasks, enabling them to become experts.

The research evidence available on such approaches to job enrichment does suggest that it can have a positive effect on reduced turnover and absenteeism, job satisfaction, and quality of production. There is little evidence of improvements in productivity or level of output, and such programmes usually involve increased costs in training time and sometimes retooling. In addition, like the theory on which it is based, this approach to job design is universalistic. In other words, it does not cater for individual differences in orientation to work and hence in responsiveness to enriched jobs. In the light of what has gone before, it is not surprising that there is considerable evidence suggesting that people do have different reactions to the increased complexity and challenge advocated by the job enrichers. This could, to a large degree, be predicted from expectancy theory.

Recent attempts to gain a fuller understanding of the circumstances under which jobs will be intrinsically motivating have therefore included not only job characteristics but also individual attributes and the psychological states mediating between the job and the personal and organisational outcomes. The model presented and tested by Hackman and Oldham[48] represents such an approach.

They suggested that five core job dimensions 'potentially' prompt three significant pyschological states which 'potentially' lead to a number of beneficial personal and work outcomes. But the strength of the link between these major elements of the model is influenced by individual differences. Reviewing research in the area, they conclude that the most important difference is in the strength of individual growth needs, (the higher order needs in Maslow's hierarchy, or the growth needs of Alderfer's classification). This was, however, seen as related to various background characteristics of the individual such as educational level, sex, age, place of work and place of residence.

The job dimensions contributing to its overall motivating potential are skill variety, task identity (the degree to which it involves doing a 'whole' piece of work) and task significance (the degree of impact on the lives or work of others). These three potentially lead to: experienced meaningfulness of work; autonomy, potentially leading to experienced responsibility; and feedback, potentially leading to knowledge of results. These dimensions then combine in the following way to provide a 'motivating potential score' (MPS).

$$MPS = \frac{(Skill\ Variety + Task\ Identity + Task\ Significance)}{3} \times Autonomy \times Feedback$$

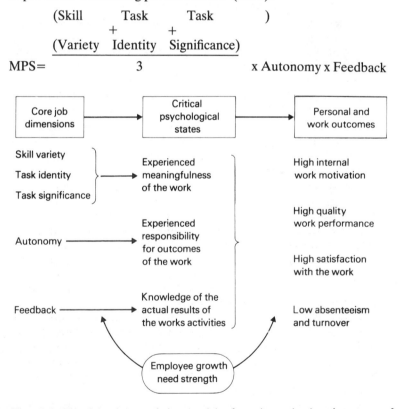

Fig. 4.4 The job characteristics model of work motivation (courtesy of Hackman, J. R. and Oldham, G. R., 1976)

The model demonstrating how the motivating potential is or is not translated into desired outcomes can be represented diagrammatically as in Fig. 4.4. The implication is that those interested in a programme of job enrichment should proceed with caution. It does not represent a universal remedy to the problems of work design. The costs may be high and the benefits arising may well be less than expected. It would be advisable to conduct some form of attitude survey before embarking on such a programme, to gain some indication of the likely expectations and preferences of those who would be affected. This may highlight areas of work where a degree of choice or flexibility can be built into certain jobs, giving the job holder more opportunity to engage in activities that are more suitable and satisfying. One way of doing this is to give more responsibility for work allocation to a group of employees.

Group working

This embraces a range of approaches or ideas, from the simple 'socialisation' of work through to autonomous/self-organising work groups. It usually includes any or all of the previous approaches but adds a social dimension to the psychological ones inherent in job enrichment. This increases the range of needs that, potentially, can be met at the workplace, and takes us a stage nearer to meeting the 'requirements' not only of the content theories of motivation (e.g. Maslow and Herzberg) but also of the process theories (e.g. expectancy theory). It involves grouping tasks in such a way as to produce meaningful 'social boundaries' rather than the artificial boundaries based on the prevailing technology. As we shall see in Chapter Six, social groups can exert powerful control over the behaviour of their members. It would seem possible to harness this power and direct it to achieving greater personal satisfaction for members and better performance in the organisation. Group working may involve, among other things: replanning work situations to bring employees closer together; re-designing equipment and machinery to allow employees to monitor their own performance; delegating to the group the responsibility for some maintenance, inspection and other activities; giving members of the group the right to elect their own supervisor; allowing members to determine the allocation of work, job rotation and the allocation of bonuses. Such a range of discretion and responsibility can enable both intrinsic and extrinsic rewards to be available on a reasonably varied basis. The implication, however, for extra training, the redesign of technology, increased pay and the redefinition of managerial work and responsibilities are not insignificant. A major advantage – apart from improved quality, improved satisfaction and reduced absenteeism – can be the freeing of managerial time to concentrate more on issues of planning, organising and controlling work at group and plant level rather than at the level of the individual employee. This approach thus embraces social, technical, psychological, economic and managerial considerations. It takes on more of a 'systems' perspective of job design and work organisation. This perspective will be discussed in Chapter Eight.

The use of group working is not restricted to job design. Other examples include Quality Circles[49], where groups of employees come together to analyse and solve problems affecting their work, using techniques of information-gathering, problem-solving and decision-making in which they have been trained, and Learning Circles[50], where managers develop themselves and their subordinates on a group basis using the training specialist as a source of support.

Returning to a more general consideration of job design, what does research tell us about the characteristics that jobs should contain, if they are to have motivational properties that lead to improved quality of working life, job satisfaction and effective performance? Much research has been carried out[51], and some of the key points we can take from it are that tasks should:

1 combine to form a coherent job
2 make a significant contribution to the finished product
3 provide variety in methods
4 provide feedback on performance
5 allow the use of discretion
6 carry responsibility
7 be controlled by the worker.

Tasks should not:

1 be paced
2 be short cycle
3 create deprivations
4 fail to use the skill and potential available
5 prevent people having a real say in what affects their work.

(Source: DE Work Research Unit)

As will be appreciated, many of the 'should' characteristics are those that are concerned with the motivational requirements of work.

Money

The importance of money as a motivational influence varies from person to person and situation to situation. Although most people go to work to earn money to survive and to achieve the luxuries they would wish to have, the motivational effect in the workplace may or may not be significant, depending on how closely financial rewards are tied to performance, how great the expectation and desire is for more money and how fair the reward is perceived to be. We can then see that content theories of motivation inform us as to how likely money will act as a satisfier (or means of achieving satisfaction) for various needs (e.g. survival, necessity, freedom to self-actualise). We can also see, from expectancy theory, that perceptions of fairness, equity, etc., based on comparisons with others, may also be important.

The way people view work will have a considerable impact on the value of money to them. There will inevitably be a wide range of individual differences in orientation[52] depending in part on perceptions, personal characteristics and circumstances, and cultural factors. It is possible, as we have already stated, on the basis of the theories discussed, to suggest a number of roles that money might play in the motivational process. These roles should not be seen as mutually exclusive.

Firstly, while it is assumed that money has no intrinsic value, it can be seen as having acquired values as a result of its perceived instrumentality in obtaining other valued objects or states. In other words, although not directly related to any of the basic human needs described earlier, it could be seen as a means of attaining satisfaction of any of them.

As perhaps the most tangible of rewards, money can be an important way of comparing personal rewards with the rewards received (or believed to be received) by others. This comparability or equity aspect of pay has become institutionalised in our industrial relations system as a major basis of collective bargaining. The precise measuring-stick attribute of money also has other implications. It may perform the role of indicating to the individual his own level of accomplishment. This may be particularly important to the high n- Ach person who requires concrete feedback on how well he is doing. In this context, it would seem that salary increases can still have an important role to play even at high income/high tax levels where the increase in take-home pay is minimal. It has also been suggested by McCelland[53] that money may function as a symbol, 'guaranteeing' a contract between two parties (employer and employee) which in fact involves more than the simple exchange of labour for money.

Following Herzberg, it may well be that for some people at least, money serves not as a positive source of satisfaction or motivation but rather as a means of avoiding or reducing dissatisfaction.

Finally, it has been suggested that, as a result of socialisation or conditioning, money may have an important reinforcement effect in its own right. In other words, by repeated association with valued goal objects, it has acquired value of its own. If this is the case, then reinforcement theory would imply that different patterns or schedules of reinforcement have significantly different affects on behaviour. For example, it seems that reinforcement at fixed intervals, such as annual increments, particularly on a set scale, does little to encourage high levels of performance. It seems unlikely that there will ever be a single universally acceptable theory regarding money. Meanwhile, to quote Opsahl and Dunnette[54]:

> Much remains to be learned before we will understand very well what meaning money has for different persons, how it affects their job behaviours, which motives it serves, and how its effectiveness may come about.

Very little research has been carried out into these issues. From research data that is available, we do know that money means different things to different people[55] – it can be seen as a source of anxiety, as being socially desirable, as being relatively unimportant – and that for money to be meaningful as a motivator it must be related to performance[56]. A tailor-made or cafeteria approach to pay and salary systems would thus seem to be an important consideration.

Other areas of potential application

We mentioned earlier that the application of motivation to training and leadership[57] would be touched on in this chapter. The choice of appropriate leadership style is discussed, in the context of groups, in Chapter Six. Here we need only make the point that the style of leadership adopted by a manager may have a significant impact on the motivation of subordinates. For example, if a subordinate has strong needs for affiliation, and the style adopted by the manager is fairly autocratic and isolationist, the subordinate may feel left out of things. Equally, a participative, involving style may do little for employees who have strong needs for autonomy. A style that is fixed and non-varying might be perceived by some subordinates as dealing with them unfairly because their differing needs require a flexible approach. The expectations as to what constitutes a 'good' style may vary with prior experiences of other managers, both good and bad. Hence, a style that fits the situation may well be an advantage. As regards training, we know that it involves learning, which is concerned with bringing about relatively permanent changes in behaviour. Unless a person wants to change – is motivated to learn – training will not be effective. We therefore have to create conditions, both on the job and in the training room, in which people will show a genuine intention to learn and from which they can receive appropriate support and recognition for their learning achievements. This demands that we assess, as best we can, the real learning needs of individuals, design stimulating and appropriate training, and give timely feedback on performance.

Finally, we would argue that motivation theory is relevant and applicable to any situation in which individuals are working or performing. The theory you use, however, very much depends on which has appeal and meaning for you and seems to fit your own particular needs. We would stress, however, that motivation theory cannot be applied solely to individuals in isolation. Most will work with other people, will interact with them and will be part of a group. It is to these aspects that we turn in Chapters Five and Six.

References

1   Example drawn from an unreported consultancy research study.
2   *The Concise Oxford Dictionary,* 1976. edition.
3   Harries, J. N. and Woodgate, R., *Making Sense of Management Jargon,* Granary Press, 1984.
4   Kretch, D. *et al., Individual in Society,* McGraw-Hill, 1962.
5   Vroom, V. H., *Work and Motivation,* Wiley, 1964.
6   Mitchell, T. R., 'Motivation – new directions for research, theory and practice', *Academy of Management Review,* **7**, no. 1, January 1982, pp. 8–88.
7   Attributed to Herzberg.
8   Cannon, W. B., *Wisdom of the Body,* Morton, 1932.
9   Murray, H. A. *et al., Explanations in Personality,* Oxford University Press, 1938.
10   The relevance of such a model is also supported by Mullins, L. J., *Management and Organisation Behaviour,* Pitman Publishing, 1985.
11   Tested and sometimes found wanting, by, for example, Hall, D. T. and Nougaim, K. E., 'An examination of Maslow's need hierarchy in an organisational setting, *Organisation Behaviour and Human Performance,* **3**, February 1968, pp. 12–35; Lawler, E. E. and Suttle, J. L., 'A causal correlational test of the need hierarchy concept', *Organisational Behaviour and Human Performance,* **7**, 1972, pp. 265–87.
12   Murray, H. A. *et al., op. cit.*
13   Maslow, A. H., 'A theory of human motivation', *Psychological Review,* **50**, 1943, pp. 370–96.
14   Maslow, A. H., *ibid.*
15   Maslow, A. H., *Toward a Psychology of Being,* (2nd edn.), Van Nostrand, 1968.
16   Lawler, E. E. and Suttle, J. L., *op. cit.*
17   Blackler, F. H. M. and Williams, A. R. T., 'People's motives at work', in Warr, P., *Psychology at Work,* Penguin, 1971.
18   Alderfer, C. P., 'An empirical test of a theory of human needs', *Organisational Behaviour and Human Performance,* **4**, 1969, pp. 142–175 (but see also ref. 11 above).
19   Cooper, C. L. and Makin, P., *Psychology for Managers,* Macmillan/British Psychological Society, 1984.
20   Festinger, L., *A Theory of Cognitive Dissonance,* Row and Peterson, 1957.
21   Taylor, F. W., *Scientific Management,* Harper & Row, 1947.
22   McGregor, D., *The Human Side of Enterprise,* McGraw-Hill, 1960.

23 Roethlisherger, F. and Dickson, W. J., *Management and the Worker,* Harvard University Press, 1939.
24 Steers, R. M. and Porter, L. W., *Motivation and Work Behaviour,* McGraw-Hill, 1975.
25 Schein, E., *Organisational Psychology,* Prentice-Hall, 1972.
26 McGregor, D., *op. cit.*
27 Argyris, C., *Integrating the Individual and the Organisation,* Wiley, 1964.
28 Likert, R., *New Patterns of Management,* McGraw-Hill, 1961.
29 Herzberg, R., *Work and the Nature of Man,* World, 1966.
30 Schein, E., *op. cit.*
31 Herzberg, R., *The Motivation to Work,* Wiley, 1959.
32 See, for example, Vroom, V. H., *op. cit.*
33 An example is Wall, T. D. and Stephenson, G. M., 'Herzberg's two-factor theory of job attitudes – a critical evaluation and some fresh evidence', *Industrial Relations Journal,* December, 1970.
34 King, N., 'Clarification and evaluation of the two-factor theory of job satisfaction', *Psychological Bulletin,* **70,** 1974.
35 House, R. J. and Wigdor, L. A., 'Herzberg's dual-factor of job satisfaction and motivation: a review of the evidence and a criticism', *Personnel Psychology,* **20,** 1967.
36 McCelland, D. C., *The Achieving Society,* Van Nostrand, 1961.
37 McCelland, D. C. and Burnham, D. H., 'Power is the great motivator', *Harvard Business Review,* March/April, 1976.
38 See, for example, the work of Lewin, K., *Field Theory and Social Science,* Harper, 1951; and Tolman, E. C., *Purposive Behaviour in Animals and Men,* Appleton-Century, 1932.
39 Georgopoulos, B. S., Mahony, G. M. and Jones, N. W., 'A path-goal approach to productivity', *Journal of Applied Psychology,* **41,** 1957.
40 Cooper, C. L. and Makin, P., *op. cit.*
41 Vroom, V., *op. cit.*
42 These are: Porter, L. W. and Lawler, E. E., *Managerial Attitudes and Performavce,* Irwin, 1968; Lawler, E. E., 'Job attitudes and employee motivation: theory, research and practice', *Personnel Psychology,* **23,** 1970; Campbell, J. P., Dunnette, M. D., Lawler, E. E. and Weick, K. E., *Managerial Behaviour, Performance and Effectiveness,* McGraw-Hill, 1970.
43 Examples of such studies are: Georgopoulas, B. S. *et al., op. cit.;* Galbraith, J. and Cummings, L. L., 'An empirical investigation of the motivational determinants of task performance', *Organisational Behaviour and Human Performance,* **2,** 1967; Porter, L. W. and Lawler, E. E., *op. cit.;* Goodman, P. S., Rose, J. H. and Furcon, J. E., 'Comparison of motivational antecedents of the work performance of scientists and engineers', *Journal of Applied Psychology,* **54,** 1970; Kesselman, G. A., Hagan, E. L. and Wherry, R. J., 'A factor-analytic test of the Porter-Lawler expectancy model of work motivation', *Personnel Psychology,* **27,** 1974; Parker, D. F., and Dyer, L., 'Expectancy theory as a within-person behavioural choice model: an empirical test of some conceptual and methodological refinements', *Organisational Behaviour and Human Performance,* **17,** 1976.
44 See, for example: Scarpello, V. and Campbell, J. P., 'Job satisfaction and

the fit between individual needs and organisational rewards', *Journal of Occupational Psychology,* **56**, no. 4, December 1987, pp. 315–28; Shalley, C. E. and Oldham, G. R., 'The effects of goal difficulty and expected external evaluation on intrinsic motivation – a laboratory study', *Academy of Management Journal,* **28**, no. 3, September 1985, pp. 628–40; Snyder, R. A. and Williams, R. R., 'Self theory – an integrative theory of work motivation', *Journal of Occupational Psychology,* **55**, no. 4, December 1982, pp. 257–68; Spector, A., 'Higher-order need strength as a moderator of the job scope – employee outcome relationship – a meta-analysis', *Journal of Occupational Psychology,* **58**, no. 2, June 1985, pp. 119–28; Spicer, M. W., 'A public choice approach to motivating people in bureaucratic organisations', *Academy of Management Review,* **10**, no. 3, July 1985, pp. 518–26.

45   See Cooper, C. and Makin, P., *op. cit.,* for a further discussion of this.

46   Bennett, R., *Managing Personnel and Performance – An Alternative Approach,* Business Books, 1981.

47   Herzberg, F., 'One more time: how do you motivate employees?', *Harvard Business Review,* **46**, 1968.

48   Hackman, J. R. and Oldham, G. R., 'Motivation through the design of work: test of a theory', *Organisational Behaviour and Human Performance,* **16**, 1976.

49   One study of the effectiveness of this approach is Bartlett, J. B., *Success and Failure in Quality Circles,* Employment Relations Resource Centre, 1983.

50   For a description of this approach, see Scriven, R., 'Learning circles', *Journal of European Industrial Training,* **8**, no. 8, 1983.

51   Some examples of research into and discussion of job design, satisfaction and related aspects are: Buchanan, D. and Boddy, D., 'Advanced technology and the quality of working life – the effects of computerised controls on biscuit-making operators', *Journal of Occupational Psychology,* **56**, no. 2, June 1983, pp. 109–120; Cooper, R., *Job Motivation and Job Design,* IPM, 1974; Paul, W. J. and Robertson, K. B., *Job Enrichment and Employee Motivation,* Gower, 1970; Kemp, N. *et al.,* 'Autonomous work groups in a Greenfield site – a comparative study', *Journal of Occupational Psychology,* **56**, no. December 1983, pp. 271–88; Wall, T. D., 'Job redesign and employee participation', in P. B. Warr (ed.), *Psychology at Work,* Penguin, 1978. The Department of Employment's Work Research Unit has undertaken or sponsored numerous studies.

52   See Bennett, R., *op. cit.,* for a discussion of how orientations vary.

53   McCelland, D. C., 'Money as a motivator – some research insights', *The McKinsey Quarterly,* Fall, 1967.

54   Opsahl, R. L. and Dunnette, M. D., 'The role of financial compensation in industrial motivation', *Psychological Bulletin,* **66**, 1966.

55   As shown by the study of Werrimont, P. F. and Fitzpatrick, S., 'The meaning of money', *Journal of Applied Psychology,* **56**, no. 3, 1972, pp. 218–26.

56   Lawler, E. E., *Pay and Organisational Effectiveness,* McGraw-Hill, 1971.

57   See Sangotta, D., *Motivational Theories and Applications for Managers,* American Management Associations, 1977.

5

Interaction with others

A key to organisational success is how well people work together, both as individuals within the work group and as groups needing to collaborate. Interaction with others is crucial to our satisfaction and satisfactoriness at work. We rely on others' approval and respect; we learn from others' instruction and example; others rely on our leadership, guidance and support. In this chapter we shall look at various aspects of interaction, such as interviewing, counselling, bargaining and negotiation.

The way we deal with others arises partly from our attitudes to them and partly from our social skills. We use social skills continuously, sometimes deliberately – as when we direct, train or persuade others – but more often than not we are quite unselfconscious about our interpersonal behaviour. Having done it all our lives, it has become a set of reflexes. One thing is sure – we do not appreciate being told that we lack social skills!

As we saw in Chapter One, social interaction is important in much of a manager's work[1]. Some studies emphasise the great amount of time managers spend interacting, often outside their work unit, in short conversations with colleagues and others, creating a vital network of co-operative relationships. A recent analysis of the activities of the most successful managers in an American sample found that 'socialising-politicking' and 'interaction with outsiders' took up significant amounts of their time, particularly among the middle managers. Obviously all this social interaction is worthy of closer analysis, as a part of management training and development[2].

The nature of social interaction

Social interaction is complex, involving both conscious and unconscious activities, creating a dynamic pattern of mutual influence. This interaction is also affected by the context in which it occurs. We are more guarded in discussing work problems with colleagues or the boss in the office than in the 'psychological safety' of a residential course, for instance, and the atmosphere of a performance appraisal discussion tends to be very different to that of everyday conversation between boss and subordinate, no matter how relaxed we try to make it.

The simplest approach to analysing social interaction is the information-processing model[3]. We act as senders and receivers of information, coding and decoding messages, sometimes failing to 'tune in' correctly so that we miss or misperceive signals, and processing information in an active but selective way, which often leads to errors. Everything we communicate is filtered by the receiver's expectations, assumptions and attitudes, so our message (and often our intention) can be misunderstood. The information-processing model helps us to focus on the components of communication; the message to be transmitted, the channels best suited to it, attracting attention (switching on the receiver), the amount of 'noise' in the system and so on. Once we apply these ideas to interpersonal communication we become aware, for instance, of the great deal of wordless communication that takes place.

Non-verbal communication

We give and receive non-verbal communication largely without conscious effort, and yet it can be a very powerful source of information. When judging what others feel we trust facial expression first, tone of voice next, and words last[4]. We sometimes try to use this powerful medium consciously, trying to hide our true feelings behind a different facial expression or body posture, or exaggerating our emotional response to make sure others know how we feel, but it is difficult to do this convincingly. Our true feelings 'leak', and there is a difference between the impression we 'give' and the impression we 'give off'[5].

Facial expression is used in normal speech for emphasis, for conveying symbolic information (a smile or a wink), and, in a complex way, to regulate conversation, such as by looking doubtful or impatient, and signalling by gaze when we are about to start or finish speaking[6]. Analysis of American politicians' TV debates revealed the extent to which viewers rely unconsciously on a speaker's mannerisms, such as blinking, pauses, nods and body-sway, in judging winner and loser. The contents of an argument may be outweighed by presentation skill. American and British politicians increasingly use drama coaching to aid television presentation.

Effectively concealing or simulating emotions requires a great deal of skill, but any time spent in studying non-verbal communication can be very useful for managers in improving their observational powers. When interviewing, bargaining and counselling we need to be alert to the various clues others give to their state of mind: posture, gesture, tone of voice, rapid or hesitant speech, direction and duration of gaze. These aspects will be explored further in this chapter.

There are simple ways in which to improve one's powers of social observation. When watching television discussions or interviews concentrate on how the participants interact, possibly turning the sound down in order to focus on non-verbal aspects. Consider how people choose clothes, furniture and vocabulary to convey an image. Privately rehearse the expressions you would use, and the way you would sit, to express interest, disinterest, anxiety, self-confidence, defensiveness, hostility, and so on. Such exercises are used in interviewer and counsellor training[7].

Self-knowledge

In Chapter Three personal construct theory was mentioned as a process whereby the individual makes sense of the world. Other people are an important part of our world, and so we develop psychological insights into how and why they behave as they do. The beliefs we assemble about others constitute our personal or 'implicit' behavioural theory. We watch what others do and where, when and why they do it, and attribute attitudes and motives to them. We learn that, at work, people behave in certain ways because their job demands it, and in other ways because of their personal temperament. To become skilled at objectively assessing or counselling others, we need first to develop insights into our own attitudes, beliefs and values, and to discover our own 'implicit personality theory'.

Unfortunately, the word 'theory' has come to mean something next to useless – the opposite of real or practical or useful. In fact, a theory is a framework on which we organise the information needed to solve a problem. The more information or detail facing us, the more we need a theory or model to help us organise information, guide our actions, and evaluate the results. People who claim that they would not dream of using 'theory' in their dealings with people are really admitting that they hold vague, implicit or hidden theories that direct their actions. Most counselling training commences by helping beginners express their implicit theory of human behaviour and then builds on it[8].

Learning in groups

Small-group exercises may be used to develop self-understanding and self-acceptance. These include developing vocabulary to describe feeling and behaviour, developing observation skills, and developing self-knowledge through other group members. Insight is gained by analysing episodes in one's experience, listing the interpersonal situations with which one copes easily, with some difficulty or with great difficulty, predicting one's own behaviour in different situations and, in more advanced stages of training, trying out new roles, new situations and new styles of behaviour[9].

The process of self-discovery and self-disclosure runs counter to the normal habit of protecting (perhaps even denying) our innermost thoughts and feelings. It needs the assistance of an experienced adviser or a reputable institution such as the Tavistock Institute of Human Relations. The methods used to help self-discovery are also somewhat unusual, because self-knowledge can only be gained by personal experience. Yet it is difficult to lay aside the defences we have built up over the years. One of the best-known methods is the T-group, or laboratory training group. Typically this involves six or eight participants in a leaderless group, with a counsellor who rarely intervenes and refrains from directing. The group focuses on process rather than on content; on how and why things are said and on people's reactions and feelings, rather than on what is said. The 'here and now' is emphasised, and 'levelling' (honesty, openness and trust in revealing feelings) is encouraged. The normal social restraints and inhibitions of the work setting are removed, and emotions and attitudes, so often ignored and avoided, are confronted and discussed.

Like a physical laboratory in which powerful reactions may occur, the human relations laboratory needs good supervision and safety precautions. Only volunteers should participate and the group should be supervised by a professionally trained consultant. Many who experience the benefits of such groups want to spread the benefits by running groups themselves, but as a client one should not assume their enthusiasm is matched by their expertise. The majority of people who participate in well-run sessions gain a great sense of achievement and enlightenment. However, a minority find such groups overstressful and unhelpful[10], particularly if the group activity is very unstructured, if the consultant is challenging and confronting, and if the participant's own personality is not conducive to receiving others' insights and possible criticisms.

A further problem with laboratory groups is that of proving their practical benefits in subsequent work performance. Early attempts to use T-groups for management training and development were criticised[11], but as the format has become more structured and work-relevant, and where work teams ('family' groups) are trained together, rather than individual managers in 'stranger' groups, there has been more transfer of human-relations skills into the work setting.

Transactional analysis

T-group activity is underpinned by psychoanalytic theory; the T-group reveals hidden motives, hidden feelings and 'hidden agenda'. The same theory underpins another well known form of insight training – TA or transactional analysis[12]. TA is a means of labelling our interactions in terms of the roles we have experienced and tend to adopt, and are determined by the ego-states from which we operate. Ego-states (ego being the conscious, executive, goal-seeking part of our personality) are listed simply as Child, Parent and Adult, and all are potentially present in the way we behave. In the Child ego-state we may be emotional, flexible, dependent, anxious. In the Parent state we may be directive, protective or punishing. In the Adult state we may be problem-solving, analytical, self-confident and objective. Each state has its positive and negative facets, but clearly we should aim to keep our work interactions at the Adult level.

The usefulness of the TA model lies in:

1 analysing one's own transactions
2 detecting problems when work transactions are 'crossed' e.g. instead of adult-to-adult transaction, parent-to-child transaction may have developed between manager and subordinate
3 detecting and unravelling the complex games that occur, where the psychological needs and satisfactions of participants become more important than effective work outcomes.

A drawback of the TA method is that it can itself become a game, lending itself to superficial point scoring among those who have learned the jargon. Paradoxically, analysis may be substituted for action. Having labelled someone's ego-state we may feel no urgency to tackle the actual work-problem that gave rise to crossed transactions. On the credit side, TA is a simple and direct model which can serve as a stepping-stone to more detailed analysis and action in solving problems of interaction with individuals at work.

Assertiveness

Much effort has gone into sensitivity training, on the assumption that managers tend to be too tough with others. In fact many newly promoted managers and supervisors find it difficult to exercise authority and control over others, and lack the interpersonal skills to deal with awkward, obstructive and aggressive people. Having a high level of professional skill in engineering, programming or accountancy does not automatically ensure success as a manager in these professions. The manager may find problems not only in dealing with subordinates, but with overbearing colleagues or superiors. One author[13] writing for supervisors makes the sad observation that rudeness and offhand treatment by managers must be expected, that one must not be surprised to receive a negative reaction to a perfectly sound idea, and that one has to learn to bear indignities gracefully.

A positive way to deal with these difficulties is assertiveness training[14]. Initiated in the United States to help raise the social competence of minority groups, the techniques have been found useful in occupational training. It is not a form of therapy, and it does not teach aggression or unethical manipulation of others. It does teach one to explore one's own unassertive behaviour and attitudes and, having adopted a new confidence in one's own rights, to express one's views and position firmly.

In order to modify our behaviour we need to examine the sources of the behaviour, and in particular what payoffs or rewards are maintaining the behaviour. Some causes may be social: aggressive men are socially acceptable, aggressive women are not; passive women are socially acceptable, passive men are not. The payoff for non-assertion may be not having to feel anxious that we appear pushy or rude and, in the short term at least, knowing that others approve of our non-assertiveness. On reflection, though, we can see that the long-term effects are damaging. To continue being non-assertive we have to downgrade our self-image. We may grow increasingly bitter at others exploiting our passivity, and they in turn may pass from approval to pity to guilt and irritation at our behaviour. Similarly, aggression offers short-term rewards: release of frustration and submission, or even admiration, from others. In the long run, aggression may lead to isolation, or to an escalation of our aggression to maintain the effect, or to others' resentment and retaliation. Assertiveness avoids the extremes of passivity and aggression, and is the action of standing up for one's rights (without damaging others' rights) and honestly expressing one's thoughts and feelings.

The methods of assertiveness training are similar to those already described. Participants describe and analyse the problems they have encountered, in group discussion. For instance, counter staff, who have to deal regularly with hostile customers or clients, role-play the difficult situations they have met, with advice and encouragement from the group and counsellor. The training can be seen as 'desensitisation'; by gradually introducing anxiety-producing confrontations in a relaxed and supportive setting, fear and withdrawal responses are unlearned and replaced by positive, successful behaviours.

You can try out these development methods without attending formal classes. For example, a simple but effective form of 'imaginal desensitisation' would be to imagine calmly the situation in all its detail as you give the management presentation you are dreading. Imagine in detail how the presentation will go very well, and the good reception it will get. Then imagine the worst that can possibily happen, a hostile and critical reception. You will realise that the worst is not so terrible, and also is rather unlikely, when imagined in detail, and that the good outcomes are more likely and quite attractive. By physically relaxing, and then approaching the dreaded situation in our imagination, we can overcome the anxiety that paralyses effective action.

Successful desensitisation depends on tackling the smallest difficulties first, establishing a successful base from the which to tackle the more difficult problems. One should list the problem situations and tackle the easiest ones first, for example refusing the extra drink you do not really want or the phone call you are too busy to take. One should also be prepared to put long-term effort into long-established problems such as changing one's general style of employee relations, since others will take time to adjust to one's new-found assertiveness.

Assertiveness training is increasingly being used in supervisory and management development, and for helping staff responsible for customer contact. The process of modifying or shaping one's own behaviour just described is a very useful approach to modifying others' behaviour, and is the basis of a staff management technique mentioned later.

Leadership skills

Leadership is a complex activity. Some writers have emphasised leadership personality[15], others task and team-management[16], and others still the one-to-one aspects of the leader's job. The manager must be able to lead a group, but also to adopt a different style for the different individuals in the team. Some writers have described the manager's job as a series of links with individual subordinates: the VDL or vertical dyadic (paired) linkage model[17]. Pursuing this idea of managing individuals, writers such as Honey[18] and Hersey[19] apply the behaviour modification approach to staff management, and Mager[20] points out its importance in the training field. The behaviour modification approach is central to the 'One Minute Manager' described by Blanchard and Johnson[21].

The behaviour modification approach requires careful observation, first of the individual and of the individual's work setting. Then, as outlined in assertiveness training, one has to understand what the behaviour is, how it falls short, how it originated, and what payoffs maintain it. The Hersey method of situational leadership suggests analysis of the individual along a scale of work-related maturity. This method stresses that the manager should not be satisfied with merely acceptable levels of work performance, but has a duty to develop the subordinate to a high level of task maturity. This is achieved by a deliberate application of leadership style along a scale composed of the two major dimensions of task-related leadership and relationships-oriented leadership. These are the two major dimensions emerging from leadership research in the 1960s and 1970s, and are used in other models of management behaviour such as Blake's Grid[22] and Reddin's

3-D Model[23]. Hersey recommends task-centred supervision initially, as the subordinate is encouraged to get to a minimally acceptable level of task performance. As this level is achieved, the manager rewards continued development by an increase in relationship aspects, by personal attention, support and encouragement. As task maturity continues to rise it is reinforced by a progressive decrease in task-related behaviour by the manager (i.e. less directive supervision). As task maturity rises to the highest levels, the manager reinforces this by decreasing his own relationship-oriented behaviour, offering even more autonomy, through delegation and trust.

This system is a dynamic one: it offers guidance on how to deal differently not only with individual employees but also with different levels of task maturity in different parts of an individual's job. The approach requires planning and consistency. Rewards are to be given only after the performance has been displayed, otherwise one is rewarding and reinforcing low performance. As a manager you can examine your conscience by asking 'Who gets most of my attention and encouragement? My best staff or my worst staff?' Perhaps it should be neither.

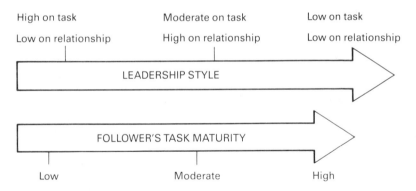

Fig. 5.1 Adaptation of the Hersey Model

Counselling

The best and the worst staff need counselling at times, and rare though these occasions may be, the manager's interpersonal skills will prove vital. Counselling is a broad term, and we shall look first at confidential counselling, later at performance counselling. Either an individual will come to the manager, often in the grip of great anxiety or other emotions, to have a private talk, or the manager may become aware of some underlying problem adversely affecting an individual's behaviour, work performance or health, and will decide to hold a private dicussion.

As such occasions tend to occur unexpectedly, it is useful to consider a general way of coping with them in advance. Firstly, the manager will have to achieve a balanced approach. Although confronted with an individual problem, the interests of the individual have to be balanced with those of the rest of the group and with the demands of the job. Balance also has to be achieved between helping too little and helping too much; phrases like 'be sympathetic but not gullible or sentimental' and 'be sympathetic but not interfering or prying' come to mind. Balance also has to be achieved between short-term solutions to the presenting problem, and the long-term welfare of the individual. Secondly, the manager should have some idea of when and where to refer the person for special help if, for instance, the problem looks like alcoholism or psychiatric illness. Whatever the problem, the manager should have enough basic skill to conduct a preliminary discussion to assemble some facts, however.

Counselling skills

Although counselling for employees was part of the Hawthorne Studies activity in the 1930s, it has been a very restricted activity in the UK. However, counselling in clinical therapy and in social welfare is a very widespread activity, and has generated a great deal of training. Career counselling, health counselling and marriage counselling are some of the areas of recent expansion. The British Association for Counselling is a resource centre and the British Psychological Society has in recent years advanced counselling as an area of research and professional interest[24]. There are many courses, of varying lengths, offered by colleges and counselling organisations, and some excellent handbooks. The emphasis is on non-directive counselling, which is appropriate in welfare and education. The needs of the manager, who is in a relationship of authority with the client, have been neglected, and counselling training has tended to avoid dealing with the grievance and disciplinary situations in the work setting.

The skills of counselling include:

1 Actively observing and listening
2 Developing rapport and empathy (seeing things from the other's perspective)
3 Preventing one's personal views and feelings from interfering
4 Being patient
5 Analysing the other's decision-making processes and progress
6 Helping the other to identify and implement solutions and strategies

Acquiring counselling skills

As with assertiveness training, the first step towards acquiring counselling skill is self-knowledge – being clear about one's own value position. This is heavily emphasised in non-directive counselling, as in Rogers' dictum of 'warm positive regard' for the client in an open, trusting relationship[25]. Other writers urge that each counsellor must develop a personal counselling model, a personal counselling theory[26]. For the manager who counsels only occasionally, a good grasp of the basic skills, together with an appreciation of the ethical issues and personal needs involved, is ample.

The needs involved are those of the client and those of the counsellor. As a manager, the counsellor will feel the need to use experience and good judgement to point out what is wrong, and to urge the most logical solutions. It is not easy to set aside these direct leadership skills. The manager must instead give priority to these aims:

1 To discover the facts, including the employee's attitudes and needs
2 To create rapport by relieving the tension, anxiety, or anger of the employee (so that the employee can eventually talk and listen calmly)
3 To help the employee identify and accept his or her own problem
4 To help the employee identify and implement solutions to the problem
5 To help restore the employee's sense of dignity and responsibility

What makes these aims difficult to achieve is that the problem as first presented is often not the true problem, and that the state of mind of the employee can make progress to these aims slow and sometimes erratic. The self-defeating needs and fears of the employee may include:

1 Not wanting to admit difficulties to oneself, let alone another
2 Not wanting to trust others, and not wanting them to judge us
3 Wanting someone else to take over our problem and tell us what to do
4 Not wanting someone else to take over our problem and tell us what to do
5 Wanting sympathy, not help with painfully unravelling and solving problems
6 Wanting to feel that our problem is unique and insoluble (and a kind of distinction we have come to depend upon)
7 Not wanting to bother others with our problem, which we would prefer to treat as trivial.

Both in confidential counselling, grievance and disciplinary cases, the employee's emotions are a major barrier to communication. This is why the counsellor's first task is to relieve the employee's tensions. If on the contrary the counsellor's own emotions become engaged through irritation, impatience or anger, the difficulties escalate into confrontation, and the counsellor also loses the ability to perceive issues clearly. A useful skill in the early stages is therefore the reflective style of communicating. Following open-ended questions such as, 'Please tell me about it', the counsellor summaries the employee's responses with reflective statements like, 'So you feel the problem started when . . .'. The counsellor signals positive interest and attention, and encourages the employee to continue, without having added any criticism, disbelief or suggested solutions. These might distract the employee from this very important process of clarifying things to oneself by talking about them. Patience on the counsellor's part is very important, as the employee may pause for thinking time, or appear to contradict their first statements. Rather than interrupting logically with 'But you said a moment ago that . . .', the counsellor should welcome inconsistencies as steps to clear thinking.

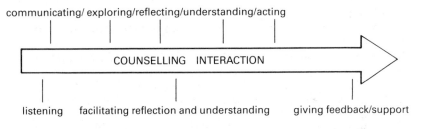

Fig. 5.2 The stages of counselling

These are only very general guidelines for the counsellor on the pattern of counselling to be followed. Ideally the employee will move through the emotional stage to exploration and understanding of the problem and then on to 'emergent directionality' and effective action. The counsellor will employ different skills at each stage and, with experience, will develop good timing. A useful outcome of counselling training is identifying one's typical style of communication, and developing an additional repertoire of styles to call upon as the situation demands[27]. Unlike a full-time counsellor, the manager has to decide whether to continue to spend time with an employee who seems to be making no progress.

If an employee has a complex problem, the manager may find it better to plan for several short sessions, rather than concluding in one marathon. The manager will also find that the non-directive style appropriate to the opening stages of counselling has to be backed up by a more directive style in later stages or, for example, in disciplinary cases, where part of the aim is to make it clear that rules have been broken and what penalties may be applied. Ultimately, however, self-imposed solutions work best. The counselling theories of later writers such as Carkhuff[28] and Egan[29] include more directive techniques than the early Rogerian theory.

An ideal counselling support for both manager and employee is the type of employee assistance programme that has developed in a number of major corporations in America and more recently in the UK, by the Post Office[30] for instance. Recognising the growing threat of stress and chemical dependency (alcohol or drug abuse) amongst employees, and recognising the major costs to the enterprise in loss of work time and skilled personnel, and lowered standards, some employers have set up confidential counselling services in addition to the usual medical and health facilities. Such counselling services stand outside the normal organisation lines of reporting in order to protect confidentiality. Some even extend their services to employees' families in such areas as marital or parenting problems, financial and legal problems. If the employer is unable to provide specialist advisers in these areas the company counsellor can provide links with external sources.

Confidential counselling systems bring their own problems of confidentiality, resistance from managers and union representatives (because they fear loss of function), difficulties in drawing the line between personal problems and work-related problems, and of resolving work-induced problems. These problems have been courageously tackled in a number of companies and some have publicly reported major benefits.

Performance appraisal and counselling

Employee report systems have existed for generations, often without the knowledge of those reported upon. Typical shortcomings of systems used in major corporations and public services were secrecy and centrality (local manager and employee were not given the results), irregularity (often, reports were made only when staff were reviewed for promotion), vague standards (ratings were done by remote raters), and vague measures (ratings of personality or general conduct rather than work performance).

In these circumstances counselling was not an issue; the information on the forms would have been of little use to the employee since it was often inaccurate, vague and came too late to be acted upon. In the post-war period some American organisations and, later, some UK organisations, instituted appraisal by immediate managers on employees' work performance, accompanied by feedback to the employees. The purpose was to improve performance and morale by letting employees know where they stood. Initial results were poor[31]. Managers were reluctant to appraise, and reluctant to discuss results with employees. Reports were filled in vaguely or not at all. Praise seemed to have little effect on performance, while criticism seemed to be counter-productive[32].

Research in the 1960s showed that the way forward was to involve the employee in self-evaluation and joint problem-solving. Participation in setting objectives for performance improvement gained much more commitment from both good and poor performers. Appraisal and counselling systems came into widespread use in British organisations in the early 1970s, and some were quite advanced in their design. One example of such a system was created from scratch in the Port of London Authority in the early 1970s, an unusually open system with training not only for appraisers but also for appraisees. Like many other appraisal systems, it failed because it was too advanced. Staff appraisal and counselling touches on the central values of the organisation, and if the culture of the organisation is against job analysis and individual accountability it will fail. Individual enlightened managers may keep such systems going for a time, but appraisal must spring from and be integrated with the organisation's general management systems and day-to-day management style in order to flourish in the long terms. In Chapter Ten we return to the issue of suiting development techniques to the organisation's culture.

The skills of counselling in staff appraisal include the observational, analytical and communication skills already covered. In addition, the manager should adopt the gradual technique, as in behaviour modification, of tackling one problem at a time. Building on an employee's existing strengths is often more productive than harping on intractable weaknesses such as shortcomings in personality. Individual appraisals should also be seen in perspective with team-building efforts (see Chapter Six). Appraisal and counselling systems are now much less of a novelty than they were in the early 1970s, though some aspects, such as rating performance continue to cause difficulties[33]. Ratings will be discussed later in this chapter. Performance counselling is an area in which computer-assisted training techniques have been used with some success. One can readily see how the system skills (form-filling and so on), though not the interpersonal aspects, lend themselves to a programmed learning approach. Nevertheless, reports[34] suggest that such training is better than none.

Bargaining and negotiation

Bargaining and negotiation enter into appraisal and counselling in subtle ways, but here we will look at their more formal aspects. As with other interpersonal skills, negotiation tends to be seen as an instinctive flair, the combination of a tough and devious personality with a competitive or even bullying style. In some books on improving success in bargaining, the writers imply that theory is a waste of time. There is obviously no substitute for real experience, but even a little time spent reflecting or theorising about bargaining and negotiation can be helpful, and there are some excellent guides[35].

Most industrial relations specialists treat the field as an elaborate set of rules and regulations, and as part of the wider scene of social and political power. Behavioural science has focused more on the detailed processes of industrial relations, such as how problems arise from conflicting attitudes and expectations, from leadership difficulties and from poor communications. Studies of industrial negotiations prove that disputes are often badly handled, with unclear aims and only partial or an erroneous grasp of the facts on both sides[36]. As in counselling, one can find that the apparent problem in dispute is not the real problem and that, although the participants treat their problem as unique, there are regular patterns and processes.

The simplest model of the bargaining and negotiation process consists of four stages. First, the parties formally and emphatically declare their own position and demands. Second, they interact less formally to explore each others positions and demands (described by one writer as probing the opponent's weaknesses while concealing one's own). Third, tentative proposals and concessions emerge on which detailed bargaining takes place. Lastly, agreements and packages are concluded and action begun. This can be used as a prescriptive model as well as a descriptive one.

Having considered the process in outline one can look in detail at the skills and effectiveness to be aimed for. The first skill is analysing the situation in terms of one's own position and needs and those of the opposition. The 'better bargaining' textbooks treat this in a combative way, but the longer-term view suggests that one should at this stage decide what sub-issues are open to integrative bargaining (I win/you win) rather than distributive (I win/you lose). The longer-term view should also consider what attitudes or expectations one hopes will persist after this particular issue has been resolved. For example, forcing a win on a trivial issue may leave a residue of resentment or mistrust that makes progress difficult later[37].

Early preparation pinpoints the maximum and minimum gains/ concessions which both you and your opponents will accept. It is important to empathise with the other party and to consider what they perceive as desirable. One has to offer what they think they want rather than what you think they ought to want! Meanwhile one has to avoid intra-organisational conflict by keeping one's client group happy. Partridge[38] has written about the struggle of shop stewards to translate their members' demands into claims which will both satisfy and unite the members and also be legitimate claims on which to negotiate with management.

The second skill is arguing one's case effectively. Forcefulness is often appropriate, but is has to be tempered with enough sensitivity to avoid causing unnecessary reactions. Emotive language or abuse and point-scoring to satisfy personal needs must be avoided. Essentially, negotiation consists of changing the opponent's perception of your case and of their own. Arguing one's case effectively will persuade the opposition of the logic and attractiveness of one's proposals and of the weakness of their case. In doing so, one can be aware of the pressures on oneself and opposition representatives: attraction to the opponent's point of view, adherence to the views of the group one is representing and pressure from the context, for example the company's financial position.

The third skill is sensing any subtle shifts in emphasis by the other party, and both signalling and receiving signals of possible compromise. Here one begins to make proposals, and must adhere to the rules of behaviour modification mentioned earlier. Reward concessions by concessions; do not reward intransigence by concessions. Make every offer conditional on equivalent concessions by the opposition. Where deadlocks occur, means of maintaining communication must be found, necessitating 'talks about talks' – at least discussing the form of the talks, if not the content. Margerison and Leary[39] have written of the use of mediators. Chapter Nine looks at organisational power, and its role in negotiation cannot be overlooked. Perception of power is more important than power itself, as can be seen in what Sheane called the 'technology of threats'. Both threats and offers must be seen as credible, and Sheane[40] discussed how to 'restructure the power dynamics' (make the opponent's power look less effective).

The fourth skill lies in packaging and concluding negotiations effectively. Attention to detail and actuarial skill are required, as well as an awareness of the dirty tricks one's opponents may adopt (amusingly described by Kennedy *et al.*[41]). In the final stages one should emphasise the expected outcomes of agreements in specific behavioural terms. Vague agreements are hard to implement. In this section, interpersonal skills of bargaining and negotiation have been examined. The broader skills of conflict management will be treated in Chapter Ten.

Interviewing

Compared with the demands of counselling, handling grievance and discipline problems, and industrial relations negotiations, the skills of interviewing are very straightforward. Provided that some preparation is made beforehand, and that the interview follows a structure, any manager can turn the interview into a very effective tool. In the fact-finding interview the interviewer should have determined beforehand which topic areas are to be covered, so that there is a framework for asking questions and recording information. The rule of thumb should be, 'short questions: long answers'. This is helped by a liberal use of 'open' questions, for example, 'Could you tell me about your job as safety representative?' These may need to be followed up by more specific questions in a 'funnel' technique; 'Could you describe a typical safety hazard you have dealt with?' or direct questions like 'What first-aid qualifications do you hold?' When asking about people's work, open questions are particularly useful for getting information on difficulties and distastes.

As an interviewee is actively seeking to create a favourable impression, a poor interviewer can be misled in many ways. More difficult than information-gathering, however, is the decision-making aspect of selection interviewing. It is vagueness in this aspect that has made interviewing appear such a weak method in much research[42]. Yet common sense suggests that if one has not clearly defined the qualities one is seeking (by job analysis and job specification), and has not conducted the interview on the basis of the specification, then the interview will not be valid or reliable.

Rodger's seven-point plan, with the headings:
 physical
 attainments
 general intelligence
 special aptitudes
 interests
 disposition
 circumstances
and Munro Fraser's fivefold framework, with the headings:
 social impact
 qualifications and experience
 innate abilities
 motivation
 emotional adjustment

are perhaps the best-known and most widely used interview checklists in the UK[43]. These can be adapted for the particular selection being carried out, and some weighting should be attempted for the different elements. In the difficult stage of final comparison of candidates, the best method is to compare them one element at a time, which avoids the 'halo' effect mentioned later.

Rating

Performance appraisal and selection interviewing demand some skill in systematically assessing and comparing individuals. Behavioural science can help in this by offering a range of rating methods and by drawing attention to the common errors of rating systems. The simplest formats are for classifying individuals into categories, or ranking them in order on certain characteristics. Next come rating scales, typically a five- or seven-point scale, which assume that all users adopt the same values for the intervals, for example outstanding, very good, good, satisfactory and poor. The fairest scales for work assessment are probably the behaviourally-anchored rating scales. These are sets of descriptions of different standards of job performance, ranked by consensus into scales. The manager chooses the descriptions of performance which match the employee being assessed. Compiling these scales is somewhat laborious and their shelf-life is limited because they have to be revised as job activities change, but they are practical and easy for the rater. Common rating errors are:

1 *Halo effect* where a good rating on one aspect of a person's performance leads to good ratings on everything; a reflection of general liking
2 *Reverse halo* where an adverse rating on one aspect adversely affects all other ratings; a reflection of general dislike
3 *Leniency* setting the criterion or level of assessment too low
4 *Harshness* setting the criterion too high
5 *Low reliability* shifting one's standards
6 *Stereotyping* using a group characteristic, such as age, as the basis of a number of judgements about an individual.

Some organisations, for example British Telecom, are well known for the care with which they train their interviewers and those acting as selectors in assessment centres. To ensure consistency, selectors can be tested for uniform standards in how they rate filmed interviewees. The trained interviewer gives more accurate and more consistent judgements[44].

References

1 See Chapter 1: Stewart (*ibid.*); Mintzberg (ibid.).
2 Kotter, J. P., *The General Managers,* The Free Press, 1982; Davis and Luthans, 'Defining and researching leadership as a behavioural construct', *Journal of Applied Behavioral Studies,* **3**, 1984, pp. 237–51;

Luthans, F., Rosenkrantz, S. A. and Hennessey, H. W., 'What do successful managers really do?' *Journal of Applied Behavioral Science,* **21**, no. 3, 1985, pp. 225–70.

3   Argyle, M., *The Psychology of Interpersonal Behaviour,* Penguin, 1981; Argyle, M., Furnham, A. and Graham, J. A., *Social Situations,* Cambridge University Press, 1981; Burnstein, E. and Schul, Y., 'The information basis of social judgements: operations in forming an impression of another person', *Journal of Experimental Social Psychology,* **18**, 1982, pp. 217–34.

4   Ekman, P. and Friesen, W. V., *Unmasking the Face,* Prentice Hall, 1975.

5   Goffman, F., *The Presentation of Self in Everyday Life,* Doubleday, 1959.

6   Buck, R., *Nonverbal Behaviour and the Communication of Affect,* Guildford, 1984.

7   Nelson-Jones, R., *The Theory and Practice of Counselling Psychology,* Holt Rinehart & Winston, 1982.

8   Hansen, J. C., Stevic, R. R. and Warner, J. R., *Counselling: Theory and Process* (3rd edn), Alleyn & Bacon, 1982.

9   Gilmore, S. K., *The Counsellor-in-training,* Century Psychology Series, Prentice Hall, 1973; Nelson-Jones, R., *Practical Counselling Skills,* Holt Rinehart & Winston, 1983.

10   Cooper, C. L., 'How psychologically dangerous are T-groups and encounter groups?', *Human Relations,* **28**, 1975, pp. 249–60; Cooper C. L. and Bowles, D., 'Hurt or helped: a study of the personal impact on managers of experiential small-group experiences', Training Services Report No. 10, HMSO.

11   Campbell, J. P. and Dunnette, M. D., (1968) 'Effectiveness of T-group experiences in managerial training and development', *Psychological Bulletin,* **70**, no. 2, 1968, pp. 73–104.

12   Berne, E., *Games People Play,* Penguin, 1964; Woolams, S. and Brown, M., *The Total Handbook of Transactional Analysis,* Prentice Hall, 1979; Wellin, M, 'Transactional analysis in the workplace', *Personnel Management,* **10**, no. 7, 1978.

13   Betts, P. W., *Supervisory Studies* (3rd edn), Macdonald & Evans, 1981.

14   Shaw and Rutledge, 'Assertiveness training for managers', Training and Development Journal, **30**, no. 9, 1976; Back, K. and K., *Assertiveness at Work: a practical guide to handling awkward situations,* McGraw Hill, 1982; Meier and Pulichene, 'Evaluation of assertiveness training', *Training and Development Journal,* **34**, no. 1980.

15   See Chapter 3.

16   See Chapter 6.

17   Graen, G. B., Danserau, F. and Minami, R., 'Dysfunctional leadership styles', *Organizational Behaviour and Human Performance,* **7**, 1972, pp. 216–36.

18   Honey, P., *Solving People-Problems,* McGraw Hill, 1980.

19   Hersey, P. and Blanchard, K. H., *Management of Organizational Behaviour: utilizing human resources* (4th edn), Prentice Hall, 1982; Lueder, A., 'Don't be misled by LEAD', *Journal of Applied Behavioral Science,* **21**, no. 2, 1985, p. 143.

20   Mager, R. E. and Pipe, P., 'Analysing performance problems: or, "You really oughta wanna . . ." ', Fearon, 1970.

21 Blanchard, K. H. and Johnson, S., *The One Minute Manager,* Collins, 1983; *Putting the One Minute Manager to Work,* Collins, 1984.

22 Blake, R. R. and Mouton, J. S., *The Managerial Grid III,* Gulf, 1984.

23 Reddin, W., *The Best of Bill Reddin,* Institute of Personnel Management, 1985.

24 British Association for Counselling, 37a Sheep Street, Rugby CV21 3BX.

25 Rogers, C. R., *Client-centred Therapy,* Constable, 1965/81.

26 Hansen *et al., op. cit.*; Nelson-Jones, *op. cit.*

27 Karoly, P. and Kanfer, F. H., *Self-management and Behaviour Change: from theory to practice,* Pergamon, 1982.

28 Carkhuff, R. P., *Helping and Human Relations: a primer for lay and professional helpers,* Holt Rinehart & Winston, 1972.

29 Egan, G., *The Skilled Helper* (2nd edn), Brooks & Cole, 1982; *Exercises in Helping Skills,* Brooks & Cole, 1982.

30 Cairo, 'Counselling in industry: a review', *Personnel Psychology,* **36,** 1983, pp. 1–18; Hall, J. and Fletcher, B. C., 'Coping with personal problems at work', *Personnel Management,* February 1984, pp. 30–33.

31 Rowe, K. H., 'An appraisal of appraisals', *Journal of Management Studies,* **1,** no. 1, 1964, pp. 1–25.

32 Meyer, H. H., Kay, E. and French, J. R. P., (1964) 'Split roles in performance appraisal', *Harvard Business Review,* **43,** 1964, pp. 123–9.

33 Landy, F. J. and Farr, J. L., (1980) 'Performance rating', *Psychology Bulletin,* **63,** 1980, pp. 751–4; Mount, M. K., (1984) 'Satisfaction with an appraisal system and appraisal discussion', *Journal of Occupational Behavior* **63,** 1984, pp. 271–9, Wexley, K. N. and Youtz, M. A., 'Rater beliefs about others: their effects on rater errors and rating accuracy', *Journal of Occupational Psychology,* **58,** no. 4, 1985, pp. 267–75.

34 Davis, B. L. and Mount, M. K., 'Effectiveness of appraisal training using computer assisted instruction and behaviour modelling', *Personnel Psychology,* **37,** no. 3, 1984, pp. 439–52.

35 Kennedy, G., Benson, J. and McMillan, J., *Managing Negotiations,* Business Books, 1980; Kennedy, G., *Everything is Negotiable!,* Business Books, 1982; Atkinson, G. N., *The Effective Negotiator,* Quest, 1975; Kniveton, B. and Towers, B., *Training for Negotiation,* Business Books, 1978; Rackham, N. and Carlisle, J., 'The effective negotiator', *Journal of European Industrial Training,* **2,** 1978, pp. 2–11; Cousins, J. Y. and McCall, J. B., 'The identification of skills in the negotiation process', *Personnel Review,* **13,** no. 4, 1984, pp. 30–34.

36 Douglas, A., *Industrial Peacemaking,* Columbia University Press, 1962.

37 Morley, I. and Stephenson, G. M., *The Social Psychology of Bargaining,* Allen & Unwin, 1977; Stephenson, G. M. and Brotherton, C. J., *Industrial Relations: a social-psychological approach,* Wiley, 1979.

38 Partridge, B. E., 'Shop stewards: the process of leadership on the shopfloor' NATO Conference Paper, Munich: Paper 29, University of Aston Management Centre; Pedler, M., 'Shop stewards as leaders', *Industrial Relations Journal,* **5,** 1973, pp. 43–60.

39 Margerison, C. J. and Leary, M., 'Managing industrial conflicts: the mediator's role', *Management Decision,* **13,** no. 4, 1975.

40 Sheane, D., 'When and how to intervene in conflict', *Personnel Management,* **11,** 1979, pp. 32–6; Bazerman and Neale, 'Improving negotiation

effectiveness', *Journal of Applied Psychology,* **67**, no. 5, 1982, pp. 543–58.

41   Kennedy *et al.,* see ref. 35.

42   Ulrich, L. and Trumbo, D., 'The selection interview since 1949', *Psychological Bulletin,* **63**, 1965, pp. 100–116; Wright, O. R., 'Summary of research on the selection interview since 1964', *Personnel Psychology,* **22**, 1969, pp. 391–413; Arvey, R. D. and Campion, J. E., 'The employment interview: a summary and review of recent literature', *Personnel Psychology,* **35**, 1982, pp. 281–332.

43   Rodger, A., *The Seven-Point plan* (3rd edn), NIIP, 1970; Rawling, K., *Notes on the Seven-Point Plan: new perspectives fifty years on,* NFER-Nelson, 1985; Fraser, J. M., *Employment Interviewing,* McDonald & Evans, 1978.

44   Keenan, A., 'Interviewers' evaluation of applicant characteristics: differences between personnel and non-personnel managers', *Journal of Occupational Psychology,* **49**, no. 1976, pp. 223–30; Bayne, R., 'Can selection interviewing be improved?', *Journal of Occupational Psychology,* **50**, no. 3, 1977, pp. 161–7; Ivancevich, J. M., 'Longitudinal study of the effects of rater training on psychometric error in ratings', *Journal of Applied Psychology,* **64**, 1979, pp. 502–8.

6

Working in groups

Why groups are important

Most of us are members of one group or another – a family unit, a club, a professional body's branch committee, the section we work in at the office or factory. We join some of these groups (e.g. a club) because of a common or shared interest with the aims of the group and its members. They help us pursue that interest. We become a member of other groups (e.g. the office section) by being appointed to do a particular job. The work we do may or may not involve formal links with others in the section. Even if it does not, the simple fact of being physically or geographically close to other people will help create close ties or interactions between the staff of the section. Usually, we will enjoy being a group member, because we can gain certain satisfactions, such as feeling wanted, friendliness and so on (see Maslow's social needs).

People will often form into groups whether or not there is a formal requirement to do so, and this is graphically illustrated by an example from an electronics company. One area of the shop-floor contained workers who assembled components for television sets. They sat in groups around work benches, but worked independently of each other. This allowed them to talk quite easily to each other. The production manager tried to get the talking stopped because of a 'company rule' against it, and his 'solution' was to reorganise the layout of the benches. In the new layout, workers sat at individual benches on either side of a long bench, all facing in the same direction. After a few weeks he was forced to revert to the original layout because, under the new one, workers got out of their seats to go and talk with fellow workers. As a result, production fell and increased supervision became necessary.

This example illustrates that people enjoy being part of a group and that, if the work situation does not allow for this, they will find a way round it, often to the detriment of performance. It is sensible to design work situations that enables people to gain what they want from being a member of a group while at the same time performing work effectively (this is one reason why some forms of job design are based on group working). This is just as true in situations where we are obliged to be a member of a group, such as when we are appointed to work on a project with a number of other people or to serve on a committee.

Thus, groups are an important means by which we achieve certain satisfactions or pursue certain interests. If we are denied these things, we may look for other ways of achieving them. We embark on behaviour that suits us but may not suit the organisation. Groups also act as important sources of control over behaviour. A second example illustrates this. It concerns a newly appointed craftsman in a factory in the south of England. He had previously worked in the north as a supervisor in a factory where black coats and bowler hats were sported. On going to his new place of work in this attire, he became the focus of much humour and ridicule by his new work-mates, who 'mistook' him for the managing director. He ignored all this, until one day he found his bowler flattened beneath a two-ton press. He never wore it to work again!

Groups are also important because they can help or hinder the use of new equipment or the implementation of change. Resistence to change is a well known phenomenon, and usually occurs when the change is seen as threatening (such as loss of jobs or lowering of earnings) or where the ties and relationships between group members are broken. Hence, in one company where job rotation was being introduced, people effectively prevented it happening by claiming that it made it more difficult to achieve a satisfactory bonus level, which it did. They also said that they did not like moving from one job to another because they never made any real friends.

Groups, then, can influence their members and, since most of us are members of groups, most of us come under the influence. Managers need to know about and understand how groups operate and how they influence behaviour in order to be effective in getting the most from the people they are managing *and* in order to help those people get the most from their work experience. This chapter explains some of the features of groups that are of importance to managers. It assumes the reader has read the previous chapters on motivation and interaction with others.

What is a 'group'?

In behavioural science, much of the study of groups is carried out by social psychologists. These are people who are interested in the behaviour of individuals in a social context. That context may involve many other people, as would be the case in a football crowd, or it may involve relatively few people, as in the case of the football team itself. Social psychologists are primarily interested in the latter. So are most managers. This chapter will, therefore, be concerned with relatively small groups, in which there is a good deal of face-to-face interaction.

The definition of a 'group' used in this chapter is based on the social psychologist's focus of interest. A group may be defined as 'a plurality of persons who interact with one another in a given context more than they do with anyone else'[1]. In addition, such a set of people form a group only if they perceive themselves to be a group. The mere physical presence of other people is not sufficient to constitute 'a group'. We are therefore talking about groups in a psychological sense rather than about groups based on other criteria (e.g. age, height, weight, location), but our definition is not universally accepted among students of small group behaviour.

Golembiewski[2], reviewing the debate in the area, recognises a range of different standpoints. At one end of the range are explanations that regard groups as having mental characteristics of their own analogous to those of individuals. The group becomes an object of study in its own right, with a 'group mind' quite separate from the minds of the individuals of which it is comprised.

At the other end of the range is the assertion that there can be no study of groups which is not essentially a study of individuals. The individual represents the only reality and the group is merely an aggregate of individuals. The whole can never be more than the sum of its parts. Thus only the behaviour of individuals, whether alone or together, justifies investigation.

Between these two extremes there are approaches that acknowledge that people behave as if groups were real. In other words, they exist in the perceptions of their members and observers. They are subjectively real, and as such can influence the behaviour of individuals, but the individual remains the prime focus of study.

Finally there are approaches which claim that for purposes of analysis the group may be regarded as real. It has a conceptual reality in its social processes and structure of relationships which can legitimately be studied without reference to the characteristics of its members.

In this chapter, while not subscribing to the 'group mind' approach, we shall be focusing not only on the behaviour and experience of the individual, but also on structures and processes at a group level. To this end we shall adopt the definition suggested by Schein, who suggested that a group is:

> any number of people who (1) interact with one another, (2) are psychologically aware of one another, and (3) perceive themselves to be a group[3].

What sort of groups are we concerned with?

We have already seen that we are not concerned with mere aggregates such as a queue in the works canteen or a number of people who happen to enter the lift together. Nor are we too interested in whole organisations or large departments which, despite possibly having some shared sense of belonging to the same unit, do not all interact with one another and are probably not all aware of each other.

What kinds of grouping are we concerned with? It is common for the distinction to be drawn between formal and informal groups within organisations. Formal groups are created to carry out some specific task or meet some organisationally required goal. Some aspects of their structure, procedural rules and membership are likely to be explicitly stated. They may be relatively permanent in nature, such as a management team, or a particular work unit on the factory floor. They may be temporary, such as a committee of enquiry or a project team. Informal groups, on the other hand, are not explicitly set up by management but arise spontaneously, possibly on the basis of friendship or some common interest which may or may not be work-related. In practice, of course, the distinction is not an absolute one. The formation of informal groups may be enhanced or inhibited by the formally prescribed relationships between people, and, as Glen points out:

> The categories of formal and informal groups . . . are often found in the same situation, as any formally constituted group of people will tend to develop informal relationships and groupings within it in the course of its normal day-to-day activities[4].

The functions groups perform

At the beginning of this chapter, we gave some examples of the importance of groups. These examples alluded to the functions that groups perform, not only for the organisation but also for the individual. It is to these functions that we shall now turn.

Groups are used to perform a number of formal organisational functions. Handy[5] presents these under ten major headings:

the distribution of work
the management and control of work
problem-solving and decision-making
information processing
information and idea collection
testing and ratifying decisions
co-ordination and liaison
increased commitment and involvement
negotiation, or conflict resolution
inquest, or inquiry into the past.

We can see from this list that groups can be and are used to carry out most managerial tasks. We shall see, however, that the effectiveness of the group and indeed the nature of the group processes will vary from task to task and situation to situation. But what of the individual group member? What does he stand to gain from his membership? We saw some answers to this question in the introduction to this chapter. Let us now take things a little further.

The first answer is organisationally related: assistance in getting a job done. Some collaborative tasks cannot be performed by one person alone. With others, however, we shall see that individuals would be more productive working alone. But the individual has other needs, and group membership can be a very important source of satisfaction of these needs. In Chapter Three we saw that individuals have varying degrees of need for affiliation and in Chapter Four it was suggested that inclusion and affection are important interpersonal needs. It is clear that, almost by definition, association with others in a group activity, be it formal or informal, is capable of satisfying such needs. Warr and Wall suggest that contact with others, such as occurs in work groups, 'is essential as a stimulus to mental activity or behaviour'[6].

The same authors, following on from the work of Festinger[7], suggest that the opportunities for social comparison provided by group membership are an important influence on the individual. The theory maintains that we all have a need to compare our opinions and abilities with others. Obviously there is a preference for hard, objective information, but this is not always available, particularly in social situations. Such situations are more likely to be ambiguous. The discomfort associated with this ambiguity can be reduced by the process of social comparison. In other words, by comparing our own beliefs with those of others we can gain a clearer definition of our social reality. For example, the young apprentice in his first week at work may not be clear as to the most appropriate way to approach the foreman. He may quickly learn from the behaviour and expressed opinion of his workmates that 'he's a right so-and-so' and should be steered clear of. One aspect of his social reality will have been made less ambiguous. A related psychological function of group membership is the opportunity to establish or test a sense of self-identity. We shall see in the next chapter how the roles we play with regard to other people influence our beliefs and feelings about ourselves.

Group membership can also provide a sense of security and greater influence over our environment, particularly our social environment – the assumption being that a number of people of like interest will be better able to achieve their own ends if they band together than if they operate separately. It has been suggested that organisations should be thought of as a coalition of such interest groups which will inevitably to a degree be in conflict with one another to some degree. This theme is discussed further in Chapter Nine.

How groups develop

As we have already seen, people come together in groups for a number of reasons. These reasons can be categorised as 'personal' or 'situational'. Under the 'personal' heading would come such items as: to achieve personal goals, to achieve satisfaction of personal needs, to develop a common interest, to seek protection from an outside threat. Under the 'situational' heading we would include: geographic location, the need to perform a given task, to communicate information among others. These factors are not only present when a group comes together; they may persist over time through the development of the group, and affect its performance. Given that these factors will exist, what characterises the development of a group?

Research and experience show that groups develop through a number of phases. These phases are often sequential, each phase having a different focus to the others. Bales[8], for example, maintains that problem-solving groups tend to follow the pattern of orientation, evaluation and control. Tuckman, reviewing the literature, was able to formulate a model representing the changes that take place in both the social and the task aspects of group behaviour. The model appeared 'to hold up under widely varied conditions of group composition, duration of group life and specific group task.'[9]. He suggests that groups pass through four main stages in a set sequence. Each stage is characterised by a dominant task issue and a dominant social issue.

Stage 1 forming. In the task dimension this is a period of orientation. Group members try to establish just what the parameters of the tasks are, how they should go about accomplishing it, what information and resources they will need and so on.

On the social dimension this is a period of testing and dependence. Members try to discover what kinds of interpersonal behaviour are appropriate. There is a tendency to look to the leader or some powerful group member for guidance in this new situation.

Stage 2 storming is characterised in the social dimension by internal conflict. There is often polarisation around key interpersonal issues. Members seem to be expressing their own individuality and attempting to resist group influence.

With regard to the task, this stage is typified by emotional responses to the demands it seems to be making on the individual, particularly where the individual experiences a discrepancy between these demands and his own orientation.

Stage 3   norming. The group develops cohesion. Members perceive themselves to be part of a genuine 'group' which they wish to maintain and perpetuate. New standards and new roles emerge and are accepted. The emphasis is on harmony at all costs. Potentially conflict producing aspects of the task are avoided.

The task activities are typified by an open exchange of ideas and opinions. There is a willingness to listen to and accept the views of others.

Stage 4   performing. The group has established a flexible and functional structure of inter-related roles. The interpersonal aspects of the group's activity have been sorted out, and now group energy can be channelled into the task.

The task dimension sees the emergence of solutions to problems and constructive attempts at successful task completion. The task and social dimensions seem effectively to have come together in this phase.

The model implies that groups must progress through the various stages before they can reach effective performance. Some groups obviously exist for a much shorter time than others. Tuckman suggests that the length of life of a group determines the rate at which these various stages are passed through. It may well be, however, that time determines how adequately the key issues of each phase are dealt with. We can take this point a bit further by reintroducing the concept of 'hidden agendas'. In other words, issues which are not truly resolved may be driven underground. If we regard group development not as linear, as Tuckman implies, but rather as spiral, we can explain the phenomenon that many managers will have come across – the re-emergence of problems which seemed resolved long ago. With this modification, Tuckman's model can provide useful insights into the complexities of group development.

A slightly different set of phases has been put forward by Woodcock[10] with reference to his work on team development. He sees a team – which is just a particular version of a group and which will be discussed later in this chapter – as passing through the stages of development shown in Figure 6.1.

What happens in a group?

So far in this chapter we have concentrated on the importance of groups, why people join them and how they develop. We have also defined the kind of group we are interested in and the various types

Stage 4

Experimentation. Risky issues debated. Wider options considered. Personal feelings raised. More listening. Concern for others.

plus

Methodical working. Agreed procedures. Established ground rules.

plus

High flexibility. Appropriate leadership. Maximum use of energy and ability. Essential principles and social aspects considered. Needs of all met. Development a priority.

Stage 3

Experimentation. Risky issues debated. Wider options considered. Personal feelings raised. More listening. Concern for others.

plus

Methodical working. Agreed procedures. Established ground rules.

Stage 2

Experimentation. Risky issues debated. Wider options considered. Personal feelings raised. More listening. Concern for others.

Stage 1

Feelings not dealt with. Workplace is for work. Established line prevails. Not 'rocking the boat'. Poor listening. Weaknesses covered up. Unclear objectives. Low involvement in planning. Bureaucracy. Boss takes most decisions.

Fig. 6.1 Summary of the four stages of team development

that exist. We now turn to some key aspects of groups; the things that take place within them. Here we are concerned with group processes. It is these processes that cause groups to be such potentially powerful sources of influence and control within organisations.

To establish what happens in a group, we need to refer back to their formation and development. Groups form for a variety of reasons but they all have one important feature – a *common purpose*. In pursuing that common purpose, members *interact* with each other, perhaps cautiously to begin with (the 'forming' stage) and more positively and vigorously in later stages. During the course of these interactions members find out what behaviour is acceptable and what is not (e.g. no smoking at committee meetings). Such acceptable levels of behaviour are referred to as group *norms*. These can be the source of powerful control. If a group member defies the norms, as was the case of the man with the bowler hat in the introduction to this chapter, he will be pressurised to *conform*. Groups expect members to obey 'the rules', and conformity is an important part of the group's process. For those who conform, the group will offer them its *support*. For example, it will help defend them against some external threat or accusation, or carry a lame duck who has been loyal to the group. The group can thus be said to be highly *cohesive*. Interaction also brings with it the development of *roles* and various patterns of *communication*. Roles refer to the expected pattern of behaviour with the group, and communication is concerned with the sharing of information, experiences and values, with the intention of achieving particular results, actions or behaviours. This can be summarised in Figure 6.2.

This brief overview of group processes serves to illustrate how much they are concerned with the behaviour of individuals within a group and, then, how important they are (or should be) to those who manage any form of a group. We shall therefore examine some of them more closely.

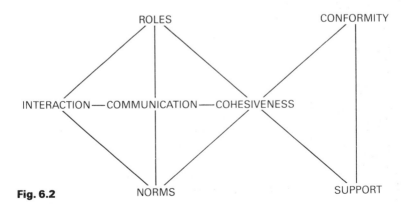

Fig. 6.2

Communication

It has often been assumed by those responsible for planning the structure of organisations that there is a logical way of arranging communication channels for maximum efficiency. Most frequently the conclusion has been that flow up and down a hierarchy is the most efficient (see Chapter Nine). Such conclusions, however, may be questioned on the basis of a considerable amount of laboratory research that has been carried out on communication networks in small groups (notably by Leavitt[11] and Shaw[12]). This research has aimed to explore the effect of imposed communication networks on such things as problem-solving effectiveness, member satisfaction, and leadership emergence. Typically it has involved a group of subjects faced with a problem to solve, but who can communicate with each other only in writing and, according to the particular network being studied, not everyone can communicate with everyone else. Figure 6.3 shows some of the different networks that have been studied. Permitted communication channels are represented by lines, and each person by a cross. It can be seen that the networks can vary in their degree of centralisation, the wheel, for example, being highly centralised (one person is more closely connected to all the others than the rest) and the circle and all-channel networks being decentralised (nobody has better access to information than anybody else) although obviously the all-channel net has greater interconnectedness. The 'Y' and chain are in between.

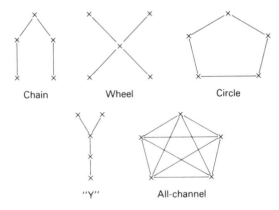

Chain   Wheel   Circle

"Y"   All-channel

Fig. 6.3

The findings from such research have been consistent. On simple problems centralised networks are most efficient but on complex problems decentralised networks are better. A leader is much more likely to emerge in a centralised network. The greater the degree of interconnectedness the higher the general level of satisfaction in the group. The more central an individual's position in the network, the higher his personal satisfaction is likely to be.

Shaw[13] suggests that the findings can be explained by two concepts – independence and saturation. Independence is valued in our society; and the greater an individual's access to information, the greater his sense of independence and so the greater his satisfaction. On complex tasks the central member of a centralised network is likely to become overloaded (saturated) by information and processing demands, so that the whole network becomes less efficient. In other words, the system suffers from the role overload of the central figure (see Chapter Five).

But such experiments are obviously rather artificial. Do they have relevance to the work organisation? Smith points out:

> Clearly they are not like the small group in which communication is face-to-face and everyone can hear everyone else. They are rather more like situations which arise in large organisations. People in different parts of the organisation are in touch with one another only indirectly, or, if directly, then only by relatively impersonal media such as telephone and memorandum, which are not necessarily shared by others. Members of organisations can communicate with one another in more personal and direct ways, but quite often they do not have sufficient time to do so . . . The provision or absence of communication links in large organisations is a key aspect of the control exercised by higher management[14].

Such patterns of communication will obviously be influenced by the physical setting, plant layout and distribution of individuals. The effect of the physical environment seems to be mediated via the communications it facilitates and inhibits. Thus, for example, proximity seems, not surprisingly, to be an important influence upon who will form a group with whom.

Even when the members of a group are all together in a single room and so potentially can all communicate with each other, the physical setting can still be influential. The seating arrangement, for example, may influence both the flow of communication and the emergence of a leader. People sitting opposite each other tend to interact more frequently than with people in other positions[15]. And there is evidence to suggest that not only do people who perceive themselves as having high status in the group choose the most favourable seating position (e.g. the head of a table), but also perhaps more significantly, people who sit in such positions tend to be regarded by the rest of the group as having a higher status and are reacted to accordingly[16].

Interaction

We have seen that direction of communication or patterns of interaction are an important group variable. Equally important is the nature or quality of that interaction. Numerous attempts have been made to find a meaningful way of categorising the various behaviours displayed by individuals in a group context. Some have been developed primarily as research tools, others have been developed primarily as aids to interactive skills training.

We saw earlier in this chapter that groups can be thought of as potentially serving two major functions; accomplishing formally prescribed tasks and satisfying various needs of the members. It has been suggested that, for a group to continue to be effective, some equilibrium between those two functions must be maintained[17]. It is common, therefore, for categorising systems to differentiate between those behaviours which seem to be performing task functions and those performing 'socio-emotional' functions. The latter term was coined by Bales[18] who developed what has probably been one of the most influential systems. He called it 'interaction process analysis'. The twelve categories comprising the system are claimed to be mutually exclusive, and any verbal or non-verbal contribution of a group member can be classified by a trained observer using the system. These are the categories.

A   Socio-emotional: Positive
1   *Shows solidarity,* raises others' status, gives help, rewards.
2   *Shows tension release,* jokes, laughs, shows satisfaction.
3   *Agrees,* shows passive acceptance, understands, concurs, complies.

B   Task: Attempted answers
4   *Gives suggestion,* direction, implying autonomy for others.
5   *Gives opinion,* evaluation, analysis, expresses feeling, wish.
6   *Gives orientation,* information, repeats, clarifies, confirms.

C   Task: Questions
7   *Asks for orientation,* information, repetition, confirmation.
8   *Asks for opinion,* evaluation, analysis, expression of feeling.
9   *Asks for suggestion,* direction, possible ways of action.

D   Socio-Emotional: Negative
10   *Disagrees,* shows passive rejection, formality, withholds help.
11   *Shows tension,* asks for help, withdraws out of field.
12   *Shows antagonism,* deflates others' status, defends or asserts self.

Bales maintained that there are a number of problems to be coped with both in the task area of activity and in the socio-emotional area. Behaviour can be further understood in terms of which of these problems it is related to. Thus in the task area, categories 6 and 7 are related to the problems of orientation, 5 and 8 to problems of evaluation, and 4 and 9 to problems of control. In the socio-emotional area, categories 3 and 10 are related to problems of decision, 2 and 11 to problems of tension management, and 1 and 12 to problems of integration. Such problems are likely to crop up at different times in the group's life and therefore the related behaviours are likely to predominate at different times. Also the type of behaviour an individual displays in a given group will influence the kind of role or roles he is seen as fulfilling.

Communication and the structure of roles

We have already seen that different communication patterns within the group can have differing affects on the satisfaction and performance according to the nature of the task. In some circumstances these patterns are predetermined, but we have also seen that they can emerge from the interaction. Such emergent patterns may be influenced by a number of things: seating arrangement and physical layout; individual differences in propensity to participate; existing status and role differences. There is in fact a dynamic relationship between role structure and communication patterns. We have already seen, for example, that the emergence of the leader role is influenced by the flow of communication.

But over time, there is a tendency for groups to become differentiated on other dimensions in addition to that of leader-follower. Even within the leader role, it has been suggested that there will nearly always be differentiation between task-leader and socio-emotional leader[19]. Although we shall be exploring the concept of *role* more fully in Chapter Seven, we must look at it here in terms of its significance for group functioning, for it is the differentiation of the group members into identifiable roles that is usually thought of as the development of group structure.

The particular role, or roles, that an individual plays in a given group will be influenced by a number of things: his position in the communication network; the kind of behaviour he typically displays with that particular group of people; his personality and abilities, and so on. It is important to mention at this stage that the role an individual develops in one group may be quite different from that he plays in other groups. The role structure is worked out, sometimes explicitly, often implicitly, between the particular group members in their particular situation. So, for example, Bales points out:

The behaviour of the person, including what he says and how he says it, in the particular group, as seen through the perceptions and evaluations of all the members including himself, and the resulting expectations of him may be called his group role. His group role is not the same as his personality. His personality consists of his relatively enduring characteristics as a total being. You see only his interpersonal behaviour which may reflect only one side of his personality, elicited by this particular group, its structure and his role in it, the expectations others have of him[20].

The part played, then, by expectations in the emergent structure is an important one. As the group gains a history, it becomes more clear to its members what kind of behaviour can be expected from each individual. The unexpected is discouraged and roles become more clearly defined and more suitable. The relative status of any particular role is likely to vary according to its relevance to the dominant group issue at any time.

The particular role structure of any group will, for the reasons we have seen, be peculiar to that group, but a number of writers have attempted to itemise the kind of roles they may develop. Bales[21] has recently extended interaction process analysis to formulate a list of 27 typical group roles. The identification of each role is, however, rather complex, based on various combinations of the major behavioural categories of his original theory.

A simpler system of classifying group roles, which has proved popular, particularly in management training spheres, was developed by Benne and Sheats[22]. Recognising, as Bales did, the need for some equilibrium between the task and social demands of group activity, they distinguished between task-oriented roles and those they referred to as oriented towards group maintenance. In addition, they suggested that some roles seem functional to the group neither in terms of task accomplishment nor in terms of group maintenance. They referred to these as self-orientated. Here are some examples from each of their three categories.

A   Some Task-Oriented Roles
Initiator-contributor: suggests new ideas or changes in the way of doing things.
Information giver: offers relevant facts or relates personal experience which is pertinent to the problem.
Co-ordinator: shows or clarifies the relationships between various ideas and tries to pull suggestions together.
Evaluator: supplies standards of accomplishment and measures group progress.

B   Some Maintenance-Orientated Roles
Encourager: praises and supports the contributions of others, indicating warmth and solidarity.

Harmoniser: mediates differences between other and attempts to reconcile disagreements.

'Gate-keeper': keeps the communication channels open, making sure that those who want to contribute can do so, and also limits over-talkative members.

Group observer and commentator: calls attention to group process, offering suggestions about problems they may be having in functioning.

C Some Self-Orientated Roles

Aggressor: deflates others by expressing disapproval of their ideas, opinions or feelings or by attacking the group as a whole.

Blocker: is negativistic and stubbornly resistant, keeps returning to issues that the group has already rejected.

Playboy: makes a show of his lack of involvement in the group by nonchalance, horseplay and raising irrelevant, mundane issues.

Help-seeker: attempts to elicit sympathy responses from all or certain group members by expressing insecurity or confusion. Depreciates self beyond reasonable limits.

Obviously this is just a sample of the many roles that may be played in a group, and as Benne and Sheats point out, one member may perform several different roles during the life of that group.

Group norms

These are shared rules or standards that designate what is acceptable and what is unacceptable in terms of group member behaviour, attitudes and beliefs. In a working context they may apply to quantity and quality of production, methods of work, interpersonal behaviour, attitudes to other groups or individuals, language, clothing or anything else regarded by the group members as relevant to their existence as a group. There is also usually an accepted set of rewards and punishments associated with compliance or non-compliance with those norms (i.e. conformity).

This process of normative influence has been of considerable interest to behavioural scientists and has given rise to a wide range of research in both laboratory and natural settings. Probably the most widely known field studies of group norms are the Hawthorne Studies[23] mentioned in the chapter on motivation. It was observed that the group had developed clearly defined norms about what represented a fair day's work for a fair day's pay. The standard was set at a level which, although acceptable to management, was well below what was possible. There were sanctions against producing too far above this level (being a 'rate-buster') or producing too far below it (being a 'chiseller'). The pressures exerted upon offenders to conform to the standard ranged from the use of derogatory names, through ostracism, to 'binging' (giving a hard blow on the upper arm). The group also applied social pressure to the inspectors and group supervisor to get them to conform to what was acceptable behaviour for those in authority.

Lupton[24] was also interested in the effect of group norms on levels of output. He found in one factory he studied that work groups were involved in an elaborate 'fiddle' aimed at regulating their output and stabilising their earnings. However, he found that, in another factory, no such restrictive norm existed. He concluded that the differences could in part be understood in terms of internal differences. But he considered that the different social and economic environments of the two factories were of prime importance. These, he implied, meant that the workers brought different attitudes to productivity into the factory with them. In other words, the group norms of production were significantly influenced by the different orientations to work.

Behavioural norms are not necessarily task-related. Roy[25] gives an interesting account of group norms which seem to be more oriented towards group maintenance. His observations were of a small work group of which he became a participant. The group was engaged in extremely simple and repetitive work; operating a punch press during a twelve-hour day. He noticed that what at first seemed disconnected and rather pointless horseplay and banter, could in fact be seen as a patterned set of rituals which were an important part of the culture the group had developed for itself. For example, the long boring day was interrupted almost hourly by 'the daily repetition in an ordered series of informal interactions'. The first such interruption each day was 'peach time' when one worker provided a pair of peaches for his mates to eat. These were always received by complaints about the quality. Peach time was followed by 'banana time'. These occasions centred around a banana brought in by the same worker who supplied the peaches, this time intended for his own consumption. Each morning another worker would steal the banana, call out 'banana time!' and eat it while the owner made futile protests. In the time Roy was with the group the first worker never managed to eat his own banana but continued to bring one for lunch every day. Similar ritualised inter-actions surrounded window time, pickup time, fish time and cake time. Roy concluded that such activities served not only to mark off the time but also to give it content and hurry it along. In this way the boredom of the work became easier to endure. In addition they served to reinforce the 'system of roles which formed a sort of pecking hierarchy'.

Probably the best known attempts to study the impact of social influence in small groups in a laboratory setting are the researches carried out by Sherif[26] and by Asch[27]. In the Sherif experiments, subjects were placed in a darkened room and asked to estimate how much and in what direction a single visible point of light moved. (In fact the light did not move but a common phenomenon known as *autokinetic effect* occurs under these conditions and the light appears to move.) It was found that individual estimates made alone varied considerably more than when made in a group where the judgements of others could be heard. In the group there was a tendency for estimates to converge on a norm. The Asch studies were slightly different. Subjects were asked which of three lines on a card was the same length as a fourth presented along with them. The task was so simple that if asked alone the subjects very rarely made a mistake. However, when subjects were placed individually in a group of people all of whom, unknown to the subjects, were confederates of the researchers, the findings were different. In this situation, when the confederates unanimously made a patently wrong choice a surprisingly high proportion of the subjects went along with it, despite the evidence of their own eyes. Even those that stuck to their own opinion showed signs of discomfort. These two studies seem to highlight two quite different kinds of group influence on the individual. In the former, the individual is in a highly ambiguous situation in which he himself is unsure. That ambiguity is reduced by information from the others. In the latter, there is no ambiguity. The individual is succumbing to the immediate social pressure to conform to the expectations of the others. There is an additional significance to the difference, in that the effects of the former type of situation seem to be relatively enduring, whereas the effects of the latter seem to be confined to that situation alone. It should be noted, however, that pressure to conform is not exerted evenly amongst group members. Hollander[28] suggests that individuals can build up an 'idiosyncracy credit' which permits deviance from group norms in certain circumstances. This idiosyncracy credit is related to status and the extent to which the individual has earlier conformed to the expected behaviour.

There is also some evidence to suggest that individuals differ in their susceptibility to social influence. Individuals high on intelligence, assertiveness and self-esteem, and low on anxiety and authoritarianism seem less prone to conformity than others. (In this context independence should be distinguished from counter-conformity or rebelliousness. The latter is paradoxically as much determined by group norms as conformity in that it always involves doing the opposite.)

Cohesiveness

This is essentially the attractiveness of the group to its members – the extent to which they would make sacrifices to maintain its existence. Following on from the last section, it is not surprising to discover that as cohesiveness increases so does the general level of conformity to group norms. The social rewards available for conformity are, by definition, more highly valued. Similarly, group members tend to be more satisfied. This is in part reflected by lower absenteeism and turnover. In addition:

> highly cohesive groups provide a source of security for members which serves to reduce anxiety and heighten self-esteem[29].

The relationship, however, between cohesiveness and productivity is not a direct one. In other words, contrary to some assumptions, high cohesiveness does not necessarily lead to high productivity. The mediating factor seems to be the group's own production norms. Highly cohesive groups seem to be more effective at achieving whatever goals their members establish for themselves, but, as we have seen, these will not necessarily be in line with those set by management[30]. Chapter Eight discusses the *socio-technical* approach to organisation design, which attempts to harness the benefits of group cohesiveness to technical efficiency.

Group and individual performance

Research shows that the mere presence of other people, whether they are a passive audience or are performing a similar task, seems to have a significant effect on the performance of the individual. The evidence, however, is inconsistent as to whether such a presence is enhancing or inhibiting. Reviewing the work done on the subject, Zajonc[31] suggested that this inconsistency could be explained by regarding the presence of others as having an arousing effect. Such an arousal can enhance the performance of simple tasks which involve little in the way of new behaviour. On more complex tasks, however, in which the required behaviour is less familiar, it can have adverse effects.

Already, then, we can see that a comparison between individual and group performance does not allow us to draw any simple conclusions as to whether the one is better than the other. As has already become clear in previous chapters, and will become more obvious throughout the rest of the book, the 'best' policy for the management of human resources will vary from situation to situation. This is certainly the case when it has to be decided whether to use groups or to pool the efforts of individuals working separately. Some of the research into this area confirms common sense, but some of findings are slightly more surprising.

It may come as no surprise that groups often, though not always, take more time to complete a task than individuals working alone. (This, of course, assumes that the task is one that can be performed by a single individual.) This tends to be the case even if measuring the total time elasped, but if we think in terms of man-hours involved, then groups may be regarded as even less efficient. This is an important point to remember if the manager's prime concern is to keep costs to a minimum. If, however, time is less important than quality or accuracy of problem solutions, the picture is different. Reviewing the research, Shaw states:

> The evidence thus strongly supports the conclusion that groups produce more and better solutions to problems than do individuals[32].

But obviously an expert individual may still do better than a group of less competent people. On the whole, however, there is likely to be more information available in a group and there is also a greater chance of mistakes or errors being recognised and corrected.

Another related area in which the picture is far from clear is in the comparison of group creativity compared with individual creativity. The technique introduced by Osborn[33] known as *brainstorming* has had its supporters and critics amongst managers and academics alike. Basically, it is a method of group participation which is claimed to generate new and radical ideas, such as new products a company might invest in or new uses for an old declining product. The basic procedure involves the group members expressing as many ideas as possible, the more far-fetched the better. No idea may be evaluated or criticised until all ideas have been expressed. Participants are encouraged to present ideas which elaborate on the previously expressed ideas of others. On the basis of their own research, however, both Taylor *et al.*[34] and Dunnett *et al.*[35] dispute the claims made for the technique. They claim that individuals working alone under brainstorming rules produce far more ideas than if working as a group, possibly because people working together are more likely to adopt the same approach or set of approaches to a problem than if they are working separately. Krech *et al.* use such evidence to suggest that:

> sometimes group membership inhibits man, constricts his creativity, and prevents self-fulfilment[36].

But Shaw points out that in both the studies quoted, the time available was limited, and it is possible that the groups were cut off in the middle of the process. He claims that there is evidence showing that:

> with longer work periods groups produce more under brainstorming instructions than do individuals. Groups continue to produce ideas indefinitely, whereas individuals run dry.

Whether or not groups are more creative then is still a question for debate, but what is clear is that both individuals and groups produce far more ideas if critical evaluation is held in abeyance until all ideas have been expressed.

One area in which research suggests that 'conventional wisdom' may be misguided is risk-taking. Many people seem to believe that decisions made in groups, committees for example, tend to be rather conservative, but according to Kogan and Wallach[38] this is not borne out by the evidence. Their claim is that decisions made after group discussion will usually be more risky than individual decisions on the same problems. This may possibly be accounted for by some diffusion of the sense of responsibility for the decision, or perhaps because in our society value is placed upon some degree of risk-taking.

But the use of groups not only has implications for the making of decisions but also for their implementation:

> People are more likely to carry out a decision that they have had a hand in making than one that has been imposed. If effective implementation is critical, therefore, it is important to involve the implementers as much as possible[39].

In general, we can say that groups may perform better than individuals on some key activities. These are:

1 for problems with many or different facets, or that require different skills, information and knowledge;
2 for decisions that require judgement rather than factual analysis;
3 for pooling and building on different ideas prior to reaching a decision;
4 for gaining acceptance of a decision and commitment to its implementation.

The use of groups may be less productive for:

1 simple, routine tasks or problems;
2 problems that have a 'correct' solution;
3 problems where it is difficult to demonstrate the solution to members;
4 problems requiring subtle, logical reasoning.

Improving the performance of groups, committees and teams

Groups can thus perform quite well at making certain kinds of judgemental, 'creative' decisions and solutions. But how can we ensure that this comes about? How do we get committees, for example, to be productive in solving problems?

Making groups effective

Zander[40] reviews the research available on making groups effective, and proposes some steps for getting the problem-solving process going:

1 clearly state the problem for the group, explain the significance of the problem and make it evident what kind of action is needed by the group;
2 keep discussion focused on the issue, stop work on a problem when consideration of it is completed and call for a vote when the time is right;
3 break a complex problem into separate parts and have members make decisions about each part;
4 help members learn how to work with others' ideas so that they do prove in a meeting that their original ideas were correct all along;
5 if no solution is clearly appropriate or appealing, make the least objectionable choice;
6 where possible, avoid the need for a unanimous decision;
7 encourage members to consider any adverse consequences from a given solution before making their final decision;
8 be sure that those who are to implement a group's decision understand exactly what they are to do.

Zander goes further and argues that groups can do a number of things to overcome ineffective decision-making. Among these are: develop special roles to overcome group-think; avoid wide differences in status among members, or help members recognise the differences and reduce their inhibitions; use brainstorming to improve participation as well as the quality of ideas; plan ahead for procedures to use for urgent/crisis decisions; protect the group from the damaging effects of external criticism but let the ideas be picked up and used; and encourage members to evaluate their group's skill and learn ways of improving it.

Better committees

In many organisational settings we use committees to reach decisions or propose solutions to problems. Here, too, social science research provides guidance for the effective management of committees, as Filley[41] argues. His thesis is that committee effectiveness can be increased by applying research findings to answer such questions as:

1 what functions do committees serve?
2 what size should committees be?
3 what is the appropriate style of leadership for committee chairmen?
4 what mix of member characteristics makes for effective committee performance?

The answer to the first question is not surprising. Committees are concerned with the exchange of views and information, recommending action, and making major decisions. Most committees, according to various surveys, are concerned with communicating information or aiding an executive's decision process. Executives reported that they often used committees to 'sell' decisions. As Filley points out, as long as members are allowed to influence and to participate, to some extent, in executive decision-making, this is probably a legitimate use of the committee.

As for size, the evidence reviewed by Filley suggests that five is ideal, if the five members possess the necessary skills (and, presumably, experience and knowledge) to solve the problems faced by the committee. Such a size also allows attention to be given to both the group and its members and enables balanced interpersonal needs to be achieved. When dealing with technical decisions, more members can be added to provide the necessary skills. Generally speaking, the evidence points to a small size of group for tasks that require interaction, consensus and modification of opinion, if performance is to be high. Where the task has clear criteria of correct performance, the addition of members may increase performance.

The role adopted by the chairman of a committee is also illuminated by social science research. This points to a need to ensure that both task and social leadership roles are performed – ideally by one person. This ideal is seldom attained. Committees require direction from the chair by a person who is somewhat assertive, who takes charge and controls the group's proceedings. Someone in the group must, however, perform the role of group-builder and monitor of social relations among members if the person in the chair is unable to do this. Both are required for effective committee performance. As we shall see in the section on team performance, other roles are needed, too.

The mix of member characteristics is taken from the standpoint of co-operation or competition between members. Co-operative membership seems to win the day. Performance can probably be improved by having members whose self-centered needs are not too intense. As for the degree of heterogeneity required, a balance would seem to be necessary. Increased heterogeneity of membership leads to increased problem-solving potential, but it can also lead to increased interpersonal conflict. The deciding factor appears to be the nature of the task and how much conflict the committee can cope with.

Improving team effectiveness

A team is a particular form of group. We come across teams in all sorts of situations: in football and many other sports, in offices, on construction sites. Project teams are frequently to be found in matrix organisation structures. These are discussed in Chapter Eight; it is sufficient for our purposes here to note that, during the life of a project, groups of people will come together at various stages to work on that project. Different specialists will make a contribution to the project at different times. Thus, in the early phases of a construction project, the architects, planners and client will be heavily involved. At later stages, surveyors, construction engineers and builders will play their parts. The project team changes its membership over time, through some key personnel remain constant and the contracting agent will play a key stabilising role. Such teams can be frustrating to manage and there appears to be little research evidence available to us on how best to manage them.

There has been, however, research conducted into the more frequently encountered 'management team'. Project teams are often of this form, and the research may well be of value to the less permanent forms of teams. We shall now turn to two pieces of research that have a good deal to say about how to achieve effective performance from teams.

The first study we shall refer to was the carried out by Belbin[42]. He developed a fairly original conception of teams that was based on many years of careful research, experiment, observation, validation and application. Indeed, the research is a good example of how behavioural science can contribute to an understanding of management, as was pointed out in Chapter One.

The findings of the study have been reported on quite extensively[43] by others. Here we shall note some of the salient findings. Perhaps the most important was that the most consistently successfully teams contained a range of roles enacted by various members. According to Belbin, 'team-role' describes a pattern of behaviour characteristic of the way in which one team member interacts with another where his performance serves to facilitate the progress of the team as a whole. Only eight useful types of contribution were discovered. These were chairman, shaper, plant, company worker, team worker, monitor-evaluator, resource investigator and completer-finisher. Each of these team-roles was associated with characteristic types of personality, as measured by the tests used in Belbin's experiments.

Belbin defines each of these team-roles in the following manner:

Chairman   controls the way in which a team moves towards the group objectives by making the best use of team resources; recognises where the team's strengths and weaknesses lie; ensures that the best use is made of each team member's potential.

Company worker   turns concepts and plans into practical working procedures; carries out agreed plans systematically and efficiently.

Completer-finisher   ensures that the team is protected as far as possible from mistakes of commission and ommission; actively searches for aspects of work which need a more than usual degree of attention; maintains a sense of urgency within the team.

Monitor-evaluator   analyses problems; evaluates ideas and suggestions so that the team is better placed to take balanced decisions.

Plant (later called innovator)   advances new ideas and strategies with special attention to major issues; looks for possible breaks in approach to the problems with which the group is confronted.

Resource investigator   explores and reports on ideas, developments and resources outside the group; creates external contacts that may be useful to the team; conducts any subsequent negotiations.

Shaper   shapes the way in which team effort is applied; directs attention generally to the setting of objectives and priorities; seeks to impose some shape or pattern on group discussion and on the outcome of group activities.

Team worker   supports members in their strengths (e.g. building on suggestions); underpins members in their shortcomings; improves communication between members and fosters team spirit generally.

To be effective, a team requires a balance of all these roles. Many of us will find we have a primary role with which we are comfortable and through which we will operate most of the time. Others will also have what Belbin refers to as a 'back-up team-role'; one, other than the primary role, with which the individual will have some natural affinity. It should be pointed out that such team-roles differ from what Belbin calls 'functional-roles' (the roles we perform because of our technical expertise or specialism).

The research identified a number of successful (and unsuccessful) teams. As we have said, the most consistently successful team had a balance of team-roles: these were referred to as 'mixed teams'. Where some roles were missing, members called upon their back-up roles. Another successful team was one containing several stable extroverts – mainly team workers and resource investigators, with company workers as back-up roles. The spread of mental ability was reasonably high. Their success was improved if a shaper took charge of things.

So, what makes a good team? Mottram[44], who worked with Belbin, reports that the *ideal team* will consist of

one chairman
one innovator (i.e. plant)
one monitor evaluator

one or more company workers, team workers,
   resource investigators or completers
specialists as required.

This is close to the mixed team. Belbin goes further and reports that a number of factors contribute to the team success. These are:

1 *Person in the chair*   patient, commanding, trust generator, ability seeker, pulls it together
2 *Existence of one strong plant*   creative and clever, producing ideas for others
3 *Spread in mental abilities*   one plant, another clever member (to spark off), chairman slightly above mental abilities of others
4 *Spread in personal attributes*   makes for wide team-role coverage, wide team-role strength
5 *Match between attributes and responsibilities*   useful job and personal characteristics fit, use of pairs, informal arrangements to achieve match
6 *Adjustment to realisation of imbalance*   group self-knowledge taking up necessary roles, understanding strengths and weaknesses.

The ideas put forward by Belbin and his colleagues have received support from the more recent work of Margerison and McCann[45]. Based on many years' research and development work, their framework is based on the notions of required behaviour and role preferences.

Their studies revealed two major aspects of *required behaviour*. These were:

1 *exploring* behaviour associated with searching, creativity, opportunity, contacting, selling, and other externally orientated activities. In short, diverging activities
2 *controlling* behaviours associated with concern for detail, precision, standards, systems, rules, regulations and ordered ways of doing things according to a plan. In short, converging activities.

The *role preferences* also had two major aspects, which were:

3 advisory roles; those that provide the invaluable support services of information, planning, research, training and other such areas that are necessary to get tasks done
4 organising roles; those that concentrate more on the mainline activities required to build and deliver a product or service.

They formed dimensions that related to each other, shown in Figure 6.4. Team members should enable each quadrant to be covered adequately. From this was developed the 'team management wheel' shown in Figure 6.5, which relates people's major work functions and skills. The team roles in brief are:

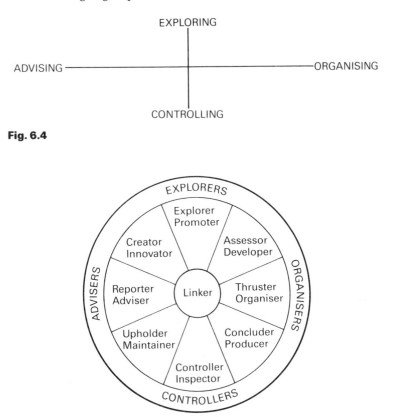

Fig. 6.4

Fig. 6.5   Team management wheel

1 *Reporter-Advisers*   They provide a support role in the organisation and typically emphasise the collection of information and resources.
2 *Creator-Innovators*   People who prefer this role will tend to enjoy thinking up new ideas. Such people will put a lot of effort into experimenting and designing new ways and approaches.
3 *Explorer-Promoters*   In any team there is a need for people to go out and publicise new ideas, bring in new resources, make contacts and chart new pathways.
4 *Assessor-Developers*   No team can work for long without people who will identify how ideas will work in practice. They therefore like to assess the viability of prosposals, often by conducting a project or making a prototype or by doing a market research assessment.

5 *Thruster-Organisers* Every team has to ensure that work gets done. Those who favour an organising kind of role will put pressure on setting up systems procedures, allocating work and making sure time and output requirements are set. In doing this they will 'thrust' forward to establish and meet objectives. They do not let obstacles stand in their way.

6 *Concluder-Producers* The completion and finishing of work is obviously critical to success. Many good ideas can fail for the want of some person who follows through and regularly produces a high standard product or service day after day. Therefore the work function of producing, needs to be linked to the emphasis on concluding.

7 *Controller-Inspectors* It is widely acknowledged that the inspection work function in a team is vital to ensure that jobs are done correctly. When they looked at the roles people played when doing such work it was clear they were putting a heavy emphasis on control.

8 *Upholder-Maintainers* In all areas of work and life it is important to maintain not only physical things such as machinery but the valuable social and organisational systems and relationships. An important part of maintaining therefore lies in upholding the cultural traditions and established ways of doing things, while at the same time seeing how new ways can be built on without disrupting the best of the past. They found a number of people who played an important role in teams working to maintain continuity and giving a direction based on strong beliefs.

9 *Linkers* All teams need people who can co-ordinate and integrate others, whatever their role preferences are. On most occasions this should be the manager. However, they recognised that others can play this vital role at times. The term Linker seemed most appropriate as the role involved not only linking people within the team but also acting as a representative for the team to other units and organisations.

This approach seems to go a stage further than that of Belbin. It links work or job functions quite clearly with the roles team members should perform. It also has implications for recruitment and selection, team building management, work allocation and counselling, and career development and promotion[46]. The authors have developed a Team Management Resource that puts the whole concept into operation.

Implications for managers

In Chapter One we stressed that management had a lot to do with working with and through people. In this chapter we have looked at some of the key aspects of a source of powerful influence over behaviour; groups (committees and teams). In some respects, the influence of the group on behaviour can be more powerful than the forces of personal motivation which, as we saw in Chapter Four, is in itself a powerful cause of particular patterns of behaviour.

We end this chapter by considering some of the implications of groups for managers. One of the clearest implications is that groups cannot be ignored. Because they have such potential for social control of members, managers must understand what happens in groups and learn to harness their power in pursuit of work-related objectives. Aligning the group's goals with your own is essential to effective management. This can be brought about by ensuring that members of the group know and understand your goals, and are consulted about them as often as is practicable. Your style of management is thus an important ingredient in the mix. Fitting your style to the needs of the group and the situation, as well as to the task, is crucial, as Fiedler[47] has shown in his contingency theory of leadership. His research led to the contention that:

> the group's performance will be contingent upon the appropriate matching of leadership style and the degree of favourableness of the group situation for the leader.

To arrive at this conclusion it was obviously necessary to find ways of measuring both style and situation. The measures actually adopted have been the subject of a fair amount of criticism and debate, but this should not be allowed to detract from the important implications of the general model.

Fiedler maintains that people can be differentiated according to whether they are primarily 'relationship-motivated' or 'task-motivated'. This differentiation is reflected in the way they score on a questionnaire measure he developed. People are asked to think of the individual with whom they can work least well and then rank that particular person on a series of scales, each ranging from an unfavourable to a favourable judgement. This provides a least preferred co-worker score (LPC). High LPC scorers, i.e. those who describe their least preferred co-worker in relatively favourable terms are said to be relationship-motivated. Low LPC scorers are said to be task-motivated. According to Fiedler:

> Current evidence suggests that the LPC scores and the personality attributes they reflect are almost as stable as most other personality measures. . . . Changes do occur, but in the absence of major upsets in the individual's life, they tend to be gradual and relatively small[48].

Fiedler chose three dimensions upon which situations could be thought of as favourable or unfavourable:

1 *leader-member relations* the extent to which he is, or feels, accepted and supported by group members
2 *task structure* the extent to which it is clear-cut and programmed with regard to goals, procedures and measures of progress
3 *position-power* the extent to which the organisation provides him with the power to reward and punish and so obtain compliance from subordinates.

If each of these dimensions is thought of as either favourable or unfavourable it is possible to combine them to yield eight different overall situational descriptions ranging from highly favourable to highly unfavourable. In very favourable or very unfavourable situations, task-motivated leaders (as measured by LPC score) seem to be most effective, whereas in moderately favourable situations relationship-motivated leaders seem to be most effective.

As has been said, Fiedler's methods have been criticised. In particular the usefulness of the LPC measure has been questioned, and indeed he himself has revised, or at least elaborated on, the original assumptions about behaviour that could be based on LPC scores[49]. In addition, it has been suggested that the three situational dimensions, apparently chosen fairly arbitrarily, although likely in themselves to be important, are inadequate to reflect the complexity of real life situations. Such criticisms may be well-founded but none the less the contingency model is important as a stimulus to look at leadership effectiveness from a new point of view and to recognise that it is not accurate to speak of a good or bad leader, but rather that an individual will perform well in one situation and not in another. His performance depends as much upon the situation to which the organisation assigns him as it does on his own particular orientation. An outstanding research team leader will not necessarily make a good production manager.

Fiedler goes further by suggesting that as a person's style is a reflection of a stable personality characteristic, it would be easier to engineer the situation to suit the man than to attempt to change the man himself. He questions, therefore, whether any current approach to management training can be expected to bring about across-the-board organisational improvememt. Furthermore, as a manager gains experience in a particular job, the level of uncertainty associated with it will possibly reduce. The situation can, in a sense, be said to become more favourable. This would imply that some leaders would be more effective in the long run, but not in the short run, whereas others may shine as newcomers but their effectiveness will reduce in time. This obviously has implications for selection and job-rotation policies.

The clear message is 'get to know your work group and how you relate to them'. If you can't change your style (should that be necessary) you may be able to change the situation.

The implications for managing successful teams would include the above. In addition, it will be necessary to assess the team roles covered by members and to seek to ensure a sufficient spread of these. Selection and development policies and practices must be thought through to ensure that newly appointed team members bring with them a needed team role as well as functional role, and that training is appropriate to both roles.

Summary — factors affecting group behaviour

In this chapter we have discussed many aspects of group behaviour. It will be helpful for analysing groups and for seeking to improve group performance to have a summary framework in mind. Such a framework has been proposed by Krech et al.[50] and has been adapted to

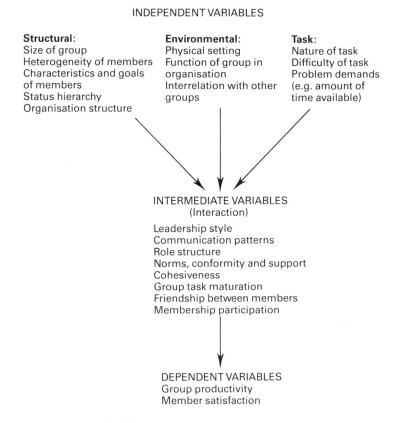

INDEPENDENT VARIABLES

Structural:
Size of group
Heterogeneity of members
Characteristics and goals
of members
Status hierarchy
Organisation structure

Environmental:
Physical setting
Function of group in
organisation
Interrelation with other
groups

Task:
Nature of task
Difficulty of task
Problem demands
(e.g. amount of
time available)

INTERMEDIATE VARIABLES
(Interaction)

Leadership style
Communication patterns
Role structure
Norms, conformity and support
Cohesiveness
Group task maturation
Friendship between members
Membership participation

DEPENDENT VARIABLES
Group productivity
Member satisfaction

Fig. 6.6 Factors affecting group behaviour

provide the summary. This framework contains three different groups of factors. The first are called 'independent variables' (or 'givens'). These describe 'what is': the existing general situation in which the group is developing and forming. The second are called 'intermediate variables' (or 'emergent processes'). These result from the interactions of the 'givens' and will lead to variations in the third group. This group are called 'dependent variables' (or 'outcomes'). These factors may be summarised as in Figure 6.6.

References

1 Sprott, W. J. H., *Human Groups,* Pelican, 1958.
2 Golembiewski, R. T., *The Small Group,* University of Chicago Press, 1962.
3 Schein, E. H., *Organisational Physchology,* Prentice Hall, 1972.
4 Glen, F., *The Social Psychology of Organisations,* Methuen, 1975.
5 Handy, C. B., *Understanding Organisations,* Methuen, 1975.
6 Warr, P. and Wall, T., *Work and Well-being:* Penguin, 1975.
7 Festinger, L. 'A Theory of social comparison processes', *Human Relations,* **7**, 1954, pp. 117–40.
8 Bales, R. F., 'The equilibrium problem in small groups', in Parsons, T., Bales, R. F. and Shils, E. A., *Working Papers in the Theory of Action,* Free Press, 1953.
9 Tuckman, B. W., 'Development sequence in small groups', *Psychological Bulletin,* **63**, 1965, pp. 384–99.
10 Woodcock, M., *Team Development Manual,* Gower, 1979.
11 Leavitt, H. J., 'Some effects of certain communication patterns on group performance', *Journal of Abnormal and Social Psychology,* **46**, pp. 38–50, 1951.
12 Shaw, M. E., 'Communication Networks', in Berkowitz, L. (ed.), *Advances in Experimental Social Psychology* Vol. 1, Academic Press, 1964.
13 Shaw, M. E., *ibid.*
14 Smith, P. B., *op. cit.*
15 Steinzor, B., 'The spacial factor in face to face discussion groups', *Journal of Abnormal and Social Psychology,* **45**, 1950, pp. 552–5.
16 Sommer, R., *Personal Space: the behavioural bases of design,* Prentice Hall, 1969.
17 Bales, R. F., *op. cit.*
18 Bales, R. F., *ibid.*
19 Bales, R. F. and Slater, P. E., 'Role differentiation in small groups', in Parsons, I. and Bales, R. F. (eds.), *Family Socialisation and Interaction Process,* Free Press, 1955.
20 Bales, R. F., *Personality and Interpersonal Behaviour,* Holt, Rinehart and Winston, 1970.
21 Bales, R. F., *ibid.*
22 Benne, K. D. and Sheats, P., 'Functional roles of group members', *Journal of Social Issues,* **4**, 1948, p. 2.
23 Roethlisberger, F. J. and Dickson, W. J., *Management and the Worker,*

Harvard University Press, 1939.

24   Lupton, R., *On the Shop Floor,* Pergamon, 1963.

25   Roy, D. F., 'Banana time: job satisfaction and informal interaction', *Human Organisation,* **18**, 1960, pp. 156–68.

26   Sherif, M., *The Psychology of Social Norms,* Harper, 1936.

27   Asch, J., *Social Psychology,* Prentice Hall, 1952.

28   Hollander, E. P., 'Conformity, status and idiosyncracy credit', *Psychological Review,* **65**, 1958, pp. 117–27.

29   Cartwright, D., 'The nature of group cohesiveness', in Cartwright, D. and Zander, A., *Group Dynamics,* 3rd edn, Tavistock, 1968.

30   Seashore, S. E., *Group Cohesiveness in the Industrial Work Group,* Institute for Social Research, University of Michegan.

31   Zajonc, R. B., *Social Psychology: an experimental approach,* Wadsworth, 1960.

32   Shaw, M. E., *op. cit.*

33   Osburn, A. F., *Applied Imagination,* Scribner, 1957.

34   Taylor, D. W., Berry, P. C. and Block, C. H., 'Does group participation when using brainstorming facilitate or inhibit creative thinking?', *Administrative Science Quarterly,* **3**, 1958, pp. 23–47.

35   Dunnette, M. D., Campbell, J. and Jaastad, K., 'The effect of group participation on brainstorming for two industrial samples', *Journal of Applied Psychology,* **47**, 1963, pp. 30–7.

36   Krech, D., Crutchfield, R. S. and Ballachey, E. L., *Individual in Society,* McGraw-Hill, 1962.

37   Shaw, M. E., *op. cit.*

38   Kogan, N. and Wallach, M. A., 'Risk-taking as a function of the situation, the person and the group', in Newcomb, R. M. (ed.), *New Directions in Psychology III,* Holt, Rinehart and Winston, 1967.

39   Schein, E. H., *op. cit.*

40   Zander, A., *Making Groups Effective,* Jassey-Bass, 1982.

41   Filley, A. C., 'Committee management – guidelines from social science research', in Huseman, R. C. and Carroll, A. B., *Readings in Organisational Behaviour – Dimensions of Management Action,* Allyn and Bacon, 1979.

42   Belbin, R. M., *Management Teams – Why They Succeed or Fail,* Heinemann, 1981.

43   Mottram, R., 'Team Skills Management', *Journal of Management Development,* **1**, no. 1, pp. 22–33, 1982.

44   Mottram, R., *ibid.*

45   Margerison, C. J. and McCann, D., *How to Lead a Winning Team,* MCB University Press, 1985.

46   Margerison, D. J. and McCann, D., 'Team mapping – a new approach to managerial leadership', *Journal of European Industrial Training,* **8**, no. 1, 1984.

47   Fiedler, F. E., *A Theory of Leadership Effectiveness,* McGraw-Hill, 1967.

48   Fiedler, F. E., 'The contingency model – new directions for leadership utilisation', *Journal of Contemporary Business,* Autumn, 1974.

49   Fiedler, F. E., 'Personality, motivational systems, and the behaviour of high and low LPC persons', *Human Relations,* **25**, 1972, pp. 391–412.

50   Krech, D., *et al., op. cit.*

7

From occupational role to the labour process

There are literally thousands of jobs in any advanced industrial society[1] and while some (Prime Minister, for example) may have only one occupant, for the vast majority there are many thousands who occupy a work role with the same title. But even the same title does not necessarily mean the same job: the title 'manager', for instance, may refer to a job involving running a betting shop, a person responsible for organising and supervising production in a large textiles factory or someone responsible for the conduct of a local branch of a high street clearing bank. The collective term we can use for these numerous and varied occupations is the 'occupational structure' and, to complicate matters further, this also changes substantially over time. For instance, Britain used to be described as a manufacturing nation but most people are now aware that this description is less true than it was. In fact, in the mid-1980s only one in four of those in employment are in manufacturing: between 1976 and 1981 a third of all manufacturing jobs disappeared and the decline has continued since. In services, on the other hand, jobs have been increasing very rapidly. In 1961 there were 11.4 million service workers but by mid-1985 this had risen to 13.6 million, that is, 2.5 times greater than the number employed in manufacturing[2].

At the same time, there are many people in occupational roles – 20.81 million in June 1985[3] – plus a large number of others, over 3.2 million in November 1985[4], who are registered as looking for a job. It is interesting to examine just how people come to occupy particular occupational roles. Clearly, given the very wide range of occupations, their differences in skill requirements and other attributes, and the large number of people shifting in and out of occupations, the processes involved are complex. Equally clearly, getting the right people (in terms of abilities or attitudes) into the right jobs can greatly enhance a country's economic performance and the sense of self-fulfilment of its workforce.

Entering the occupational role

Behavioural scientists have long been interested in occupational placement both for intellectual reasons and to help industry allocate people to the occupational roles to which they are best suited. The initial running was made by psychologists and the focus of interest was very much on how individuals choose occupations, linking this very closely with individual personality characteristics and development. In the early formulations, dating back to the early 1900s, the emphasis was on individual abilities, character, dispositions etc., and how these are matched to different occupations. The assumption was that people had relatively fixed personalities and, equally, that occupational roles had clearly distinguishable requirements.

Criticisms of early theories of occupational choice concerned their over-static approach and neglect of factors external to the individual. In addition, the assumption that people have relatively fixed personalities has come increasingly under attack on several grounds. For instance, many early psychological theories concentrated on the emerging personality of the child or young person, implying that this would provide clear predictions of adult personality over the entire life span. More recent psychological thinking emphasises that people are involved in a learning process throughout their lives, which may involve considerable change in attitudes, aspirations and the development of further skills and abilities. Notions of social learning bring into consideration the individual's environment and the impact of factors external to the individual. The social world that individuals occupy is an enormously important source of influences on how people see themselves, and of encouragement or discouragement to develop or display particular attitudes and attributes. Education, especially, might be seen as a very potent source of such influences, with 'education' being defined broadly to encompass not only full-time attendance at educational institutions but also all forms of formal and informal training received in adulthood.

A further problem of *differentialist* approaches to occupational choice, as the above theories have come to be called⁾, is that they rely heavily on the notion of *personality traits*. The latter refers to special and distinctive characteristics argued to distinguish the kind of person who occupy different occupational roles. But recently the whole trait approach in psychology has come under attack. Just what a personality 'trait' is seems extremely difficult to establish – is it inherited, acquired, permanent or temporary, is it neurologically based or physicochemical in origin? Further, there is the problem of the correlation between the measurement of a trait (however defined) and actual behaviour: the correlation reported in studies has often been very low and this poses the question of whether traits and their associated behaviours are elicited in all situations the individual experiences or only in some limited range of situations[6].

For the above and other reasons, the differentialist approach to occupational choice became supplanted by the *developmental approach*. This assumes that rather than being an *event* occurring at a single point in time, occupational choice is, in fact, a *process* which begins early in childhood and involves a complex, continuous inter-action between the person and environment. Ginzberg *et al.*[7], among the best known of the early proponents of this approach, suggested that children start this process with fantasies about their future adult occupations. Gradually, however, these give way to a recognition of what is possible given their own accomplishments and available opportunities. In other words, people become 'occupationally mature' by developing through a series of stages as they grow older. An even better known and very influential formulation in this tradition is the work of Super[8].

Individuals, according to Super, develop a 'self-concept' which gradually integrates with their occupations. Consistency between self-concept and occupation is seen as crucial to job satisfaction, for example. Personality traits remain important in this approach but are seen as developing and changing as a result of the influences and experiences of growing up. A major aim of this approach, as with earlier work, was to develop a set of predictors linked with occupational choice which, in principle, would have considerable importance for vocational guidance and selection.

However, despite further refinements of developmentalist perspective and of other psychological contributions to occupational choice linked to decision-making and expectancy theories[9], criticisms still abound. First, although a large number of studies have now been conducted within these traditions, results have often been criticised for methodological inadequacies or because results have been difficult to interpret unequivocally. For instance, many samples chosen for study, particularly in the USA, have been seen as unrepresentative because they concentrate on young people from white, middle-class back-grounds. Similar criticisms have been made of research in Britain[10]. Many of the studies of the process of occupational choice have been cross-sectional – respondents have been interviewed at only one point in time – so that the process as it occurs has not been studied. Instead, researchers have had to reply on respondents' memories. Such reliance is known from a wide range of behavioural science studies[11] to be questionable.

If methodological weaknesses are revealed, results must always be in doubt, but even where results have been established more firmly, the conclusions have been rather general. For instance, research on personality differences suggests that schoolchildren opting for arts subjects are distinguishable from those opting for science subjects and parallel differences have been recorded for undergraduates. Similarly, research on expressed interests has concluded that these are related to preferred occupations but the relationship is weaker when correlated with jobs actually obtained[12].

In other words, only very broad links between personality and occupation have been at all well established and then for only limited samples. This is hardly a firm basis for a systematic application of behavioural methods of selection. Yet something of an 'industry' has developed here with consultants offering advice to both individuals and companies on individuals' suitability for specific occupations. Much of the advice offered is common sense or based on rule-of-thumb experience. However, this is often dressed up in behavioural science terminology or accompanied by psychological tests of one kind or another. Measuring the success of these approaches is difficult. Even inexperienced interviewers, for example, would eliminate grossly unsuitable applicants and, in any case, many of those who take on a particular occupational role may be expected to 'grow into it' with experience even if they were initially not ideally suited. Rigorously conducted longitudinal studies of the results of this kind of advice are rare.

Sociological approaches to occupational choice

Sociologists have also had a good deal to say about occupational choice, though they came on to the scene rather later. Initially, sociologists were highly critical of psychological approaches for their failure to take into account social and economic influences on occupational choice. While developmental approaches did allow for interaction between the individual and the environment, the latter was defined in a very limited fashion to refer mainly to immediate experiences.

One of the most forceful sociological arguments was that offered by Roberts[13], who first attacked the very notion of occupational *choice*. One of the illusions of modern industrial society, he argued, was that people had freedom of occupational choice. Parents, teachers and others close to young people ask repeatedly 'What are you going to do when you grow up/leave school/graduate?' Young people are often encouraged to believe that the world is their oyster although, in reality, they often have little or no firm idea about what kind of job they want or will subsequently get. Roberts' argument implies that young people may be wiser than adults, since he argues that, in practice, the kind of occupational role an individual comes to occupy is determined by the 'opportunity structures' they encounter. Social class and parental background, education, gender, ethnicity and local and national employment markets all combine to limit the kind of job which might eventually be taken.

Moreover, individuals' job aspirations – the jobs they say they would like or feel they might be successful in obtaining – are also highly influenced by these structural influences. Social class background has been shown by a wide range of studies to influence the level of occupations to which young people aspire. Typically, young people whose fathers are unskilled or semi-skilled leave school earlier and are less likely to go on to higher education, even if their ability is higher than average[14]. The effect of ethnicity has been shown to be equally marked. Asian children have been found to be considerably more ambitious than other ethnic groups (including whites) and to have higher occupational aspirations[15].

In other words, the idea that individuals 'choose' their occupations may be an overstatement. It might be more accurate to use the phrase 'occupational *placement*'. These arguments are even stronger in the 1980s when prevailing levels of unemployment are taken into account. As Chapter Two pointed out, for much of the early 1980s, almost one in four young people were unable to obtain conventional employment in the formal economy. For young West Indians in inner city areas, this proportion has been substantially higher. Further, economic restructuring, including the shift towards a service economy, has resulted in large numbers of older people being made redundant, often with little chance of ever securing another occupational role in the formal economy. Other sociologists have developed the analysis of structural influences on occupational placement still further by pointing out that another major weakness of earlier theorising and research was that it paid little or no attention to the other half of the employment relationship, the employer. Employers themselves have preferences for certain kinds of employees, so the study of occupational placement has to take these into account if the processes involved are to be fully understood[16]. Again, this point is even more important in the 1980s when employers can be more choosy about whom they employ than in the full employment decades of the 1950s and 1960s.

Economists have also had a long-standing interest in the analysis of the labour market – the ways in which labour prices are established through the processes of demand and supply for particular kinds of employees. Sociologists and some economists have built upon this approach to develop a sociology of the labour market that takes into account the attitudes and behaviour of employees (potential and actual) and employers as well as structural influences associated with social class, education, gender, ethnicity and the economy as a whole[17].

Generally, the sociology of the labour market approach to occupational placement has concentrated more on employer behaviour and structural influences on occupational placement than on individuals' behaviour. Special attention has been paid to ethnicity to show why it is that, even where ethnic minority members share the same culture as other members of society and attain the same level of educational achievement, they still persistently fail to do as well as whites in obtaining well-paid, secure work[18]. What this research has shown is that the complexities of individuals' relations to the occupational placement process are matched by an equally complex set of influences emanating from employers' attitudes and behaviour and the structural features of the economy itself.

A further issue which has recently attracted considerable attention is relationships between gender and occupational placement. That women have been treated in a less than equal manner by employers has been accepted for some time, as the Equal Pay Act, 1970 and Sex Discrimination Act, 1975 bear witness, together with the establishment of the Equal Opportunities Commission under the latter Act[19]. There is also a considerable amount of research which establishes gender as a key factor in determining occupational placement.

It should be stressed that gender influences on occupational placement are not simply the results of employers' attitudes and behaviour. Socialisation into gender stereotypes begins at an early age as a result of parental behaviour and other influences on the formation of children's views. An American study of 540 kindergarten children, for example, found that 97 per cent of the girls selected occupations conventionally seen as female while 85 per cent of the boys selected traditionally male occupations[20]. Research in Britain attests to the continuation of these processes in later stages of education[21]. In short, where employers make gender an important consideration in employee selection, they are reflecting to some extent widely held gender stereotypes in society. Curran, in a study of the recruitment of clerical workers, for example, found that 43 per cent of recruitment respondents made a reference to gender in describing the requirements of jobs for which they were recruiting[22].

Other stereotypes, especially those connected with age[23], are also of some importance in occupational placement. Employers often show strong preferences for younger employees. This appears to be particularly marked among small firm employers[24], but the study noted in the above paragraph found that three-quarters of a wider employer sample expressed a requirement or preference mentioning age and, of those mentioning a maximum age, 87 per cent wanted employees aged 40 or younger[25]. In a society where average age is rising and where economic and technical change means that more people may expect to have to change jobs more frequently as they get older, age influences on occupational placement will undoubtedly increase in importance in the future.

It may be that the sociological approach to the study of labour markets and occupational placement has moved too far away from consideration of the individual to over-stress the importance of structural factors and employer influences. The strong implication in this approach is that the individual job seeker is of little importance in explaining how people end up in particular jobs. But, of course, people are not simply collections of personality traits or passive reactors to external influences but purposive, acting individuals who seek to change their situations or to circumvent barriers which they perceive as inhibiting them from realising their goals. Willis[26], in an extremely influential study of young male working class respondents, showed that disadvantaged youths may develop a complex counter-school culture which needs to be taken into account in studying attitudes to getting a job as well as the kind of work they will do. Equally, despite the disadvantages particular groups may suffer, individual members may well strive hard to overcome these barriers even when they recognise their existence.

In the work role

When people enter an organisation and a work role, they enter into a complex set of social and economic relations. Just how the individual is linked to the organisation, however, is not that easy to explain. Organisational theorists, as Chapters Eight and Nine show, seem to be happier analysing the organisation as an entity in itself, making references to the individual from time to time, but rarely taking the individual as their starting point[27]. This is partly a reflection of a more general problem in behavioural science – how to link the individual to the wider social structure (in this case the work organisation) and vice versa. One well-established solution to this problem is the use of the interpretive framework known as role theory. Role theory is not a theory in the sense that a natural scientist would use the term, that is, it does not make predictions on the basis of assumed relationships between variables which may be confirmed or disproved by experiment. It is a framework or model involving a battery of concepts based on the usefulness of the concept of *role* as an articulating concept linking the individual to the social environment. Individuals occupy or perform a wide range of roles in every area of social life, but here we are concerned primarily with roles within the formal economy.

It is useful to distinguish initially between *role* and *position* (or status)[28]. 'Accountant', 'husband', 'mother', 'secretary' are examples of positions. In a sense they are labels or titles which, strictly speaking, tell us little about what is involved (however much we may think we know what they involve). It is only when a position has rights, norms, duties and responsibilities attached to it, and is acted out in terms of these, that it constitutes a role. The written job specification which is frequently created for a new occupational role or where an existing role is advertised, is only a brief description of the role in that it usually lists only the principal duties and responsibilities attached to the job.

To make this important distinction clearer, the position of policeman exists in most societies but the role of the policeman in, say, Britain and South Africa or Saudi Arabia will differ. Equally, as Chapter Eleven emphasises, the position of 'manager' in a small enterprise differs considerably from that in a large enterprise in terms of the way the role is perceived by the holder, the way the role is performed and the expectations of others with whom the manager normally interacts of how the role will be performed. In short, individuals occupy positions but perform roles.

Two rather different notions of role have developed within behavioural science[29]. In the first, the assumption is that the role is imposed upon or adopted by the individual in a virtually complete form. In the business organisation, for example, it is assumed that a person takes on an occupation role which is fully specified and his or her performance may be judged in relation to how effectively that specification is met. Some of the 'people-less' versions of systems theory models of the organisation, previously popular in management teaching, embody this notion of occupational role. Individuals are assumed to be of little real importance in the sense that 'people may come and people may go but the organisation goes on'.

The alternative concept of role sees it as largely a creation of the particular role holder. There may well be written job specifications (though in far fewer instances than might sometimes be assumed[30]) but on close examination these are rarely comprehensive in any strict sense. Most end with some vague catch-all phrase such as '. . . and such duties as his/her superior may from time to time, prescribe'. In practice, however, individuals create a large part of their role performance through injecting their own ideas, skills and abilities and, more basically, because of all the situations the role holder will encounter which simply cannot be predicted in advance.

The role holder, however, does not unilaterally create the role against the background of the given role specification defined by management. He or she is also involved in a *role set*, which Merton[31] defined as the network of role relationships in which an individual is involved by virtue of occupying a particular position or status. The individual occupying the role of 'manager', for example, is automatically involved in relationships with other managers in the organisation, with supervisors, often with shop floor employees, clerical workers, worker representatives such as shop stewards and very often people outside the organisation also such as customers, suppliers, trade union officials and civil servants.

The notion of the role-set has been particularly helpful in training situations. People can be asked to act out both their own and the roles of others in their role set. Normally, people rarely get the opportunity to see how the world looks from the viewpoint of others: the manager, for instance, may never experience the frustrations of a customer waiting for an order delayed without explanation or of a secretary having to cope with a seemingly endless chain of interruptions while still getting a long report typed to a deadline. Even though role set training of this kind is simulation rather than reality, it has proved to be of enormous value both in the academic setting and in in-company training. One of the best examples of role-set training is negotiating exercises based around industrial relations issues. Managers can take on the role of the union negotiator, gaining insights into how the union official sees his situation which, in turn, improves their performance in the managerial role later in real life. Case study exercises that involve a group of participants adopting a complete role-set of positions and later switching roles can have considerable training value. In-company exercises based on this concept can be resource expensive – especially in executive time – and may be politically sensitive where those involved have to resume their usual roles after the exercise, but they can be a valuable way of enhancing interpersonal social skills and developing new ways to increase efficiency.

A central notion in role theory is *role conflict*. Role conflict may take two forms. First, an individual in a particular role may find that others in his or her role set have developed differing and conflicting expectations in relation to that individual's role. A much cited example of this form of role conflict is the role of supervisor. The supervisor may find that senior managers expect their directives to be carried out strictly and productivity maximised. On the other hand, the supervisor also has to maintain good working relations with subordinates. Yet subordinates may strongly resent senior management's notions of what constitutes a proper working pace and level of productivity[32].

A second form of role conflict occurs where an individual occupies two (or more) roles whose expectations are in conflict with each other. The best contemporary example of this phenomenon is the married career woman. Out-of-work role set members – husband, children, relatives etc. – may well have expectations which are impossible to meet if the expectations of the woman's employment role-set are that she be available and totally committed to their shared tasks.

In practice, those subject to role conflict of either form may adopt a variety of solutions to solve or cope with the resulting situation:

1 It may be possible to ensure that in *intra-role conflict* (the first of the two forms) the holders of the conflicting expectations do not become aware that conflict is occurring or that their expectations

are not being met. The supervisor, for example, may become very skilled at not letting management know that their directives are not being met fully and so win subordinates' goodwill. Providing the department runs well and productivity is reasonable, the supervisor can, in effect, keep everybody happy.

2   Role set members may occupy different levels of power or have varying levels of interest in the role holder's performance. Those with the least power or interest can be partially ignored and their expectations need not be met as fully as those of others in the role set. For instance, a supervisor may give more attention to his or her seniors' demands if subordinates are unorganised.

3   Competing sub-groups within the role set may neutralise each other, giving the role holder greater autonomy. Thus a supervisor may find that managers from different departments are in conflict with each other and can be played off against each other to reduce overall management demands on the supervisor role.

4   The role holder can divert the attention of others in the role set away from him or herself and towards each other. A supervisor, for example, may arrange for workers' representatives to meet directly with senior management to thrash out their differences so that they no longer use the supervisor as a conduit for their conflict.

5   The role holder may forge a coalition with others to increase his or her bargaining power within the role set. Since the mid-1960s a large proportion of supervisors have joined trade unions; one reason for this, it has been suggested, is that many supervisors have felt they needed their interests protected and represented in their relations with management and with subordinates who were also increasingly union represented[33].

6   Finally, a role holder may actively go on the offensive to rearrange the role set and so reduce the severity of the conflicting expectations. For instance, a supervisor may seek to undermine the authority of a particular manager whose demands are considered to be intolerable. The manager may be discredited in the eyes of other managers so that either the demands made on the supervisor are reduced or the manager's career prospects are badly damaged[34].

There is no guarantee, however, that any of these strategies to reduce role conflict will be successful. It may be that the only solution is withdrawal from the role. This is not always possible: people may feel, for all kinds of reasons, that whatever the disadvantages, they must stay in their present role. The result may well be *role stress*, the psychological reaction to role conflict which impairs the mental and physical well-being of the person concerned. Stress resulting from employment experiences has become a fashionable issue in the 1980s[35]. Role theory provides a way of integrating this discussion into a wider examination of work activities.

Role ambiguity is a widely used phrase, but it is difficult to define clearly. One view states that role ambiguity exists where there is:

> . . . discrepancy between the information available to the person (role holder) and that which is required for adequate performance of his role[36].

Another attempt at a definition claims:

> Role ambiguity results when there is some uncertainty in the minds, either of the focal person or of the members of his role set, as to precisely what his role is at any given time. . . . If his conception of his role is unclear, or if his conception of his role differs from that of others in his role set, there will be a degree of ambiguity[37].

As noted earlier, job specifications are never and cannot ever be complete, particularly for high level roles in the organisation. Chairmen of nationalised industries, for example, are judged in terms of several criteria – making a profit comparable to a similar sized private enterprise, providing a cheap, efficient service to the public, and providing stable employment for their large number of employees, especially where the industry is the dominant local employer. In recent years, these criteria have frequently been in conflict, making it virtually impossible for the role holder to achieve any widely acknow-ledged degree of success in the role[38].

Role-taking and role-making in the organisation

In the initial discussion of the notion of occupational role the distinc-tion was drawn between a role as something imposed in a virtually complete form on the holder – a puppet conceptualisation of role – and a role as something created by the role holder over time in relation to, and in negotiation with, others in the organisation. A more satisfactory conceptualisation combines these notions: the individual takes or accepts a role in the organisation, which comes with certain role prescriptions – duties, responsibilities etc. – imposed by the employer. But at the same time the individual is able, and is often *required*, to devise further important elements in the role performance in order to be judged as adequate or a success.

Every occupational role, even the humblest post room assistant or delivery driver, has a built-in requirement that the holder will use their initiative, that is, will act in ways which enhance the aims of the organisation (as defined by top management) whenever unforeseen difficulties occur. In some higher level roles – in marketing or accounting and finance, for example – people are employed to be creative in ways which cannot be defined precisely in advance. Top managers are often defined as role holders whose main task is to cope with uncertainty and pilot their organisations through an unpredictable, even hostile environment. All these requirements refer to the process of *role-making*.

In many ways, the distinction between role-taking and role-making parallels the familiar distinction in organisational analysis between the formal and the informal structures. The formal structure refers to the total collection of roles and their interrelationships in the organisation as defined and prescribed by top management – the elements of every role which comprise its *role-taking* aspects. The informal structure refers to the often larger part of roles and their interrelations which are created by role holders themselves and which may or may not be approved of by top management – the process of *role-making*.

In most organisations, these two aspects of the occupational role work in harness for much of the time. People use their initiative to devise more efficient ways of achieving management-defined aims. Other aspects of role-making, however, may be relatively unconnected with the formal aims of the organisation – people form personal relations, clubs for leisure pursuits and so on as part of the process of filling out their occupational roles[39]. Other elements of role-making may be in conflict with the aims and procedures defined as the formal structure of the organisation. For instance, fiddling, the misappropriation of monies and goods is common in business organisations at all levels[40]. In some industries such as catering, it has become an institutionalised, permanent feature of the industry to the extent that it might be doubted that the industry could continue in being in its current form if it were eliminated[41]. Other forms of anti-management role-making include participating in groups or associations to counter management authority or individual acts which are intended to undermine managerial authority[42]. These expressions of role-making are no less important in understanding occupational roles than the others discussed above.

The usefulness of role theory

Role theory, as we said earlier, is not a theory in the strict sense and it cannot make any claim to direct explanatory power. It is, however, useful as a framework for organising data and ideas to further the understanding of the individual in the organisation. It also has heuristic usefulness in suggesting hypotheses which can be tested empirically – for example in how people cope with situations of role conflict or ambiguity – and it has proved very effective as a training vehicle for sensitising people to an appreciation of the difficulties and strategies of others in the organisation. It is a pity that role theory has fallen somewhat out of favour among contemporary behavioural scientists since, despite its limitations, its potential for exploring the articulation of the individual to the organisation is far from exhausted. Indeed, some of the more recent developments in theorising and research, such as ethnographic approaches (see Chapter Two) might benefit from reviving a framework that allows the researcher to link people to each other systematically.

Labour process analysis

Both occupational placement and the analysis of the individual in the occupational role have been tackled in a rather different way by an enormously influential perspective developed by theorists and researchers since the early 1970s. It has pushed aside concern with some of the earlier focal concepts of behavioural scientists, such as alienation, and has offered other ways in which the articulation of the individual to the organisation can be explored.

Labour process analysis, as this more recent perspective is usually termed, began essentially with the publication of a seminal study by Braverman[43]. In a sweeping historical analysis, he argued that the logic of development of industrial society imposed on management a need to increase efficiency and maximise profit and capital accumulation through the workings of the economy's competitive dynamic. In other words, managers were not only responsible to shareholders and owners but, in a more fundamental sense, to the market itself. Unless managers responded successfully to ever-increasing standards of efficiency, profit levels and capital accumulation, the enterprise (and the managers' and shareholders' interests) would perish.

Yet at the same time, Braverman argued, a major barrier to effective managerial responses to these external constraints was the very means through which the enterprise functioned – its employees. This contradiction arose because production always requires human beings – employees – hired not just for their brute energy but much more for their very specific and unique human attributes, their creativity, problem-solving abilities and imagination. These qualities, used to further management aims, can ensure the success of the firm – indeed, they are a necessary condition for its success – but they may also be a source of profound resistance to management.

Braverman noted that in the nineteenth-century enterprise, employees often had very considerable autonomy. Management, usually in the form of the owner-manager of the small enterprise, might have little direct knowledge of how employees carried out their tasks. Employees would jealously guard their 'secret knowledge' for it gave them independence in their dealings with management. In other words, while employee creativity and problem-solving skills were a tremendous potential source of support for management aims, they were also the source of management's major headache since the beginning of the modern enterprise: employee recalcitrance. Employees, because they are purposive, acting human beings with their own aims and goals, frequently do not share management aims.

The tension between employees striving to retain independence and managers seeking to serve the interests of shareholders and respond to the pressures of the market, grew more acute as ownership and management became separated and business organisations grew larger. At the turn of the century, the large business organisation, often with several thousand employees, posed severe problems for management attempting to co-ordinate their activities. Scientific management, particularly in the pioneering work of Taylor (see Chapter Eight) is seen by Braverman as the most influential and eloquent initial solution to these managerial problems.

Put briefly, Taylor's solution was to reduce, even minimise, employee autonomy and to shift decision-making firmly into the hands of management. By a process of de-skilling, management power would be enhanced, the enterprise rationalised and efficiency maximised. Braverman suggests that the enormous influence of Taylor's ideas, both in and outside the United States, was not so much due to their intellectual and scientific rigour but because they offered the prospect of a solution to an increasingly hard-pressed management stratum[44].

What was suggested in this thesis, therefore, was that the major trend built into the development of employee roles in the twentieth century was a gradual but inevitable de-skilling process and reduction in employee independence. Management strategies led to the proliferation of mass production work roles where employees became interchangeable labour units requiring only a few hours' or weeks' training to carry out their work tasks.

While manual employees, especially craftsmen, were the first targets of this transformation of work roles, Braverman suggested that in the latter half of this century, clerical workers would suffer a similar fate[45]. The introduction of computers and other forms of office mechanisation allows the de-skilling and stripping away of worker autonomy, already experienced by manual workers, to be repeated. In other words, de-skilling gradually ascends the hierarchy of occupations in the business organisation, extending even to professional roles such as accounting, which were being partly routinised by conversion to computerised solutions.

True, scientific management had been followed by human relations with its attempt to restore human interest and job satisfaction as important motivational bases of worker performance. But, in fact, despite all the energy and research devoted to human relations, in Braverman's view its real impact was never very great. Scientific management had remained clearly dominant even where mingled with human relations strategies. True, also, employees had organised themselves into trade unions to reassert their autonomy and bargaining power but again, according to Braverman, in the long term they had not defeated the fundamental advance of de-skilling.

Braverman's thesis has particular salience in the 1980s, since this is a period of fundamental economic restructuring and technological innovation in advanced industrial societies. The ability of management to dictate the context of occupational roles is further enhanced by the recession, reducing trade union and employee bargaining power.

Since Braverman's contribution, the labour process perspective has developed a good deal further through the contributions of a number of other theorists and researchers. For instance, there has been a detailed examination of the emergence of managerial roles in industrial society, particularly in the nineteenth century, which has questioned the necessity of the form in which they have emerged[46]. Managerial roles, in the form that we know them, it has been argued, developed not simply because of the need for efficiency or out of any inevitability but rather out of the historical configurations of ownership of the means of production in the industrial revolution. In short, there are potentially a large number of ways in which production could be efficiently organised and managerial functions exercised – the dominant privately owned enterprise with managers primarily responsible to outside shareholders is only one form.[47]

Braverman's original thesis has, however, been the subject of a number of criticisms. First, it has been argued that he exaggerated the levels of autonomy and skill among nineteenth-century workers. In focusing on the craft worker, the great majority of ordinary employees in unskilled or semi-skilled work with little freedom or autonomy were left out of consideration. This led to an overstatement of the extent of de-skilling in this century. However, it has also been pointed out that there was a good deal of internal sub-contracting in many nineteenth-century enterprises: owner-managers delegated the supply and control of particular forms of labour to a contractor who would be usually paid a lump sum[48]. Again, therefore, owner-managers would be distanced from their employees and unable to closely supervise or organise their labour.

It has also been argued that the thesis overstates the power of management. Management may well be under strong market pressure to increase efficiency and control labour performance but it would be wrong to assume that employees are always and entirely unsuccessful at resisting management efforts to further their aims. The history of trade unionism and other forms of individual and collective worker resistance cannot be dismissed as easily as Braverman appears to argue. The original thesis was based very much on an analysis of American experience, but trade unions have been rather more effective in other individual societies such as Britain. But, it has been argued, even in the United States, worker expressions of autonomy have been much more effective than Braverman implies[49].

This criticism is also important in relation to the more general issue of new technology, Popular views tend to see the introduction of new technology as inevitable: to try to stop such change is to stand in the way of 'progress' and to be a Luddite. In practice, new technology and other organisational changes introduced by management are often resisted and resisted successfully, at least to the extent of imposing limits and conditions on the exact form in which such changes will be accepted[50]. Moreover, employee resistance strategies may take time to bear fruit, so that the apparently successful introduction of new techniques and procedures may be undone later. Also, the public acceptance of change by employees, bolstered by managerial claims of its successful introduction, sometimes looks rather different when informal relations and procedures at the shop floor level are examined more closely[51].

What has emerged from recent thinking on this currently important set of issues is the recognition that organisations are first and foremost political structures (see the discussion of power and conflict in Chapter Nine) and the processes involved can only be fully understood by linking this point to the analysis of technological change. The introduction of any new technology or procedure threatens the position, reward, status and future of many of those in the organisation: equally, for others such changes may have the opposite effects. Management and non-management alike are affected in these differing ways by change. Resistance, usually not in the form of outright opposition but aimed more subtly at minimising perceived disadvantages, turns on the ability of those affected to form factions and exercise political influence. It will also depend on the current distribution of political power and bargaining opportunities in the organisation.

In other words, predicting the outcome of technological change is often far from easy. New technology and organisational change can often be introduced in a variety of ways which are more or less substitutes for each other in relation to management strategies. Which technology is selected, how it is implemented, what organisational structure and role changes result and, not least, the extent to which it successfully serves management aims in the long term, are all likely to rest on the outcome of complex political bargaining between those involved. Looking at the past, at the introduction of 'new' technology at every stage of the industrial revolution, it was ever thus.

External influences are also important in understanding technological and organisational change. First, there are market pressures that arise initially from the activities of other firms in the market, producing a competitive environment. Currently, these have grown more complex (and more severe for British firms) as the market in real terms has become global, particularly in manufacturing and high technology products. Formerly non-industrial countries have developed manufacturing capabilities exerting massive influences on older established industries and firms in industrial societies such as Britain and the United States, often to a point where, despite all attempts to respond to challenge, the older established enterprises have collapsed.

A further important external factor since the mid-1970s has been recession. This has not only increased the pressures on management to remain competitive but has also greatly undermined the bargaining power of labour, thus enabling management to cut labour costs more easily through reduced manning – a reorganisation of the work role structure in the enterprise – and to force through the introduction of new technology and procedures with less resistance than would have been the case a decade or so before. Historically, however, this situation may not persist: as in the past, periods of recession and weak employee bargaining power may be followed by periods where employees' power increases and they are able to claw back some of the autonomy and rewards lost previously[52].

A final criticism of the original Braverman thesis which is worth discussion surrounds the notion of skill. Braverman discusses skill (and the associated term de-skilling) as if it is a non-problematic notion. But, in fact, considerable ambiguity surrounds our ideas of skill: the term 'skill' may, for instance, refer to the intrinsic requirements of a task or set of linked tasks or, in contrast, it may refer to the capabilities of the individual. A job may be de-skilled; that is, the inherent difficulties of performing the job may be reduced by introducing new technology, but this does not necessarily mean that the worker is de-skilled if 'skill' refers to the worker's own capabilities. The worker may be able to transfer to a different occupation, perhaps in another industry, where these personal skills can be applied with equal effect[53].

Others refer to what they term 'the social construction of skills', by which they mean that attaching the label 'skilled' (or 'semi-' or 'unskilled') to a job and the person who performs it, may be more or less determined by negotiation (often of a tacit kind) between employers and employees and sustained by either or both because it serves their interests. For example, organised groups of workers in engineering or the early cotton industry, were able gradually to extend the range of tasks defined as 'skilled' and which only they would be allowed to perform. Their organised power forced management to recognise these tasks as 'skilled' and, by the same token, that other tasks performed by other workers, were to be deemed 'semi-' or 'unskilled'[54].

Conversely, employers may themselves create hierarchies of work grades labelled as 'skill' or 'career' grades as a personnel strategy. The creation of internal labour markets within the enterprise, with career paths described in terms of skill grades, may have a number of advantages in the eyes of management. For instance, they are a source of motivation to employees who may feel that being able to strive to reach a higher grade gives their work more purpose. Such strategies may also help to tie valued workers more closely to the enterprise, particularly where higher grades carry rewards and benefits not easily obtainable elsewhere in the external labour market. Just as in the instance where employee power successfully imposes the label 'skilled' on groups of workers and their tasks, the creation of internal skill grades by management may be unrelated, in any strict sense, to the actual skills intrinsic to the tasks performed or possessed by the particular individuals[55].

Trade unions may well go along with management-initiated skill hierarchies because members like the advantages and because they provide a solid basis for negotiating pay and conditions. Management may find advantages in accepting union-initiated definitions of skill in relation to particular work roles. Labour force turnover may be reduced, thereby cutting training costs, and employee loyalty to the union (resulting from the latter's success in negotiating with management) may reduce unofficial disputes and stoppages. These arrangements, regardless of who initiates them, are, however, inherently unstable: changes in bargaining power, management objectives, and especially economic and technological conditions, may lead to attempts to reconstruct definitions of skill[56].

In short, any thesis positing a relatively straightforward and inevitable unlinear trend towards de-skilling as industrial society develops, is grossly over-simple. There may be a tendency towards an overall de-skilling of work roles as part of managerial strategies to cope with the problems of controlling human contributions to the enterprise but, clearly, a proper analysis needs to take into account a whole range of other factors. Among the latter are the emergence of new skills (however defined), employee responses to management strategies which are by no means easily predictable, and short- and long-term influences linked to economic change and technological discovery[57].

Implications of the labour process perspective

The above account by no means exhausts the contribution of labour process analysis to the discussion of work roles and employee-employer relations in the enterprise[58]. Enough has been said, however, to indicate the important implications of this perspective for several key issues of interest to other behavioural scientists. For example, it has obvious links with the dynamics of labour markets examined earlier in this chapter. The construction of internal labour markets and notions of skills are directly connected with employers' recruiting strategies, as are gender and occupational placement[59]. Or again, the central employee-management relationship at the heart of the labour process perspective, as explored and analysed by Braverman, Edwards and Friedman, for example, offers a major input to organisational theories and organisational analysis as well as to the examination of organisational power and conflict, and industrial relations more generally. Finally, as the above account stressed, the labour process perspective offers important insights into the analysis of technological change in the enterprise.

In contrast with the more traditional role theory approach discussed in the middle of the chapter, the labour process perspective offers certain advantages. It offers a systematic way of linking vertically the major role networks within the firm: traditional role theory, while excellent at examining horizontal relations between work role holders and some vertical relations (usually those with immediate superiors), has rarely been able to suggest an analytical and explanatory framework which would situate role sets within the firm as a whole or in the wider macro-economic environment. The latter is especially needed in the 1980s, when fundamental economic restructuring and technological change are affecting all enterprises and role relations within them.

Role theory, on the other hand, retains superiority in two important respects. As a training aid, sensitising individual role accupants to their own thoughts and feelings about their involvement in the firm, and, even more importantly, increasing their appreciation of the ways in which others in the enterprise perform their roles, role theory remains central. Secondly, role theory analyses have shown a capacity to explore how particular human beings think, feel and define their involvement in formal work roles in a way which has not yet been matched by labour process perspective studies[60]. In the latter, the individual is often lost sight of, becoming an unthinking foot soldier in the processes of economic life and change[61].

This chapter has shown that work roles, in terms of how people enter them, structure and perform them and how work roles are constituted as an enterprise-wide network, are central to behavioural science contributions to understanding the economy. Other forms of analysis discussed at length elsewhere in this book can all be said, in a sense, to begin with the work role. Work meanings, motivation, interaction with others, work groups as well as organisational analysis, the examination of power and conflict including industrial relations, all ultimately centre on the work role and its holder.

References

1 See, for example, *Classification of Occupations and Directory of Occupational Titles,* HMSO, 1978, for an illustration of the number and range of jobs to be found in Britain.
2 All data and calculations in this paragraph derived from Handy, C., *The Future of Work,* Blackwell, 1984, p. 21 and *Labour Research,* 75, no. 1, 1986, p. 38.
3 *Labour Research, ibid.*
4 *Ibid.*
5 For a general discussion of these approaches and some of the further theories discussed below, see Lancashire, R., 'Occupational choice theory and occupational guidance practice' in Warr, P. B. (ed.), *Psychology at Work,* Penguin Books, 1971 and, for a more up to date assessment, Clarke, L., *Occupational Choice: A Critical Review of Research in the United Kingdom,* HMSO, 1980.
6 Chell, E., *Participation and Organisation: A Social Psychological Approach,* Macmillan, 1985, explores this issue in greater depth.
7 Ginzberg, E., Ginsberg, S. W., Exelrad, S. and Herma, J. L., *Occupational Choice,* Columbia University Press, 1951.
8 Super, D. E., 'A theory of vocational development', *American Psychologist,* 8, 1953, and Super, D. E. and Hall, D. T., 'Career development: exploration and planning', *Annual Review of Psychology,* 29, 1978.
9 For a critical discussion of more recent developments see Clarke, *op. cit.*
10 *Ibid.*
11 The alternative, and potentially more satisfactory approach, the longitudinal study, has been employed but, at least in Britain, the results have not been generally acceptable methodologically. The data collection has usually been too infrequent or too general to provide a detailed picture of the development of respondents' occupational choice patterns. Clarke, *ibid.* discusses this at greater length.
12 Clarke, *ibid.* pp. 10–14.
13 Roberts, K., 'The developmental theory of occupational choice: a critique and an alterative' in Esland, G., *et al.* (eds.), *People and Work,* Holmes McDougall/Open University Press, 1975.
14 Clarke, *op. cit.,* p. 7.
15 Clark, *ibid.,* p. 2.
16 A good example of the reasoning and research behind this development is provided by the studies of small and large firm employee-employer behaviour discussed at length in Chapter Eleven.
17 A set of papers covering a wide range of aspects of the sociology of labour markets is contained in Kalleberg, A. L. and Sorensen, A. B., 'The sociology of labour markets', *Annual Review of Sociology,* 1979. For a detailed empirical study in Britain, see Blackburn, R. M. and Mann, M., *The Working Class in the Labour Market,* Macmillan, 1979. For an economist's overview of recent theories, see Nolan, P., 'The firm and labour market behaviour' in Bain, G. S. (ed.), *Industrial Relations in Britain,* Blackwell, 1983.
18 This analysis has been especially well pursued in the United States. See,

for example, Gordon, D. M. *et al., Segmented Work, Divided Workers,* Cambridge University Press, 1982.

19   A very full account of sex discrimination in Britain is offered in Chiplin, B. and Sloane, P. J., *Tackling Discrimination at the Workplace, An Analysis of Sex Discrimination in Britain,* Cambridge University Press, 1982. See also, Curran, M. M., 'Recruiting gender stereotypes for the office' in *Equal Opportunities Research Bulletin,* no. 9, Spring, 1985, which, somewhat unusually, also examines carefully the views of employers on recruiting males and females for different jobs. The *Bulletin* also contains other papers relevant to this topic and 'A compendium of research into women and employment' compiled by Speakman, S. and Spicer, J.

20   Rily, P. J., 'The influence of gender or occupational aspirations of kindergarten children', *Journal of Vocational Behaviour,* **19,** 1981.

21   See the thoughtful introduction and papers in Deem, R., *Schooling for Women's Work,* Routledge and Kegan Paul, 1980.

22   Curran, M. M., *op. cit.,* p. 13. Of course, it may be argued that a study of recruiting clerical workers would be more likely to produce evidence of gender stereotyping than a study of recruitment for a wider range of occupations, but occupational segregation by gender is very widespread in Britain. See Dex, S., *The Sexual Division of Work,* Wheatsheaf Books, 1985, pp. 95–99.

23   Besides age, religion is worth mentioning, particularly for the study of occupational placement in Northern Ireland. Accent may also be a factor, although this has probably become less important in Britain in recent years and should probably be assimilated into social background influences on occupational placement.

24   Curran, J. and Stanworth, J., 'Self-selection and the small firm worker – a critique and an alternative view', *Sociology,* **13,** no. 3, 1979.

25   Curran, M. M., *op. cit.,* p. 10.

26   Willis, P., *Learning to Labour, How Working Class Kids Get Working Class Jobs,* Saxon House, 1977. See also for a similar analysis of girls who were also from an ethnic minority, Fuller, M., 'Black girls in a London comprehensive school', in Deem, *op. cit.*

27   There are, of course, exceptions, most notably in Britain. Silverman, D., *The Theory of Organisations,* Heinemann, 1970. For a more general discussion of this point, see Clegg, S. and Dunkerley, D., *Organisation Class and Control,* Routledge and Kegan Paul, 1980, pp. 273–95.

28   Linton, R., 'Status and Role' in Coser, L. and Rosenberg, B., *Sociological Theory: A Book of Readings,* Collier-Macmillan, 4th edn, 1976, pp. 276–81.

29   This distinction was initially elaborated by Turner, R. H., 'Role Taking: Process Versus Conformity' in Rose, A. (ed.), *Human Behaviour and Social Processes,* Routledge and Kegan Paul, 1971.

30   In the study by Curran, M. M., *op. cit.,* for example, only one third of recruiter respondents had produced any kind of written job description.

31   Merton, R. K., 'The role-set: problems in sociological theory' in Worsley, P. (ed.), *Modern Sociology: Introductory Readings,* Penguin Books, 1970.

32   For a general discussion of this form of role conflict based on a recent

study see Child, J. and Partridge, B., *Lost Managers, Supervisors in Industry and Society,* Cambridge University Press, 1982.

33   In practice, the situation is more complex than this, as the discussion and analysis in Child and Partridge, *ibid.,* Chapter Eight, makes clear, but the general point made here is broadly borne out.

34   These six ways of coping with role conflict are derived from the discussion in Merton, *op. cit.* Similar analyses could be provided for coping with *inter role conflict,* the second form discussed earlier.

35   See, Cooper, G. and Davidson, M., *High Pressure: Working Lives of Women Managers,* Fontana, 1982, especially Chapter One, which briefly reviews the literature on occupational stress. The remainder of the book offers a multitude of examples of role conflict of both kinds.

36   Kahn, R. L. *et al., Organisational Stress: Studies in Role Conflict and Ambiguity,* Wiley, 1964, p. 73.

37   Handy, C. B., *Understanding Organisations,* Penguin, 1976, p. 56.

38   Chapter Eleven offers a common example of role ambiguity, where small enterprise owner-managers refuse to define clearly other roles in the enterprise and frequently change managerial strategies without informing their juniors who are, hence, often unaware of what is required of them or what goals they should be striving to meet.

39   See, for example, Henry, S., *The Hidden Economy,* Martin Robertson, 1978 and Roy, D., 'Banana time: job satisfaction and informal inter-action' in Salaman, G. and Thompson, K. (eds.), *People and Organisations,* Longman, 1977.

40   Henry, *ibid.;* Ditton, J., 'Perks, pilferage and society: the historical structure of invisible wages', *Theory and Society,* 4, 1977; Mars, G., *Cheats at Work,* Allen and Unwin, 1983.

41   Mars, G. and Nicod, M., *The World of Waiters,* Allen and Unwin, 1984. For an example from another industry, see Ditton, J. 'Alibis and aliases: some notes on the "motives" of fiddling bread salesmen', *Sociology,* 11, May, 1977.

42   Taylor, L. and Walton, P., 'Industrial sabotage: motives and meanings' in Cohen, S. (ed.), *Images of Deviance,* Penguin, 1971, offers a rare glimpse of a form of behaviour which is probably a good deal more common than research can easily establish. For a more extended discussion see Brown, G., *Sabotage,* Spokesman Books, 1977.

43   Braverman, H., *Labor and Monopoly Capital, the Degradation of Work in the Twentieth Century.* Monthly Review Press, 1974.

44   *Ibid.,* especially Chapters 4–6.

45   *Ibid.,* especially Chapters 15 and 16.

46   See, for example, Marglin, S., 'What Do Bosses Do? The Origin and Functions of Hierarchy in Capitalist Production,' reprinted in Nichols, T. (ed.), *Capital and Labour,* Fontana, 1980, as 'The Origins and Functions of Hierarchy in Capitalist Production' (abbreviated from the original) and Edwards, R., *Contested Terrain, the Transformation of the Workplace in the Twentieth Century,* Heinemann, 1979.

47   For instance, a number of contemporary writers have pointed to the producer co-operative as an alternative form of economic organisation where the functions of management may still be performed by managerial specialist but the latter are primarily responsible to other members of the

enterprise rather than outside shareholders.

48 For a brief discussion of these practices and their implications for Braverman's arguments see Littler, C., *'Deskilling and Changing Structures of Control'* in Wood, S. (ed.), *The Degradation of Work? Skill, Deskilling and the Labour Process,* Hutchinson, 1982.

49 An important British example of this criticism is Friedman, A. L., *Industry and Labour, Class Structure at Work and Monopoly Capitalism,* Macmillan, 1977.

50 A 'classic' study of such successful resistance in Britain is briefly reported in Trist, E. L., and Bamforth, K. W., 'Technicism: Some Effects of Material Technology on Managerial Methods and on Work Situation Relationships', in Burns, T. (ed.), *Industrial Man,* Penguin Books, 1969. More recent examples are offered in Wilkinson, B., 'Technical Change and Work Organisation', *Industrial Relations Journal,* Summer, 1983 and *The Shopfloor Politics of New Technology,* Heinemann, 1983.

51 Child, J., 'Managerial strategies, new technology and the labour process' in Knights, D. *et al.* (eds.), *Job Redesign, Critical Perspectives on the Labour Process,* Gower, 1985, and for a wider discussion, the same author's *Organisation: A Guide to Problems and Practice,* Harper and Row, 2nd edn, 1984, especially Chapter Nine.

52 See, for example, the papers in Poole, M. *et al., Industrial Relations in the Future, Trends and Possibilities in Britain Over the Next Decade,* Routledge and Kegan Paul, 1984, and Mackay, L., 'The macho manager: it's no myth', *Personnel Management,* January, 1986.

53 Lee, D. J., 'Skill, craft and class: a theoretical critique and a critical case', *Sociology,* **15**, February, 1981.

54 Moore, C., 'Skill and the survival of apprenticeship' in Wood, S., *op. cit.* It should be stressed that the same processes operate in relation to higher level work roles and, most notably, in those occupations labelling themselves 'professions', the debate on solicitors' skills in conveyancing being a notable recent example.

55 Firms which have been seen as relying heavily on this approach to managing employees include IBM, Polaroid and Marks and Spencer. See Edwards, R., *op. cit.,* Chapter Eight and Purcell, J. and Sisson, K., 'Strategies and practice in the management of industrial relations' in Bain, G. S., *op. cit.* It is also sometimes associated with management attempting to prevent unionisation of their enterprise. See Brown, W. and Sisson, K., 'Current trends and future possibilities' in Poole, M. *et al., op. cit.*

56 Knight, *et al., op. cit.,* contains several papers analysing this form of internal enterprise change.

57 The best single source account of the labour process perspective to date is Thompson, P., *The Nature of Work, An Introduction to Debates on the Labour Process,* Macmillan, 1983.

58 Other notable contributions to the perspective include Burawoy, M., *The Manufacturing of Consent, Changes in the Labour Process Under Capitalism,* University of Chicago Press, 1979; Littler, C. R., *The Development of the Labour Process in Capitalist Societies: A Comparative Analysis of Work Organisation in Britain, the USA and Japan,* Heinemann, 1982. Thompson, *ibid.,* discusses a large number of shorter studies.

59   For a clear but brief discussion of this aspect, see Dex, S., *op. cit.,* pp. 99–104.

60   There are, however, studies that do bring the individual much closer to the forefront of labour process analysis, most notably Burawoy, M., *op. cit.* Other studies by researchers sympathetic to the labour process perspective, might also be added to this list. See, for example, Nichols, T. and Beynon, H., *Workers Divided, A Study of Shopfloor Politics,* Fontana, 1976.

61   A final point that may be made in favour of the labour process perspective is that it introduces history as a behavioural science which can make an importat contribution to our understanding of the enterprise and the economy. On the whole, history has not been prominent in helping those involved in the enterprise to devise more effective ways of realising their aims and goals, yet a sense and understanding of the past can positively inform our interpretations of the present and plans for the future.

8

The organisation of work

This chapter is about organisations, and their influence on behaviour. The principal emphasis is on the design of organisations. It provides a synthesis of attempts to design better organisations that promote greater efficiency and higher levels of motivation. Like other chapters in this book, however, it does not 'stand alone'. Important aspects of organisation theory and organisation design are picked up and developed in the ensuing two chapters. Because organisations are such a persuasive influence in our society, and provide the context for managerial work, most of the chapters in this book contain references to the constraints on behaviour imposed by organisations.

Organisations play an increasingly significant role in our society. Most of us work in organisations, are educated in organisations, interact with other organisations both at work and play, and spend much – perhaps too much – of our leisure time coping with the demands and paperwork set up by both public and private sector organisations. Those of us who have moved from one organisation to another will have experienced the differences in behaviour to be found between people in different organisations, illustrating the point that our behaviour at work is not only the outcome of our own personalities, and that of our work groups, but is also heavily influenced by the type and nature of the organisation concerned. We may also have experience of different organisations engaged in the same line of business, where one organisation is clearly more competitive and efficient than another. Such an organisation may be, and usually is, more exciting and challenging to work for.

An emphasis on the design of organisations may seem somewhat remote to many managers. After all, few managers, at least until they reach a very senior level, have much influence upon the design of their organisation. A higher proportion can perhaps have some influence upon the design or improvement of a part of their organisation, possibly within their own department. But the main reason for taking an interest in organisation theory has already been hinted at, namely the interaction between organisation structure and behaviour. If managers are to lead successfully, and influence the behaviour of individuals and groups, they need to understand the constraints and opportunities provided within different organisations. What is possible and desirable in a fast-moving, consumer-orientated private company may not be successful in a slower moving bureaucracy. And between two fast-moving, consumer-orientated companies there may exist wide differences in what can be achieved, and in the behaviour of their employees. Some aspects of this are picked up in the ensuing chapter where reference is made to differences in 'culture' between organisations, but 'culture' and 'structure' are strongly interrelated.

This chapter includes a review of the major approaches to the design of organisations developed during this century. Such an historical approach might initially seem inappropriate in a book devoted to the latest ideas and practices concerning behaviour and management, and it is in contrast with physical sciences, which concentrate on the most recent discoveries. But when Henry Ford described history as 'bunk' he was ignoring at least two important factors. Firstly, scientific ideas frequently take considerable time to be developed, first as hypotheses, then to be tested, and finally to be translated into practical applications. The first computer was developed in the last century, but computers have only recently advanced to the stage where they can control the production lines of the Ford Motor Company. Secondly, recent history shapes our ideas and attitudes. Henry Ford was a product of his times, and we as managers are surrounded by other managers and specialists whose ideas and attitudes about organisations and the way people should behave in organisations have been shaped by the course of recent events. We need to recognise the basis on which others are operating in order to pursue our goals more effectively.

The term 'organisation' has a number of different meanings and so requires definition. By 'organisations' we mean formal organisations that employ people, have a name or title, and are usually recognised in a law as corporate bodies. Such organisations are social systems by virtue of bringing people together, who then act and react as individuals, groups and departments in a recognisably social manner. Organisations are frequently economic systems as well, having to pay for goods and services and raise funds for this purpose. Sometimes their overt aim is to produce and sell goods and services for profit, sometimes to provide a public service, sometimes to serve the recreational or spiritual needs of members.

We begin with the early years of this century. Shortly before the First World War a book was published in the United States that was to have a profound effect upon management thinking about the organisation of work. Its author was Frederick Winslow Taylor, probably best known as the pioneer of Work Study, and the book was called *The*

Principles of Scientific Management[1]. Taylor was to become a leading figure in the so-called 'scientific management' movement, whose ideas remained influential until the middle of this century.

The Scientific management movement

The advent of the Industrial Revolution and the growth in size of industrial corporations created a need for principles upon which to base the organisation of people at work. In the past there had of course been large military, religious and civil organisations, but these provided little guidance to the leaders of industry. So rule-of-thumb methods prevailed, based mainly on the division of labour and a belief in hierarchical structures.

At the same time exciting developments in the physical and biological sciences were taking place, and it seemed logical enough to try to develop a science of management along similar lines. Taylor and his followers tried to do this and failed. What they came up with was a set of general statements about the way in which organisations ought to be set up and run. These statements had the merit of being fairly systematic, and appealed to what then seemed common sense. (Rather like the quest for the Holy Grail, the search for a science of management has attracted many since those days and still continues to do so. Unfortunately such people are frequently confused as to what the term 'scientific' really means.) Major contributions were made to the Scientific Management movement by such prominent authorities as Gulick in the United States and Urwick in England[2], and Fayol[3] in France. In time, a general synthesis took place, of which a representative set of statements is given below. Some of these still have a familiar ring:

1 Employees should be formally grouped and organised in specialist functional departments.
2 These departments and the persons within them should occupy a hierarchical structure, with authority emanating down from the board of directors.
3 An organisation chart should be produced to show this structure, with lines depicting the chain of command and the proper channels for official communications.
4 Each employee should report to only one superior.
5 The span of control of subordinates by superiors should be limited to permit effective supervision. This number was unlikely to exceed eight.
6 Jobs should be described and the nature of the duties prescribed, preferably in writing.
7 The number of levels of authority in the organisation should be kept to a minimum to ensure effective control and communication

in turn from director to manager to supervisor and to worker.

8   Authority should be commensurate with responsibility.

9   Departments could be categorised as either 'line' or 'staff'. Using a military analogy, line departments were depicted as those directly responsible for success in the market place, and therefore included production and sales. The function of staff departments was to give specialist advice and services to line departments, but they should never usurp the authority of lie managers over their own functions. Typical staff departments might be Work Study or Personnel.

Implicit in the statements emanating from the scientific management movement were assumptions about human behaviour. These assumptions have been parodied as the 'rabble' hypothesis, as they assumed that work people behaved like a rabble of isolated individuals motivated chiefly by a desire to earn money. The authority of management to give orders, and the generally hierarchical nature of society, were also taken for granted.

We can see how a number of the principles put forward by these writers appeal to common sense. It is difficult to argue with the idea that authority should be commensurate with responsibility, because it would be unfair to give one without the other. It is of course much harder to define either of these terms, let alone weigh them quantitatively in order to achieve a balance. Two of the 'principles' appear to conflict with one another. The more we limit the span of control, the more we widen the gap between workers and management by increasing the levels of authority.

In their time these 'principles' probably helped a large number of managers and contributed to increased efficiency. In other cases the reverse may have been true for reasons we shall discuss in the rest of this chapter. By the 1920s empirical evidence that questioned the basis of many of these principles was already accumulating. For example, successful organisations containing very wide spans of control were revealed. Advances in the social sciences led to criticism of the behavioural assumptions of these theories. Psychologists suggested that workers were influenced by many more factors than money. Sociologists began to question their assumptions about social order at the place of work.

One of these sociologists was a contemporary of Taylor, although their paths never crossed. He was the German sociologist Max Weber, whose work we have already met in Chapter Two, but whose writings did not become widely known and influential until a quarter of a century later. Probably best known today for his writings on bureaucracy and the Protestant ethic, his description of bureaucracy with its hierarchical and impersonal structures has some similarities with the 'principles' of scientific management. And his description of the Pro-testant ethic[4], which extolls thrift, hard work and a sense of duty, reminds us that large organisations run on traditional lines rely far more than is often recognised upon an inculcated set of values. Yet in spite of the many criticisms of scientific management, large formal organisations still use some of their guidelines. This is nicely embodied in the slogan 'simple form, lean staff' used by Peters and Waterman[5] following their study of 'excellent' American companies.

Human relations

Organisations are composed of people. This simple truth is frequently overlooked because questions of finance and production take pride of place. But it does mean that human relations at the place of work have long been the subject of speculation. During the 1930s and 1940s a number of prominent writers and researchers were led to place great emphasis upon the significance of human relationships at the place of work and their impact upon productivity, laying particular stress upon group behaviour, joint consultation, and the 'informal' organisation.

In the 1920s, psychologists had already begun taking an active interest in what went on at the place of work. It was a team of psychological researchers from Harvard University who carried out the famous investigations into the Hawthorne plant of the Western Electric Company in Chicago, subsequently described by their leaders Roethlisberger, Dickson[6], and Elton Mayo[7].

Most interest in this particular piece of research has centred on two of the investigations. In the first, a small group of female operators whose task it was to assemble telephone relays, was transferred to a room by themselves along with their equipment, and asked to continue with their task. This they did, while the researchers made changes to their working conditions in order to see whether these had any appreciable affect upon output. The workers continued to be paid by the company on an incentive system. In one set of experiments, the quality of lighting was improved in stages and in another, rest periods and refreshments were introduced. It was found that output increased significantly compared with previously recorded levels as these improvements were made. What was far more startling was that it remained at this high level even after a return to the original condi-tions. Furthermore, sickness and absenteeism decreased. The workers themselves had no clear explanation of why they worked so much faster, nor were they conscious of a speed-up or increased productivity.

In a second investigation by the researchers at Hawthorne, discreet observation was kept on male workers in the bank wiring room in the factory. Here again, the workers were on individual incentive schemes. However, instead of exerting maximum effort, they worked well below their real capacity. Individuals who showed signs of outpacing the rest were brought into line and made to conform.

From this and other studies made in the 1930s the general conclusion was drawn that the key to increased output lay not in individual incentive schemes and traditional authoritarian management, but in fostering better relations upon the shop floor. As higher output seemed to require the active co-operation of employees, supervisors had to be trained to show greater consideration and a more democratic style of leadership. Stress was laid upon better communications, interpreted as passing on more information as well as operating counselling programmes, and the creation of good morale in work groups. Put at its most simple, the human relations school advocated putting a human face to capitalism, with the promise of a payoff to all concerned.

This emphasis upon the individual and the work group continued during the 1950s and 1960s under the impetus of the American behavioural scientists mentioned in earlier chapters, such as Maslow[8], Likert[9], McGregor[10], Argyris[11] and Herzberg[12]. In its modern, sophisticated form, this approach is more correctly referred to as neo-human relations. Emphasis is placed upon the factors we have already discussed of job satisfaction, group dynamics, participative leadership styles and motivation. While this important approach to behaviour at work (which in turn is very relevant to the organisation of work) has been dealt with in appropriate detail elsewhere in this book, it is important to note that their general message with regard to organisations was and still is to the effect that the proper place for intervention when trying to modify the behaviour of workers and increase productivity is at the level of human relations on the shop floor or in the office.

From this group of American behavioural scientists we single out for special mention the work of Chris Argyris. Writing as a psychologist, he shows concern for the well being of people working in organisations. In consequence he underlines the dangers inherent in situations where psychologically healthy individuals are constrained to work in formal organisations run on traditional lines. By definition, a psychologically healthy individual will be 'predisposed toward relative independence, activeness, use of their important abilities, control over their immediate work world'. But this is 'not congruent with the requirements of formal organisations, which tends to require agents to work in situations where they are dependent, passive, use few and unimportant abilities, etc.'. Note that Argyris emphasises the concept of an ideal type of psychologically healthy individual. This begs the question of who has the right to define just who is psychologically healthy and who is not. But more important in this context, it demonstrates the manner in which experts tend to judge human institutions from within their own frame of reference.

Bureaucracy

For many people the term 'bureaucracy' is synonomous with 'organisation'. Most of us grumble from time to time about bureaucracies, faceless bureacrats, and endless form-filling. Bureaucracies appear to be a general characteristic of modern industrial societies, whatever their political creed or ethnic populations. The word 'bureaucrat' is often used as a term of abuse.

It may therefore seem somewhat surprising to us that Max Weber[13] depicted bureaucracies as an 'ideal' type. He did not mean ideal in the sense of being functionally perfect, but ideal in the sense of describing an extreme type of structure useful for comparative purposes, a kind of model or standard. As we have noted, bureaucracies are not very different from the form of organisation advocated by the scientific management school. But do bureaucracies actually work efficiently? Is it right that so many work organisations today should be bureaucracies? The criticism levelled by the Human Relations school at scientific management can also be levelled at extreme bureaucracies. Most of us know from personal experience that they can be impersonal and inflexible and neglect the psychological needs of employees and clients alike. Insight into their actual efficiency is given by two case studies.

In the first example, Alvin Gouldner[14] described the imposition of a bureaucratic structure upon a gypsum company, a small plant employing just over 200 employees in a semi-rural community in the United States. In this situation kinship meant a great deal, and family relationships were important both outside and inside the plant. Local people were united in their distrust of outsiders. A so-called 'indulgency pattern' of relationships operated in the plant, which meant that supervisors were not strict, management frequently turned a blind eye to petty misdemeanours, and tradition and custom were highly valued. A sudden change was precipitated when head office appointed a new manager, with institutions to make the plant more efficient. This was interpreted as a requirement for more bureaucratic procedures and stricter controls. The indulgency pattern was attacked. Work study, production control, paperwork procedures and formalised promotion and selection methods were imposed. As can be imagined, there was immediate resentment and increased tension. In order to counter this, supervision was made even tighter, which in turn generated further tension. The outcome was a series of bitter disputes and a wildcat or unofficial strike. Eventually an uneasy peace was established, but the immediate consequence of imposing bureaucratic procedures was a decline in efficiency. It is important however, to note the circumstances. The new manager had to act out a role imposed upon him by head office. The local workers were also acting out roles. In this particular case bureaucracy did not work because individual expectations were not taken into account.

In contrast, Peter Blau[15] describes a situation where the workers were accustomed to bureaucratic procedures. This was in a public employment agency in a city where the interviewers he described worked in two sections, A and B. Their duties were alike, and involved finding suitable jobs for job seekers. However, there was considerable competition between interviewers, particularly in section A, to see who could achieve the largest number of satisfactory job placements. In a period of job shortages this competition took the form of trying to utilise job openings as they were notified before anyone else did. Instead of leading to greater efficiency, this led to subterfuge by interviewers in section A in order to boost their own individual success rate. For example, incoming notices about job vacancies were concealed or deliberately amended in order to confuse other interviewers. Members of section B were more co-operative, and helped each other with placements. When a productivity index was created, it showed section B to be better than section A. Interpersonal competition had the effect of reducing the efficiency of part of that bureaucracy.

The effect of more recent studies, such as that by Burns and Stalker[16], has been to shift the focus of interest away from the internal workings of bureaucracies to the question of their appropriateness to their economic and social environments. Because bureaucracies tend to be both inflexible and particularly adapted to a prevailing set of circumstances, they may well provide the most efficient (defining 'efficient' in a fairly narrow economic sense) form of organisation at the time. But should circumstances begin to change, then trouble ensues, as Burns and Stalker highlighted. The recent economic history of this country is littered with examples of large organisations which have failed to adapt to the rapid change in markets and technology, and have therefore gone to the wall.

Technology and behaviour at work

Why is it that some industries seem to be the focus of industrial unrest and others are rarely in the news? Should work be organised in exactly the same way in mass production forms, oil refineries, hospitals and civil services? How much attention should we pay to the way technology dictates the nature of work? Can the contents of a job so alienate the worker that no amount of human relations technique will make him satisfied? Some see the key to these and related questions in an analysis of the technology of work.

A simple approach to the technology of work is to classify organisations on the basis of their production technology. This has been used to great effect by Robert Blauner[17] in the United States and Joan Woodward[18] in England. Concentrating on industrial production methods, we can follow Blauner in classifying work according to whether it is:

1 a 'craft' industry such as printing
2 'Machine-minding' in industries, such as textiles, with considerable standardisation and mechanisation
3 'Assembly line', such as the car industry, where workers carry out repetitive unskilled work
4 'Process' industries using continuous process methods, such as in chemicals and oil refining.

Of these four kinds of work situation the assembly line probably has the most notorious reputation. Blauner was much concerned with the problem of alienation already discussed in Chapter Two, which he defined in terms of workers' feelings of powerlessness, meaninglessness, isolation and self-estrangement. His conclusion, after investigating a large sample of workers in the United States, was that alienation increases as the degree of mechanisation of work increases, up to a peak when the assembly line is reached, and then improves considerably as continuous process methods take over in the technologically advanced industries.

If this is true, forms of organisation structure that create harmony and high output in a craft industry might well prove a failure in a mass production situation. Evidence along these lines was produced by Joan Woodward as a result of a study of 100 firms in south-east England. She used a similar method of classification, categorising the firms as to whether they used unit, mass or process production methods. Like Blauner, she found evidence of the greatest tension between workers and management in the mass production firms. But what is of greater significance is that she also analysed the organisation structures of the firms concerned, using many of the headings put forward by the advocates of scientific management, such as span of control and number of levels of authority.

Her findings dealt a serious blow to the claim of the scientific management writers that the application of their principles would promote the success of the organisation, irrespective of type of place. What she did find of a positive nature was that the outstandingly successful firms had one feature in common. Many of their organisational characteristics approximated to the media of their production group. For example, in successful unit-production firms the span of control of the first line supervisor ranged from 22 to 28, whereas in successful mass production firms it ranged from 45 to 50. Also, mass production firms who conformed with the principles of scientific management appeared to do better than the mass production firms who did not, although this did not apply to firms in the other two production categories.

The lesson here appears to be that conformity and a 'follow-my-leader' approach to organisation structures pays off, at least in an industrial context. But this is a very crude rule of thumb. Findings from other studies, in particular that conducted by Tom Burns and G. M. Stalker into the organisation of the electronics industry in Scotland in the 1950s and already referred to, underlined the importance of the marketing and social environment in which a firm operates. A firm operating in a fairly bureaucratic (sometimes termed 'mechanistic') manner had a good chance of remaining stable and successful if its product market also remained stable, but a turbulent economic environment required a far more informal organisation that could quickly produce the appropriate multi-disciplinary task orientated work groups to meet the challenge of change (this is sometimes referred to as an 'organic' structure). The principles of reporting to only one boss, hierarchical and rigidly separated functional departments, detailed job descriptions and little delegated authority appear to mitigate against rapid change.

Ensuing work on technology and behaviour at work has concentrated on the actual task which workers were expected to carry out, including factors such as variety of work, skill and control over pace of work. Taken in conjunction with the work of American behavioural scientists such as Herzberg, already referred to in Chapter Three, emphasis has been placed on the nature of the work performed and its relevance to a personal sense of achievement in order to increase motivation. This found expression in this country and the USA in the job enrichment programmes already alluded to, and the more recent emphasis on job design. In northern Europe a more broadly based and long-lasting approach has come about through the application of a 'socio-technical' approach, developed within a 'humanistic' cultural and political framework. This is discussed in the next section in the context of systems theory.

The systems approach

The systems approach treats the organisation as a system of inter-related parts. These parts constitute a whole which in turn has goals and interacts with its surrounding environment in an attempt to maintain its existence and achieve its goals, the primary one usually being survival and/or growth. The concept is simple enough, and natural to much of our thinking when we are concerned to see both the wood and trees. However, its development and applications have led to considerable advances in management thinking, as well as in other fields such as biology and engineering. For example, changes frequently have to be made within work organisations that affect, say, a major process or department. Too often such changes are implemented without adequate consideration for their repercussions on other parts of the organisation, and possibly on customer service. Or organisations go out of business because the leaders have not identified or controlled the manner in which they should interact with the environment, represented perhaps by customers or the government. A startlingly high production of the household names of 20 years ago no longer feature amongst the top 100 of contemporary business.

Credit for original thinking must be given to von Bertalanffy[19], who developed a theory of open systems in physics and biology some 40 years ago. Open systems theory underlines the relationship between the organism (or organisation) and its environment, and as such is particularly relevant to work organisations. As interpreted by Katz and Kahn[20], open systems are seen as having nine important characteristics – importation of energy, throughput, output, cycle of events, negative entropy (the attempt to counter the 'running-down' of the system), information input (or feedback), and a steady state (interpreted as 'dynamic equilibrium'). To this should be added the concept of a goal, or goals, already alluded to. That such a list is not mere academic quibbling, but can be applied in a vital way to the success or failure of work organisations, can be seen by applying these nine characteristics to both successful and less successful organisations to show where the shortcomings and successes lie. The two diagrams shown in Figure 8.1 contain a simple illustration of work organisations viewed as systems.

Two developments of systems theory have particular relevance to organisation design. The first is the 'socio-technical' approach of the Tavistock Institute in this country, and the second is 'contingency theory' developed in the United States.

Socio-technical systems

The socio-technical approach emphasises the need to consider the interrelationship between social and technological factors when planning and carrying through changes in work methods and organisation structure, instead of, as is too often the case, implementing new technology and work methods in a manner which causes resistance and unrest. In a classic study in this country in the 1940s[21], social scientists from the Tavistock Institute observed some technical changes carried out in the coal mining industry in Durham. The object of these changes was to mechanise the system of extracting coal underground, thus enabling coal to be extracted with a longwall method. This replaced

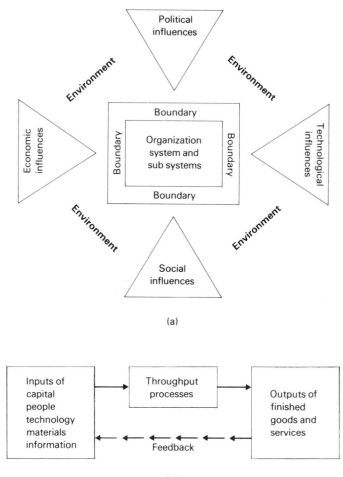

Fig. 8.1 (a) Simple system model (b) essential processes in organisation viewed as a system

the old single place working method where a small group of miners worked their own place in the coal seam. Each miner had formerly been an all-rounder, and belonged to a self-selecting group of miners with strong interpersonal ties. The new method replaced this with shift working, each shift specialising on a different task, namely preparing, cutting, or loading. The new system proved unsuccessful because of lack of co-operation within the shift and between shifts, resulting from specialisation. Technical change had taken place, but an appropriate social system had not been developed to match this change. What was needed, in the opinion of the social scientists, was a socio-technical systems approach. Applied to this particular problem, this approach led to the development of the 'composite longwall method', where a multi-skilled role was re-introduced, shifts carried out composite tasks, and social cohesion was restored.

It is in the application of socio-technical systems ideas to industry in northern Europe that most *interest is shown* today. True to form, the British have failed to exploit the idea themselves, and in this case have left the Germans and Scandinavians to make the most of it. Out of the socio-technical approach has emerged in northern Europe the idea of semi-autonomous 'work groups' and 'team working', which has affinity to the 'quality of working life' and 'job enrichment' approaches described in the earlier chapters on motivation and work groups. Taken in conjunction with the emphasis on democracy at work, and on worker participation, this has found expression in such well-known schemes as the Volvo and Saab-Scania works in Sweden. Contrary to wishful thinking by many British managers (and trade union leaders) a large proportion of these initiatives have been successful, and have made a significant contribution to wealth creation, as well as to greater job satisfaction. However, many practical problems have to be overcome before group working can be successful.

The pioneer project in applying a socio-technical system in conjunction with group working was initiated at Norsk-Hydro in Norway in the late 1960s. Advised by the Norwegian Work Research Institute, management agreed with unions on work changes in a section of a chemical plant where new equipment was being installed. After some discussion involving a project committee and 'brainstorming' sessions with workers, a scheme was agreed whereby process workers took on greater responsibilities and worked on shifts in semi-autonomous groups of about 12. Each group contained people with different skills and, as their experience increased, more flexible and integrated work patterns emerged. People were paid for what they knew and could do under a new grading structure and benefited from a plant bonus scheme. Initially, individuals attended a 200-hour course designed and run by process operators, maintenance supervisors and foremen. The course included elementary chemistry, industrial processes, mechanical syllabus and instrumentation. The charge-hand acted in a new role as a troubleshooter and the position of assistant foreman was abolished. The simpler maintenance work was undertaken by the shift teams and the number of skilled craftsmen reduced. Unskilled jobs were abolished. Specialist and service departments were decentralised to encourage autonomy on individual, group and plant level. A new philosophy of management was initiated, emphasising participation in decision-making at all levels. The outcome was improved productivity and better labour relations. However, as a word of caution, Emery and Thorsrud[22] comment:

> The creation of better conditions for personal involvement in company affairs is heavily dependent on the ability of management to gain a relatively high degree of control over boundary conditions (the interdependence between a company's internal conditions and external environments). Otherwise, it is impossible to define the conditions within which individual persons or groups can exercise self-management . . . our tentative conclusion is that the establishment of semi-autonomous groups is strongly dependent on the ability of management to shift its primary attention from internal co-ordination and control to the regulation of the company's boundaries. In a way, this point is in conflict with the traditional view of the task of management.

Contingency theory

Contingency theory is a refined version of open-systems theory, concentrating on the management of key contingencies critical to the successful functioning of organisation. It has proved popular in the United States, largely because it can provide practical guidelines to the design of more effective organisations. Two leading exponents are Paul Lawrence and Jay Lorsch[23], who comment:

> In order to perform its task of converting inputs to outputs, an organisation essentially engages in two types of processes; maintenance and task performing. The maintenance process is essentially those activities which the organisation engages in to remain viable. It must build and maintain staff, plant, etc. in order to perform any task at all. The second set of processes, task performing, are the actual activities by which raw materials are transformed into finished products. Finally, there are import and export processes across the organisation boundary, as organisation members gather resources and distribute products or services.

This version of contingency theory underlines the need for the degree of specialisation, and the consequent need to co-ordinate and integrate the specialist, to match relevant facets of the environments. Thus more finalised and centralised methods of integration are appropriate to stable and less complex environments, whereas the opposite may be true for turbulent and complex environments. This is illustrated in Figure 8.2, adapted from Lawrence and Lorsch.

John Child[24] labels this type of contingency theory the 'task contingency approach', because of its intitial focus on the tasks to be performed within an organisation, paying subsequent attention to such

Industry	Environment Diversity	Actual Differentiation	Actual Integration	Integrative Devices			Conflict Management Variables		
				Type of Integrative Devices	Special Integrating Personnel as % of Total Management		Hierarchical Influence	Unit Having High Influence	
Plastics	High	High	High	Teams, Roles, Departments, Hierarchy, Plans, Procedures	22%*		Evenly Distributed	Integrating Unit	
Foods	Moderate	Moderate	High	Roles, Plans, Hierarchy, Procedures	17%*		Evenly Distributed	Sales and Research	
Container	Low	Low	High	Hierarchy, Plans, Procedures	0%*		Top High Bottom Low	Sales	

Fig. 8.2 Environmental factors and organisational characteristics of effective organisations (adapted from Lawrence, P. R. and Lorsch, J. W., Addison Wesley, 1969)

contingencies as environment, diversity, size, technology and type of personnel. He contrasts this with 'political contingency', where emphasis is given to power and politics in the design of organisations. Relevant aspects of power and politics are examined in the next chapter.

Ways of classifying organisations

Scientific progress requires the development of adequate systems of classification. The physical, chemical and life sciences all rest on logical systems of classification. Early writers on organisations tended to use over-simple methods of classification, but when we consider organisations as diverse as the Civil Service, a general hospital, a school, ICI or the local youth club, we can see the need for a more sophisticated system. We have already touched on some of the simpler methods of classifying organisations, including the following:

by ownership, e.g. public versus privately owned
by size, e.g. large versus small
by 'ideal' type, e.g. similarity to Weber's ideal type
of bureaucracy
by membership, e.g. is membership voluntary or compulsory?
by technology, e.g. unit production or mass production?

Clearly an adequate system of classification will have to take account of these and other significant facets of organisations. One of the best known modern attempts to classify organisations from a sociological perspective was that made by Etzioni[25]. He used compliance as the major source of differentiation. Put quite simply, an organisation would cease to exist if it did not achieve a degree of compliance on the part of its members. Etzioni sees compliance, and the authority which exerts compliance, as resting on the way in which the individual member becomes and remains involved in the organisation. This may come about because of coercion, desire for financial reward, or moral or normative feelings. If, suggests Etzioni, coercion is the basis of authority, then compliance will be alternative. If remuneration is the basis, then compliance will be utilitarian or calculative. And if moral feelings and norms are the basis, then the compliance itself will also be moral. Etzioni further suggests that there will be a tendency for alignment or 'congruence' between authority and compliance, such that organisations will tend to be one of three types: coercive-alienative, remunerative-utilitarian, or normative-moral. Also, congruent types would be more 'effective' than non-congruent types. Examples of these three types would be, respectively, prisons, work organisations and voluntary associations.

This typology is valuable in that it reminds us of the dependence of organisations upon compliance, a fact which is often skated over, particularly by management. However, it still leaves a number of questions unanswered. These include the significance of technology, the way in which organisations might become 'incongruent', and certainly as to the meaning of 'effectiveness'. Practical difficulties have also been found in applying this system of classification to a wide range of actual organisations[26]. Some organisations show a diversity of involvement on the part of their members. Individuals join and work in organisations for a variety of reasons. Etzioni's system of classification then does not fit the bill, although it reminds us that the manner of involvement of its membership is crucial to the classification of an organisation.

A highly systematic approach to the classification of organisations has been put forward by Pugh and Hickson[27]. They have attempted to blend ideas highlighted by such diverse authorities as Max Weber, Wilfred Brown (a British industrialist), Henri Fayol (a French industrialist), and Bakke (an American writer on organisations). Five dimensions of organisation structure, or 'primary variables' are elucidated. These are:

specialisation
standardisation
formalisation
centralisation
configuration

Most of these variables reflect terminology used every day within organisations. We speak of the degree of specialisation within a job, the standardisation of procedures and methods, the formalisation of official rules on communication channels and procedures, the degree of centralisation of decision-making at head office, and finally, the shape of configuration of the organisation chart, including spans of control and distance between the chief executive and the shop floor worker. Scales are put forward for measuring these variables. Other variables are also introduced into their scheme in an attempt to do justice to the complexity of the problem. For example, the context in which an organisation operates is given special treatment, including factors such as size, technology, ownership, and location.

This 'dimensional' approach was tried out on work organisations in the West Midlands using a sample of 52 medium and large firms employing a variety of technologies. It was shown that structural profiles could be drawn up, using the primary variables described. This suggests that we have the basis here for a rather more satisfactory system of classification than has been available hitherto. At present it still remains a basis rather than a fully developed scheme, although it has been used in some empirical studies[28]. Part of the problem in developing a fully worked out and comprehensive system of classification is of course the considerable time, resources and co-operation of management required. Because the Pugh and Hickson approach combines so many of the significant variables we are concerned with in studying organisations, their scheme, which forms the basis for further research is shown in Figure 8.3.

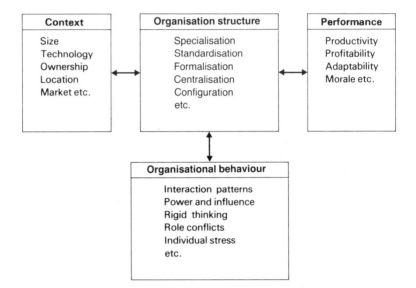

Fig. 8.3

Recent interest in culture has led to further systems of classification. Culture is a subject dealt with in the next two chapters, but at this stage it is worth noting the classification system used by Charles Handy[29], which has proved popular in this country. This gives a fourfold system, namely power, role, task, and person. Power cultures embody a strong central power source, as can be found in small entrepreneurial organisations, 'robber-baron' companies of nineteenth-century America, and some trade unions. Control is exercised from the centre through a few key individuals. Role cultures operate as bureaucracies, emphasising work roles based on specialism and rationality. Task culture is project orientated, dedicated to getting on with the task. Personal expertise is more important than hierarchy, and people work in groups containing requisite skills. Person culture is based on the cult of the individual, and such structure as exists serves only to assist individual members. Examples include barristers chambers, hippy communes and families.

Limitations to systems theory

Versions of open systems theory remain the dominant paradigms in the field of organisational design, but they possess serious limitations, both practical and theoretical. This can be frustrating to managers who look for packaged solutions, but by taking note of these limitations, better and more realistic decisions can be made. Social scientists remind us of the danger of reifying an organisation; treating an organisation composed of many human beings as if it was one being with a mind of its own. Only individual humans can have goals; to speak of an organisation having a goal or goals is just a short-hand way of saying that some person or persons have decided what the goals of the collective body should be. To assume that these goals apply to all participants can lead to a form of collective state, with the consequent suppression of the individual or deviant group. A useful antidote to this form of thinking is provided by the 'social-action' approach in the social sciences, which is derived largely from the work of Max Weber, and was referred to in Chapter Two. Individuals construct their own 'realities' and define their situations in ways which may not accord with the thinking of managerial elite. Wise managers attempts to find out about such attitudes when restructuring organisations, in order to take them into account.

Whilst research has lent some support to the validity of systems theory and, in particular, contingency theory as a form of scientific explanation or as a framework for organisation design, the evidence is limited. Khandwalla[30], in a major study of American manufacturing firms, found that profitable firms were those that had in definable respects adjusted their structures according to the mass output orientation of their technology, thus echoing Woodward's earlier findings. Sophisticated controls are applicable under standardised conditions within relatively stable environments. Child[31] found that the pattern of specialisation in production and ancillary areas such as production control and maintenance was predictable in terms of the technology employed.

However, the discovery of a simple correlation between level of performance and the match of an organisation to its contingencies does not demonstrate conclusively that organisation is the causal factor. It is possible that non-organisational variables may provide a better explanation for success or failure. Channon[32] and Rumelt[33] suggest that financial performance is more strongly influenced by strategic decisions on diversification and growth, whilst Franko[34] concluded that, for a sample of successful European firms, structural changes had not closely followed changes in product strategies. It is reasonable to assume that contingencies may represent more of a constraint for some firms than others; some firms have monopolistic powers or political protection that free them from constraints. There also remains the practical problem for managers following the advice of Lawrence and Lorsch in balancing the resources devoted to differentation and integration. The higher the degree of intra-organisational structural variation, the greater the cost of maintaining integration to overcome potential conflict between sub-units. Also, different contingencies may require different structures and systems, creating a dilemma for the firm in deciding which contingencies are the more critical. Finally, the issues of power and politics taken up in the next chapter may override rational consideration based upon analysis of contingencies in the design of organisations.

Matrix and project structures

Traditional forms of organisation structure based on hierarchy and specialisation can be inimical to co-operation and flexibility, because employers can at times identify so strongly with their own departments that the interests of the organisation suffer. This applies particularly where projects have to be completed to a dead-line that requires co-operation between different skills. Using a matrix approach, a project leader is appointed for the duration of the project who draws resources from different functional specialisms, over whom he has direct authority. Upon the conclusion of the project, or their contributory task, these personnel revert to their own departments and come once again under the authority of their functional head until their next project assignment. This type of structure has been found to work well in engineering construction and design. However, it works well only when the system is supported at the top, project managers are accorded due status and resources, promotion and rewards are linked to project work and training in group working is provided.

Matrix structures have been used in other situations as well, for example, in divisionalised structures within international conglomerates. Here managers may find themselves reporting to more than one boss, perhaps in different countries. The net result may be a blurring of lines of command and communication, and the evidence is that matrix structures can be inappropriate. Davis and Lawrence[35] advise 'If you do not really need it, leave it alone. There are easier ways to manage organisations'. To this can be added the comment 'If you really need it, then take the trouble to make sure it works effectively. It is no easy panacea'.

Divisionalisation and the trend to decentralisation

As organisations have grown larger and larger, they have experienced problems with communications, motivation and morale. Employees have felt alienated and managers have not been able to be held accountable for specific results. One popular solution has been to create divisions based on products or geographical areas. Each division then contains its own functional specialisms, and operates as a 'firm within a firm' for day-to-day purposes. In this way profit responsibility can be assigned to heads of divisions, leaving head office to concentrate on strategic planning and the allocation decisions can be taken nearer the point of action. Managers are then motivated by greater involvement and participation in decision-making and by less 'red tape'.

Once again, divisionalisation is not an easy recipe for success. There may be no clear product groupings. The divisions, once created, may come into conflict with each other, either through bidding for resources, or through marketing to the same consumers. Customers of one large computer firm in the UK were recently confused by calls from sales representatives pressing, in one case, the merits of its large computers, in the other case, those of its small computers, until this was rectified by new customer-based divisions whereby the sales representatives sold a range of products. Sometimes divisions grow so large that they dominate the whole group, and further regrouping has to take place.

Divisionalisation has proved popular in this country in recent restructuring exercises by large organisations, as shown by a survey reported by Evans and Cowling[36]. The climate affecting such decisions also appears to have been influenced by the slogan 'small and beautiful', representing a swing from the trend to bigger institutions and conglomerates in the 1970s. While in many organisations there is a strong case for the decentralisation of certain aspects of decision-making, at the same time retaining centralised control of others, we need more and better research evidence concerning its contribution to effectiveness and profitability[37].

References

1 Taylor, F. W., *The Principles of Scientific Management,* Harper and Brothers, 1911.
2 Gulick, L. and Urwick, L. (eds.), *Papers on the Science of Administration,* Institute of Public Administration, New York, 1937.
3 Fayol, H., *General and Industrial Administration,* Sir Isaac Pitman and Sons Ltd, 1949.
4 Weber, Max, *The Protestant Ethnic and the Spirit of Capitalism,* Urwin University Books, 1965.
5 Peters, R. and Waterman, R., *In Search of Excellence,* Harper and Row, 1982.
6 Roethlisberger, F. J. and Dickson, W. I., *Management and the Worker,* Harvard University Press, 1939.

194   *The organisation of work*

7   Mayo, E., *The Human Problems of an Industrial Civilisation,* The Mac-Millan Company, 1933.
8   Maslow, A. H., *Motivation and Personality,* Harper and Row, 1954.
9   Likert, R., *New Patterns of Management,* McGraw-Hill, 1961.
10   McGregor, D., *The Human Side of Enterprise,* McGraw-Hill, 1960.
11   Argyris, C., *Integrating the Individual and the Organisation,* John Wiley and Sons, 1964.
12   Herzberg, F., Mausner, B. and Synderman, B. B., *The Motivation to Work,* John Wiley and Sons, 1959.
13   Weber, M., *The Theory of Social and Economic Organisation,* Free Press, 1947.
14   Gouldner, A., *Wildcat Strike,* Harper, 1965.
15   Blau, P. M. and Scott, W. R., *Formal Organisations,* Routledge and Kegan Paul, 1963.
16   Burns, T. and Stalker, G. M., *The Management of Innovation,* Tavistock, 1961.
17   Blauner, R., *Alienation and Freedom,* University of Chicago Press, 1964.
18   Woodward, J., *Industrial Organisation, Theory and Practice,* Oxford University Press, 1965.
19   Bertalanffy, L. von. 'The theory of open systems in physics and biology', *Science,* **3**, 1950.
20   Katz, D. and Khan, R. L., *The Social Psychology of Organisation,* Wiley, 1966.
21   Trist, E. A. and Bamforth, K. W., 'Some special and psychological consequences of the longwall method of coal getting', *Human Relations,* **4**, no. 1, 1951.
22   Emery, F. and Thorsrud, E., *Democracy at Work,* International Series on the Quality of Working Life, E. Stenfert K. Rose, Leiden, 1976.
23   Lawrence, R. P. and Lorsch, J. W., *Developing Organisations: Diagnosis and Action,* Addison Wexley, 1969.
24   Child, J., *Organisations,* 2nd edn, Harper and Row, 1984.
25   Etzioni, A., *A comparative Analysis of Complex Organisations,* Free Press of Glencoe, 1961.
26   Hall, R. H., Haas, J. E. and Johnson, H. J., 'An examination of the Blau-Scott and Etzioni typologies', *Administrative Science Quarterly,* **12**, no. 1, June, 1967.
27   Pugh, D. S. and Hickson, D. J., 'The Comparative study of organisations' in Pym D. (ed.), *Industrial Society,* Penguin, 1968.
28   Warner, M. and Donaldson, L., 'Dimensions of Organisation in Occupational Interest Groups; some preliminary findings', working paper, London Graduate School of Business Studies, 1971.
29   Handy, C., *Understanding Organisations,* Penguin, 1976.
30   Khandwalla, P. N., 'Viable and effective organisational design of firms', *Academy of Management Journal,* September, 1983.
31   Child, J., 'Managerial and organisational factors associated with company performance', *Journal of Management Studies,* 1975.
32   Channon, D. F., *The Strategy and Structure of British Enterprise,* Mac-Millan, 1973.
33   Rumelt, R. P., *Strategy, Structure, and Economic Performance,* Harvard Business School 1974.

34 Franko, L. G., *The European Multinationals,* Harper and Row, 1976.
35 Davis, S. M. and Lawrence, R. P. (eds.), *Matrix,* Addison Wesley, 1977.
36 Cowling, A. and Evans, A., 'Organisation Restructuring and the Role of the Personnel Department' in *Personal Review,* Winter, 1985.
37 Child, J. and Kieser, A., 'Organisation and managerial roles in British and German companies' in Lammers, C. and Hickson, D. J. (eds.), Organisations: *Like and Unlike,* Routledge and Kegan Paul, 1979.

9
Power, authority and conflict

Within their own organisations managers are formally entrusted with power and perceived as having authority. This goes with their responsibility for achieving results, decribed in detail in Chapter One. They are of course not the only holders of power; in many British organisations people such as shop stewards, quality control inspectors, computer analysts and technical experts also wield power and influence. Managers sometimes see themselves as involved in a continuous struggle to maintain their power and authority vis à vis other groups and individuals, and there is often rivalry and competition between managers. Where clear goals and consensus do not exist, damaging conflict may result.

Power influences behaviour. In fact, power can at times dominate the behaviour of both individuals and groups. Until a decade or so ago power was frequently neglected by behavioural scientists, particularly those belonging to the human relations school of organisational behaviour. Power was seen as a rather unpleasant feature of life that was not the province of the psychologist operating in a nicely detached and balanced scientific manner, and besides, it was, and remains, a factor that is hard to define and measure in precise terms. The same was not true of the sociologist, who despite his limitations, recognised from the outset that power was a critical variable in the analysis of society and its institutions. In this chapter we shall examine definitions of power and look at practical ways of measuring it. We shall also consider the sources of power available to managers, and then go on to analyse the conflict within organisations that creates obstacles for the manager and may undermine the viability of the organisation.

Definition of power

Examples of naked power are rare in modern work organisations. Few executives are accompanied by bodyguards. On the surface, most organisations give an impression of civility and calm. However, those working within organisations are usually well aware of where the centres of power lie, and how much pressure can be exerted when occasion warrants. Power can be inferred and measured by its consequences rather than by direct observation. This gives us one of our most popular definitions of power, provided by Robert Dahl[1] 'A has power over B to the extent that he can get B to do something B would not otherwise do.' Power is the ability to change another's behaviour. Max Weber[2] provides us with further insight by reversing this definition, and placing it in a social context: 'Power is the probability that one actor within a social relationship will be in a position to carry out his own will, despite resistance, and regardless of the basis on which this probability rests.' In using the word 'role' Weber is also reminding us that power is frequently attributable to a position rather than an individual, which led him to an examination of the concept of authority in relation to power, a point developed further below. The low visibility of power is brought out in another definition by Bierstedt[3], who said: 'Power is latent force. . . . Power itself is the prior capacity which makes the application of force possible.' Powerful individuals rarely have to demonstrate their power, and in fact too overt a demonstration of power can be interpreted as a sign of weakness. The successful school-teacher, army officer or company manager rarely has to display his power except in emergency. The weak supervisor is constantly having to buttress his position by claims to authority. But Machiavelli[4] gives us a word of warning in a book which has become a classic for students of power and politics: 'One can make this generalisation about men, they are ungrateful, fickle, liars and deceivers, they shun danger and are greedy for profit; while you treat them well, they are yours. They would shed their blood for you, risk their property, their lives, their children, so long, as I said above, as danger is remote: but when you are in danger they turn against you. Any prince who has come to depend entirely on promises and has taken no other precaution ensures his own ruin!' Managers, beware!

Examinations of power within organisations requires a broader sweep than a focus only on individuals or 'princes'. While formal definitions of power have tended to be restricted to the individual, they can be extended to groups of individuals, departments or divisions. More powerful departments can get their own way at the expense of weaker departments, and one group or clique of managers can pressurise another group into actions they would prefer not to take. We shall examine departmental power after a closer examination of sources of personal power.

Sources of personal power

Those who work in organisations see the sources of power all round them. These include:

1   financial rewards, e.g. pay increases and fringe benefits
2   non-financial rewards, e.g. time off, praise, transfer to more inter-
    esting work
3   punishment, e.g. dismissal, fine, transfer to unpleasant work, with-
    drawal of a trade union card, sending to Coventry
4   physical coercion, e.g. aggressive strike picketing, calling in the
    police
5   respect for authority, e.g. referring to a trade union official or
    director's 'authority'
6   interpersonal skills, e.g. persuasive language, force of personality,
    manipulation of group dynamics
7   technical expertise, e.g. demonstrating special knowledge which is
    in demand
8   resources, e.g. control of needed physical, financial and human
    resources.

A number of these sources of power have been touched in earlier
chapters discussing motivation and leadership; the ability to motivate
or lead, for example, is a manifestation of the power to change
another's behaviour in a desired direction. In practice, a manager may
be able to draw on a number of sources of power simultaneously; a
subordinate might obey an order for a combination of the reasons
listed above. Arising from social change, these sources of power are
also changing. Legislation and bureaucratisation have noticeably constrained the first four power sources listed above. New knowledge has
enhanced power sources six and seven. But it is probably in the area of
authority that the greatest changes have taken place in recent years.

The concept of authority has frequently been associated with that of
power, because it has been thought that authority permits the exercise
of power without the necessity for coercion. In his classic treatment of
the subject, Weber[5] interpreted the term in much the same way. To
him, compliance with authority was a voluntary act that rested on a
common value system, and he analysed the term under the three
headings of traditional, charismatic and legal authority. Legal
authority rests on a belief in the right of those in high office to give
orders and to be obeyed. Charismatic authority rests on the personal
influence of the individual, giving him power over devoted followers.
Traditional authority is based on a belief in the traditional order of
things, including respect for those in authority.

A number of attempts have been made to improve on Weber's
typology of power. A generally satisfactory example by French and
Raven[6] is based on the determinants of interpersonal power as they
influence the relationships between power holders and power reci-
pients. Their typology covers five perceived determinants of power:
'reward', 'coercive', 'legitimate', 'referent' and 'expert' power.

Reward power is based on the ability to offer a reward attractive to the recipient, coercive power on the ability, perceived or real, to punish, legitimate power on an acknowledgement by the recipient of the authority of the power holder, referent power on the admiration the recipient has for the power holder, and expert power on special knowledge and expertise. This typology of power has been adapted by Etzioni[7] in order to develop the typology of organisations referred to in the previous chapter. The three forms of power Etzioni observed to be particularly relevant to modern organisations were coercion, remuneration, and normative, to which he added three forms of involvement by members of organisations termed calculative, moral and alienative. The principal virtue of this approach probably rests in its reminder that the power of a reward to induce a change in behaviour is dependent on the involvement of the employee in his job, career, and organisation. The power to facilitate promotion only carries weight with the ambitious subordinate.

Two relevant examples of the influence of power and authority are provided by Pelz[8] and Milgram[9]. The first concerns leadership. As noted in Chapter Six successful leadership is contingent on a number of factors, including power. Pelz reported that the power which supervisors were perceived to hold by their subordinates influenced their success. Holding constant such variables as size of the work group, kind of work, and length of time on the job, Pelz found that relations between supervisors and subordinates differ from the expected pattern. For example, 'giving honest and sincere recognition for a job well done' depressed morale in groups of white collar workers. Further analysis showed that these perplexing findings were due to the amount of power which the leader was perceived by his subordinates to possess. When supervisors perceived to have 'influence upstairs' followed supervisory practices generally considered to represent effective leadership behaviour, workers tended to respond favourably, but when supervisors lacked such influence they secured far less favourable results.

The second example concerns authority and obedience. Milgram conducted an experiment to test whether individuals would carry out acts dangerous to others in obedience to the orders of someone perceived as being a technical expert. Subjects were invited to participate in an experiment concerning learning under the stimulus of electric shocks. The subject was in one room along with the expert, whilst the learner was supposedly seated in a chair next door wired to electrical terminals. The learner was asked questions, and when he got the answer wrong the subject was instructed to administer an electric shock. With each mistake the voltage was increased in a manner visible to the subject, and clearly marked at the different stages of slight, moderate and dangerous levels of shock up to 450 volts. When the subject pulled the generator switch following each mistake the generator lighted up and buzzed, but unknown to him, no shock was actually transmitted to the learner.

It was observed that subjects were willing to carry on administering shocks to the unseen learner even after the danger level had supposedly been reached. At these levels the learner could be heard screaming and pounding on the walls, and thereafter lapsed into an ominous silence. At this stage most subjects turned anxiously to the instructor, who advised them to treat no response as an incorrect response and to proceed with the administration of the shocks. Out of forty subjects, all proceeded past the very strong shock readings and some even proceeded beyond 450 volts, although most were visibly disturbed and under stress. When the experiment was repeated with forty new subjects, it was found that the absence of the experimental instructor from the room, using a telephone to communicate his orders, led to a dramatic fall in obedience, although some serious shocks were still administered.

Departmental power

That some departments have more power than others can be observed from the distribution of resources and perks within an organisation, and which departmental representatives take the dominant role in meetings and decision-making. In general, it is the so-called 'line' departments who wield the greatest power, because they are seen as crucial to the success or failure of the enterprise, and are responsible for the generation of profits. Thus the marketing and production functions in traditional private enterprise organisations have a major say in what goes on. However, the picture is frequently more complex than this. For example, the finance department can become dominant, even though they technically perform a staff function. This usually happens at times when the financial environment becomes turbulent. Other staff on specialist functions can wield seemingly disproportionate power, simply because of superior expertise or clever politicking. Outside the traditional private enterprise sector it can be difficult to define and highlight the line functions, and consumer interests can be relegated below those of the producers. This can lead to powerful vested interest groups with no direct interest in the quality of products or service. Sooner or later this leads to economic ruin, deteriorating services, or both.

Departmental power can arise from the very structure of the organisation, as noted in the previous chapter. Traditional organisations are hierarchical in structure, and power is seen in 'vertical' terms, descending through the organisation by a process of delegation. Power can be retained at the centre, or decentralised to the operating units.

The reality can of course be different, with low status departments acquiring and retaining considerable power. A typing pool can acquire power because of its control over a desired resource which is in short supply, causing busy executives to expend much time and energy in pleading for favours to speed up the production of their letters and reports. A nice example of power residing in a low status department was provided by the French sociologist Crozier, who investigated the tobacco industry in his own country[10]. The industry was operating as a state monopoly, based in Paris, where most of the high status executives were located. Given the assurance of a guaranteed outlet for their products, the main problem was one of continuity of supply. This in turn depended on the smooth running of the twenty-three small tobacco plants located some distance from Paris, where maintenance personnel held the key to continuous production. In turn, this meant that considerable power was vested in the maintenance personnel, who controlled the repair of machine breakdowns. This led Crozier to suggest that power is related to 'the kind of uncertainty upon which depends the life of the organisation'. This led him to propose a 'strategic' model of organisations as systems in which groups strive for power.

This emphasis upon the uncertainty which threatens the future of the organisation, and the ability of particular departments to cope with it, and hence acquire power, has been developed further. Findings from a number of research studies that underlined the disparities of power which exist, as it were, horizontally across the organisation chart has led to a 'strategic contingencies' theory of power. Perrow[11] investigated twelve firms in the United States, asking the question, 'which group has the most power?' He found that the sales departments were invariably perceived as having the most power, as illustrated by the graph in Figure 9.1.

Perrow argued that this came about because sales possessed the most critical function in such industrial concerns. 'As the link between customer and producer, it absorbs most of the uncertainty about the diffuse and changing environment of customers.' The influence of attempts to adapt to a changing environment on organisation structures, and hence on matters of power, authority and loci of decision-making were discussed in the previous chapter. Studies of particular relevance in this context include those by Burns and Stalker[11], and Lawrence and Lorsch[12]. Burns and Stalker put forward the concepts of 'mechanistic' and 'organic' organisation structures, the former being appropriate to a stable environment and the latter to an unstable one. In the former, power and authority were likely to be retained at the top of the management hierarchy, whereas in the latter they were delegated to the appropriate task groups. Lawrence and Lorsch pay considerable attention to the extent of differentiation

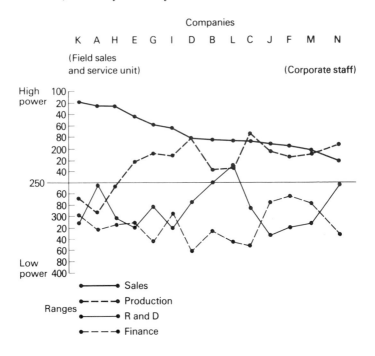

Fig. 9.1 Overall power of departments in industrial firms (courtesy of Charles Perrow, 'Departmental power and perspective in industrial firms', in Zald, Mayer N. (Ed.), *Power in Organizations*, Nashville, Tenn., Vanderbilt University Press, 1970)

between departments and functions within a firm, in relation to the needs of the system to adapt to environmental demands. They found that in their most differentiated industry, plastics, the perceived amount of influence was spread evenly amongst the six highest levels of management. But in the container industry, operating within a more stable environment, influence was concentrated at the top. Where a diverse environment existed, such as in plastics and food, the research and sales divisions were perceived to possess greater power than production. In a stable environment, power might be vested in production.

In this country, Hickson and Hinings[14] developed a comprehensive 'contingency' model for analysing and explaining departmental power, with an emphasis on coping with uncertainties perceived as a threat to the organisation. This is brought out in Figure 9.2. Their expression 'centrality of work flows' means the degree to which the department possesses skills relevant to the organisation at that period of time.

Machine maintenance may be critical to a tobacco firm enjoying a guaranteed market, but is less important when markets are uncertain and have to be fought for. The key to their model is 'coping effectiveness', indicating that to retain power a department has to visibly demonstrate its effectiveness to all and sundry. Figure 9.2 shows the results of an investigation in a brewery, where each major department was asked to rate the other three major departments. As can be seen, production was perceived as possessing greatest power. This is explained as a consequence of its demonstrated competence in coping with the contemporary contingencies for a successful brewing company, namely a guaranteed supply of good quality beer. It is likely that if this research were repeated at a time when beer sales had levelled off and the market was more turbulent the balance of power would have shifted away from production, as was the case with the firms investigated by Perrow and shown in the earlier diagram.

Decision-making and organisational politics

A powerful politician is reported as saying, 'I don't care who does the electing, as long as I have the power to do the nominating.' Certain decisions can be of great importance to an organisation, and light can be thrown on the wielding of power by a study of how major decisions are taken. Frequently, such decisions are not taken in an overt and rational manner by one particular individual or department, but are the outcome of a series of compromises and bargains between pressure groups who have a vested interest in the outcome. This was illustrated by a study by Pettigrew[15] of a large shoemaking firm in Britain that had decided to purchase and install a large new computer system. The management services group was asked to recommend which of six computer manufacturers should receive the order. The head of the management services group and his two subordinates, one in charge of the programmes and the other in charge of the systems analysts, each preferred a different computer system. Each one could and did put forward legitimate reasons for choosing his own preferred system, but the head of the department was able to have the decisive influence in determining the board of directors choice by controlling the nature and flow of information from his subordinates and the computer firms to the directors. As a result, the final decision was not a dispassionate, rational one, based on complete and up-to-date information, but reflected the power structure acquired through hierarchical position and control of information, as shown in Figure 9.3.

Pettigrew's findings were similar to those of an earlier study made in the United States by Cyert[16] and a more recent Swedish study by Norman[17]. Carter traced major decisions in an American computer company, and concluded that 'by bargaining within the departments

17 ISSUES, as allocated to task areas (or functions)

SUBUNITS	Sales area					Engineering area		Production area				Finance area			Personnel area (salary training)			OVER-ALL MEANS
	marketing strategies	introduction of new products	product packaging	price	interpretation of liquor regulations	obtaining equipment	operating performance of equipment	obtaining raw materials	product quality	product efficiency	overall production plan	overall capital budget	overall non-capital budget	reviews of the non-capital budget	salary revision	personnel training and development	personnel and labor relations	
Accounting	1.5	1.5	1.5	4.5	2.75	2.75	1.75	2.0	1.0	2.25	2.75	4.0	3.75	3.5	3.25	3.5	3.25	2.7
Engineering	1.25	1.75	3.25	1.00	1.5	4.25	5.0	2.25	1.75	4.75	2.5	3.5	2.75	2.5	1.75	2.75	1.5	2.7
Marketing	5.0	5.0	3.5	3.0	4.5	1.75	2.0	2.0	2.75	2.0	2.25	2.75	2.75	2.5	2.25	3.0	2.25	2.9
Production	3.25	3.75	4.0	2.0	2.5	4.5	4.5	5.0	5.0	5.0	4.0	3.5	2.75	2.5	2.25	3.25	3.0	3.6

Fig. 9.2 Received power (weight) of four subunits in organisation S (brewery). On each of 17 issues, means of the questionnaire ratings of every subunit by heads of all 4 subunits (scores at or above the mean for the table underlined) (courtesy of Hinings et al, 1974)

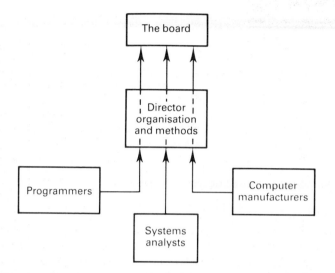

Fig. 9.3 Information flow for computer decision (courtesy of Pettigrew, Andrew M., *The Politics of Organizational Decision Making*, London: Tavistock, 1973)

the staff would pre-process investments to ensure that projects submitted for the president's considerations filled the wishes of the members of the department'[18]. Lindblom coined an appropriate phrase to describe what frequently went on, in his title 'The Science of muddling through'[19]. The optimum decision made in a detached way by exact calculation from all relevant information, uncontaminated by political and social processes, does not happen outside text books and mathematical exercises.

Line managers develop their own methods for controlling specialist advisers who are perceived as gaining too much power and influence. Pettigrew[20] has drawn up a list which will draw rueful smiles from some readers of this chapter:

1 *Straight rejection* The staff man and his report are dismissed without further consideration. Needs power and self-assurance on the part of the executive.
2 *'Bottom drawer it'* The report is praised but then left unused. The specialist, grateful for the praise, may not press for utilisation.
3 *Mobilising political support* The executive calls on support from colleagues with similar interests.
4 *The nitty-gritty tactic* Minor objections to fact or inter-pretation

are raised to discredit and delay implementation.

5 *The emotional tactic* 'How can you do this to me?' or '. . . to my chaps?'

6 *But in the future . . .* The report is fine for today's conditions but unlikely to work in the (hypothetical) future.

7 *The invisible man tactic* The executive is never available for discussion when wanted.

8 *Further investigation is required* The report is sent back for further work on it.

9 *The scapegoat* Someone else (e.g. head office) won't like it.

10 *Deflection* The executive directs attention to the points where he has sufficient knowledge to contradict the specialist.

Politics and power

Nearly all social activities exhibit some form of politics, usually bound up with the quest for power by individuals, groups, or parties. In a democracy the study of politics in relation to government is usually concentrated on political parties with open forms of membership and constitutions. In organisational life, politics is more concealed, encompassing shifting alliances of individuals and departments seeking to influence decisions and the distribution of resources. Many managers resent such internal politics, seeing it as a diversion from the main task and a means whereby pressure groups can bring about bad decisions that weaken the effectiveness of the organisation. Mayes and Allen[21] define organisational politics as 'the management of influence to obtain ends not sanctioned by the organisation'. Hellriegel, Slocum and Woodman[22] take a different view, seeing politics as a means to both good and bad ends, and state that 'politics is the use of power to get things accomplished, both good and bad. Politics emerges where there is uncertainty and conflict'. Zaleznik[23] reflects the experience of many managers when he makes a distinction between 'coalitions' and 'collusions'. Managers may join together in coalitions to push things through and to acquire more power, or they may react defensively in collusion to block new initiatives which they dislike.

Where power is seen as a 'zero sum' within the organisation, the politics is likely to be fiercer. A zero sum situation means that an increase in power by one group necessarily leads to an equivalent loss in power by another group. In some situations it is possible to change the equation and achieve outcomes which will lead to increased power for all concerned, by methods explored in the next chapter in the context of organisation development.

In one research study, reported by Gandz and Murray[24], 428 managers were asked to rank organisational decisions from the most to the least political. Top of their list as most political came inter-departmental co-operation, promotions and transfers, and delegation of authority. It was argued that decisions in these areas are charac-terised by lack of established rules and procedures and the existence of subjective, ambiguous decision criteria. Bottom of the list as least political came personnel policies, hiring and disciplinary penalties, as there were seen to follow established policies and more objective criteria. Over 90 per cent of these managers reported that organi-sational politics was more frequent at the middle and upper levels of management. Another recent study[25] identified the tactics used within organisations as featuring attacks on others, use of information, image building, developing base of support, integration, power coalitions and associating with the influential.

Some managers are able to take a more detached view of politics than others, and some relish the cut and thrust of political activities. This is reflected in Mintzberg's[26] view of organisational behaviour as a power game in which various players seek to control the organisation's decisions and actions. These players are seen as 'influencers', who are attracted to work in organisations as a vehicle for satisfying some of their own needs. He notes the choices which Hirschman[27] presents to participants in a social system as:

1 Stay and contribute. This is seen as loyalty, or, as he says, to 'shut up and deal'
2 Leave, meaning to 'take my marbles and go'
3 Stay and try to change the system.

These are choices which readers of this chapter have probably faced on numerous occasions. Karen Legge[28], in a book addressed to personnel managers but deserving a wider audience, suggests that those who do stay and try to change the system have two choices. They can either work as 'conformist' innovators, accepting the dominant values and relationships within the organisation and attempting to demonstrate the contribution of their activities to organisational success criteria, or they can become 'deviant' innovators. Deviant innovators attempt to change things by gaining acceptance of different criteria for estab-lishing organisational success, and of their contribution to this. At a high level this could influence strategy and commercial success, as with the turn-round of the Burton group in this country by individuals with a new vision of what was required and the political skills to push things through in a crisis, or at a humbler level in a quest for greater influence by a staff department.

Power and structures

In the preceding chapter we examined the principles of organisation design, putting forward a selection of rational models that could lead to greater effectiveness. However, the picture would not be complete without an acknowledgement of the part that power and politics can play in the shape of organisations. While the intitiative for major changes in structure frequently comes from individuals, particularly the chief executive, coalitions of managers will fight for control over decision on organisation design. Contingency factors such as size, technology and environment will act as a constraint, but the outcome will still be considerably influenced by negotiation and politics. Given that organisation design is not an exact science, and there can be reasonable debate about the ends and means, 'the critical question becomes' says Pfeffer 'not how organisations should be designed to maximise effectiveness, but rather, whose preferences and interests are to be served by the organisation'[29]. Figure 9.4 portrays this as a power control model, emphasising the role of the dominant coalition in the outcome, given the existing constraints.

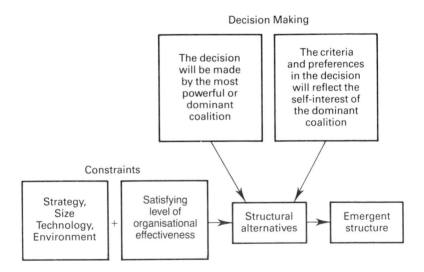

Fig. 9.4   The power-control model

The legitimisation of power and authority

Managers form an elite in society. Sidney Webb, the socialist historian, acknowledged that "Under any social order from now to Utopia a management is indispensable and all enduring. The question is not: 'Will there be a management elite?' but 'What sort of elite will it be?'' '

Peter Drucker, probably the best known writer on management topics, who has a very different political orientation, attempts to place management in a social context. He sees society as becoming increasingly dominated by organisations, which means that managers now occupy an important role and are at the centre of the stage. 'Management is the means through which a given society makes productive its own values and beliefs.'[30]

To individual managers caught up in day-to-day pressures at work and their own internal politics, the question of their role in society and the legitimacy of their authority may seem rather philosophical questions. Certainly some managers find an expression for their social consciousness in such activities as the 'Round Table' or in fund-raising for charities. But there are occasions when their authority is directly challenged, either by a political party, or by trade unionists at work, or simply by their own subordinates. It is not enough to say that their authority emanates from higher management or from their technical competence if they are seen as lackeys of an unacceptable face of capitalism, or, for that matter, of town hall patronage.

The nature of management and managing was examined in the first chapter of this book. Most attention has been paid to 'top management' in our society, the supposed decision-makers in both public and private sectors of our economy, but in recent years account has had to be taken of the swelling ranks of 'middle' and 'junior' management who control day-to-day operations, and who can bring considerable collective pressure to bear when major decisions are taken. In this section attention is given to the three principal perspectives used by behavioural scientists when considering the nature of management in the context of the issues of power, authority and conflict. This, in turn, constitutes an examination of the control managers are in a position to exert over the means of production in our society, the function of managers within work organisations, and the typical day-to-day behaviour of managers in different positions of responsibility.

The debate on the influence that managers are in a position to exert in society and on the means of production conducted by economic historians and political writers as well as by social scientists stems from changes that have taken place in our economy over the last hundred years. In the course of our industrial revolution the legal ownership of most business organisations has passed from private hands to share owners by means of the stock market.

Because of share-owning public, made up of a large number of individuals and institutions, is rather diffuse and not concerned with the control of the business in the same way as the founding fathers, it has been suggested that a divorce has taken place between ownership and control, and that control has effectively passed into the hands of managers. These managers are likely to be more interested in feathering their own nests and building up their power than in serving the interests of shareholders. This has given rise to that much quoted phrase 'the managerial revolution', used as the title to James Burnham's well-known book[31]. In recent years the debate has been taken a stage further by writers such as J. K. Galbraith[32] who have warned of the influence of giant organisations on our daily life, and suggested the need for some 'countervailing power'. The general situation in Britain today with regard to control of the means of production is somewhat confused because it is a 'mixed economy'; large sections of the economy are under direct public control, and the remaining parts are heavily influenced by government directives.

This brief excursion into economic and social history may at first seem surprising in the context of a discussion of power, authority and the manager. However, its direct relevance swiftly comes across to any manager who has had his authority to make decisions questioned by articulate shop stewards, particularly if they have challenged the legitimacy of his position. We shall return to this point again shortly.

A systematic examination of the relative influence shareholders and managers are in a position to exert in publicly quoted industrial concerns has been provided by Sargant Florence[33] in a study of 268 large English companies over the period 1936–51. He analysed the composition of shareholding groups and concluded that about two-thirds of these companies were not owner-controlled by the end of the period, and that the trend was towards greater divorce of ownership from control. Widely distributed shareholding can of course mean that considerable scope exists for control to be exerted by a minority interest.

Evidence on how decisions are made by boards of directors and senior management committees is very limited and understandably hard to come by. Some sociologists have suggested that evidence showing that both managers and shareholders come from the same social class is sufficient to establish that this section of society both owns and controls the means of production, although the objectivity of some sociologists on questions of this sort is open to serious question. Theo Nichols[34], in a study of senior managers and shareholders in a northern English city claimed to find a considerable overlap in the financial interests of business owners and managers, suggesting that both ownership and control remained in the hands of a traditional elite. Richard Whitley[35] examined the network connecting directors of financial institutions in the 'City' with directors of forty large industrial companies and found evidence of a common educational background based on wealth, common membership of expensive clubs and overlapping directorships. 'This suggests', Whitley concluded, 'that the financial institutions play the central role in co-ordinating companies' policies, and that seemingly disparate industries may be united through the financial elite.' In contrast, he also noted that eleven out of eighteen directors of Marks and Spencer, GUS, Thorn Electric, Sears, and Tesco for whom educational data was available, did not go to public school and were relatively unconnected with the City.

In recent years, the influence of institutional shareholders such as pension funds, insurance companies, and government holding companies has grown, in spite of government attempts to widen the spread of share ownership in our society. As reported in *The Times* in November, 1985[36], Cable and Wireless shareholders, with five hundred shares at the time of issue, today represent only just over 1 per cent of the total equity, while shareholders with over one million shares represent 58 per cent. Total small shareholding in British Telecom represent only 1.5 per cent of total equity. *The Times*[37] reported that proportion of net financial assets held by the personal sector through pension and life assurance schemes will have grown from 44 per cent in 1980 to almost 70 per cent by 1988. We are in danger of moving to a situation where managers are servants of organisations run for the benefit of large financial institutions and pension funds. While this has the advantage that ordinary people can see the benefit of protecting their future livelihood in the form of pensions and savings, it diminishes the say that individuals feel they can have in the future of their organisations, whether as shareholders or employees. This can lead to further alienation among the apathetic and resistance to management by organised groups of employees who question the legitimacy of managerial authority.

An alternative source of legitimisation is provided by demonstrating competence. Managers can lay claims to authority by virtue of their competence, an issue touched on in the first chapter. Though a number of British organisations are acknowledged to be run by competent and successful managers, there is still too much evidence that many managements lack both status and competence, and this is related to a lack of ability and training. At a recent British Institute of Management conference, Lord Young, the Employment Secretary, deplored the fact that 40 per cent of our three and a half million managers and supervisors had no qualifications at all, and 80 per cent had no qualifications relevant to management. The situation is slowly improving, but too slowly in relation to our competitors.

Consideration of authority and the legitimacy of management to give orders leads naturally to an examination of conflict. Conflict can exist at all levels in the organisation, and is not simply a matter of 'us and them', or 'management versus the rest'. Conflict is more widespread than the system of industrial relations and collective bargaining, although these are major elements which have attracted the attention of behavioural scientists.

Conflict and the organisation

Aspects of conflict have already been examined in earlier chapters of this book dealing with interpersonal relations and group behaviour. Conflict can exist at a number of different levels – individual, group, organisational and inter-organisational. In the concluding part of this chapter we are primarily concerned with organisational conflict; conflict between groups of employees within an organisation. Some ways of coping with this conflict will be examined in the following chapter.

Conflict has in the past been overlooked by behavioural scientists, in much the same way as power was overlooked, except by industrial sociologists. This was partly because it was felt that conflict was damaging to the organisation, and that emphasis should be put on measures to create harmony. However, conflict is now treated very seriously as a key to the proper understanding of organisational behaviour. At the same time there has been a realisation that not all conflict is harmful, and a certain level of conflict is inevitable. Attempts to sweep conflict under the carpet will only create greater problems at a later date. The emphasis has to be on a proper understanding of the causes of conflict, and the development of constructive measures to control and harness the energies released by conflict.

Following our examination of organisational structure in the previous chapter, conflict within an organisation can be said to be either horizontal or vertical, reflecting the structure of the typical hierarchical functional structure. Horizontal conflict is concerned with interdepartmental conflict, as well as line-staff relationships, whereas vertical conflict describes conflict between different status levels. Examples of the latter are disputes between supervisors and managers, or between unionised workers and employers. We shall look first at horizontal types of conflict.

Early studies by behavioural scientists found considerable evidence of conflict between so called 'line' and 'staff' managers. Line managers were usually held directly accountable for results, and tended to be long-service employees who had 'come up the hard way'. They frequently showed resentment at the form and manner of the advice they received from better educated younger staff experts. In one of the best known studies of line-staff relationships, Melville Dalton[38] found that staff managers also tended to be more concerned with correct dress and manners, and to show greater concern for theory. Line managers held greater power in controlling promotion procedures, whilst hiding their anxiety that the staff managers might come up with bright ideas that would embarrass them. Turnover was rather higher among staff managers, who showed impatience at not making faster progress.

As the standard of education and training of line managers has improved in recent years, this cause of tension has decreased. Interest has shifted to the related problem of professional-organisational relationships. A proportion of managers consider themselves to be 'professional' by virtue of belonging to the accepted professions such as accounting or engineering. Studies by Kornhauser[39], Box and Cotgrove[40], and Hall[41] have shown that most such 'professional' managers are strongly committed to their work, without necessarily being committed to their own organisations. In place of this they identify with the persons regarded as their professional peers and take a pride in membership of their professional institute. This can result in conflict between what is perceived as good professional practice, in combination with an internalised need for a measure of autonomy, and the discipline of complying with the procedures that characterise the bureaucracy for which they work. At the same time the professional is anxious about his career prospects because senior positions tend to go to the good all-rounders and competent administrators.

The ever-present reality of conflict and internal politics for managers is well illustrated by the following example provided by Charles Handy[42]. When a group of middle managers were asked to comment on conflict and the major problems facing them in their work:

1   87 per cent felt that conflict was rarely coped with, and attempts to solve conflict were inadequate
2   65 per cent thought that the most important unsolved problem of the organisation was that top management appeared unable to help them overcome inter/group rivalries, lack of co-operation and poor communications
3   53 per cent said that if they could alter one aspect of their superior's behaviour it would be to help him to see the dog/eat/dog communication problems that existed in middle management.

Katz[43] identified three psychological bases of conflict within the organisation. The first is 'functional conflict induced by various subsystems within the organisations'. Certain departments in a typical work organisation are concerned with internal procedures: they 'face inward in their organisation and are concerned with maintaining the status quo'. Other departments face outwards to the world and so develop different norms and priorities. Hence the seeds of conflict between cost accountants and sales personnel. The second source of conflict arises from similarity of function, leading to competition for power and status. The final form of organisational conflict arises from interest group struggles for status, prestige and money. Subgroups join forces to increase their power base, which can lead to workers versus managers ('us and them') or inter-departmental factions.

Cohesiveness within groups leads to conflict between groups, as referred to in the earlier chapter on group behaviour. The very success of management in creating effective groups in which members identify strongly with team goals can lead to conflict. This is shown, for example, in competition between football teams on the sports field, and there are too many painful reminders that, unless properly controlled, sporting rivalry can lead to public disorder and unacceptable conflict. Within work organisations, members of a group can develop pride in their accomplishments and compare themselves with other groups in terms of 'we' and 'they'. One strength of Japanese management is that they are able to create superordinate goals for such groups, channelling these energies into co-operation against external competitors, whereas Britsh and American industrial cultures can on occasion foster harmful internal competition within organisations.

Sociology reminds of the influence of structure on behaviour within organisations. The technology of work may frequently lead to conflict. Joan Woodward reported after her South East Essex study[44] that the level of conflict and the 'tone of industrial relations' appeared to be related to technology, and commented that, 'In firms at the extremes of the scale [of technology] relationships were on the whole better than in the middle ranges. Pressure on people at all levels of the industrial hierarchy seemed to build up as technology advanced, became heaviest in assembly line producmion and then relaxed, so reducing personal conflicts.' The technology of the assembly line has frequently been blamed for the high incidence of industrial disputes in the car industry. In the United States, Kuhn[45] investigated the relationship between technology and 'fractional bargaining' (the unauthorised pursuit of demands backed by unofficial sanctions) and concluded that, 'the incidence of fractional bargaining is greatly influenced by the technology of production'. In an investigation into human relations in the Durham coalfield by Trist[46] and his colleagues, already referred to in earlier chapters, the general conclusion was that changes in technology of work had had major social implications for work groups (a socio-technical situation) which led to considerable conflict between different shifts.

Wedderburn and Crompton[47], after researching into the attitudes of workers employed on a large chemical manufacturing complex in the north-east of England, reported that the different technologies used in three works in close proximity to each other (labelled works A, B and C), particularly as they affected the control workers had over their tasks, influenced attitudes and hence the level of conflict. Works C provided least satisfaction to the workers in this respect. Wedderburn and Crompton comment: 'In the case of Works C, we would argue that the constraints imposed by the technology were predisposing factors making for discontent which expressed itself around the bonus and pay levels.'

Industrial conflict is the most pronounced feature of horizontal conflict within an organisation. At its simplest it is portrayed as an 'us and them' situation, workers versus management, the underdogs against the top dogs. Its best known form of expression is the strike and lockout, but there is a wide range of manifestations on the employees' side, from collective withdrawal of labour to go-slow, working to rule, spoiled production and individual actions such as absenteeism and dissemination of anti-management propaganda. Bad industrial relations have frequently been blamed for low levels of productivity and lack of competitiveness in the British economy.

The behavioural sciences provide us with a better understanding of the causes and nature of the problem, without necessarily coming up with all the answers, though some will be pursued in the following chapter. It is in this area that industrial sociology makes perhaps, its greatest contribution, because of its ability to place conflict in a social context. The psychologist provides an insight into the human interactions which are part and parcel of the negotiating and bargaining in industrial relations, but it is the sociologist who points us to more fundamental issues. This can sometimes be irritating to managers, who are under pressure to come up with packaged solutions to their problems, but the history of industrial relations is littered with the ill-fated consequences of managerial actions based on superficial analysis and short-term measures.

Our understanding of what is happening in the sphere of industrial relations can be helped by viewing it as a system, in much the same way as organisations were viewed as systems in the previous chapter. This provides a more balanced approach than analysis entirely dependent on psychological or social-action frames of reference. A general model has been provided by Stanley Parker[48], which attempts to isolate the significant variables and demonstrate their interrelationship. This is reproduced in Figure 9.4.

This model has been confined to five clusters of variables, and the sub-headings illustrate the major part the behavioural sciences have to play in our understanding of industrial relations. The further relevance of this model to the subject of conflict is made clear by reference to the cluster headed 'quality of industrial relations', which features 'level of conflict'. The level of conflict can then be seen as influencing, and being influenced by, all the other clusters in the diagram. Parker adds the caution:

> This [does] not imply any necessary causal connection between the absence of conflict and good industrial relations. The absence of conflict may be a sign, not of positive agreement between management and workers about ends to be achieved or means to achieve them, but disengagement or alienation of one or both sides from the problems of the other or of the whole enterprise.

Such a model provides a useful tool for the manager anxious to get to grips with an industrial relations situation, with a view to effecting an improvement. Much contemporary interest in industrial relations is focused upon work groups, as these are seen as a key to the understanding of what happens at plant or office level. Hugh Clegg's[49] major exposition of the industrial relations system in this country commenced with a chapter headed 'Work Groups and Shop Stewards'. Conflict also needs to be considered in terms of group behaviour; aspects of inter-group rivalry and hostility were discussed in Chapter Six. Group behaviour was also examined in Chapter Eight when discussing the human relations approach to organisations. It will be remembered that the research team investigating the Hawthorne Electrical Works drew attention to the importance of work groups on conduct at work, and how in the bank wiring room group norms effectively restricted output. Leonard Sayles[50], in a major study in the United States of the behaviour of 300 industrial work groups employed over a wide area of the manufacturing industry (referred to in Chapter Five), noted that the behaviour of work groups was influenced by a wide variety of factors, including technology, status and the nature of the task. Lupton[51] came to similar conclusions following his study of work groups in an electrical-engineering workshop and in a garment producing workshop in this country.

An examination of industrial conflict and industrial relations inevitably drags us into political considerations, at the level of both the organisation and the state. We have already noted that political considerations with a small 'p' are a fact of life in all organisations. Political

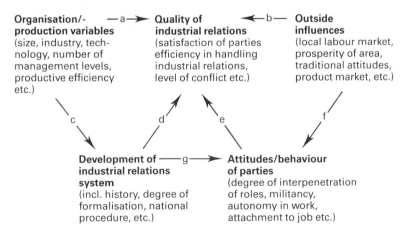

Fig. 9.5 General model of scope of workplace industrial relations (courtesy of Parker, Stanley, *The Sociology of the Workplace*, Warner, M., (Ed.), Allen & Unwin)

considerations with a capital 'P' have come about largely because successive governments have intervened in the industrial relations system. This can again be frustrating to managers who simply want to get on with the job, although many managers welcome the legal framework that has been set up to control the level of conflict. Analysts of the industrial relations scene tend to borrow from sociology in order to make sense of what they observe, and find it useful to use a frame of reference for this purpose. A Marxist will use what he describes as a 'radical' framework, which largely rests on the notion of conflict of interest between capitalists and workers, whereas a functionalist will analyse and explain events in terms of function and structure at the level of firm and society. Ultra-conservatives will complement the Marxists by simplifying issues into 'us' and 'them', blaming conflict on 'reds under the bed'. Pragmatists may see the issues in terms of setting up adequate bargaining structures and improving communications.

The Donovan Commission, set up to consider relations between management and employees and their representatives in this country in the 1960s, which has had a large impact on our industrial relations practices, saw the principal cause of our problems as the 'bifurcation between a formal, orderly, industry-wide system, and an informal, disorderly system based on largely autonomous managers and the power of industrial work groups led by shop stewards at the plant and company level'[52]. That this level of analysis was inadequate is borne out by the increase in the number of stoppages in the 1970s, which were only brought to a halt by the severe economic recession of the early 1980s. Both Donovan and the post-Donovan era were much influenced by Alan Fox's research paper[53], which criticised what he described as the 'unitary frame of reference' adopted by many managers. The unitary frame of reference, a term borrowed from social psychology, sees the organisation as one unit, with all employees properly concerned to achieve common goals laid down by management. With a benevolent management this would take the form of aiming for a 'happy family' atmosphere, or to use another analogy, of 'all pulling together' in the same boat. Fox claimed that this was unrealistic, because it didn't take account of real life situations in which interests diverged. He therefore urged that the industrial enterprise should be treated as a 'pluralist system', arguing that:

> The full acceptance of the notion that an industrial organisation is made up of sectional groups with divergent interests involves also a full acceptance of the fact that the degree of common purpose which can exist in industry is only of a very limited nature.

One example of the application of a pluralistic frame of reference is provided by attempts to improve collective bargaining machinery, endorsed in this statement by Kessler and Weekes[54]:

Once it is accepted that collective bargaining consists of a rule-making process by independent organisations of work people and management, then this has to be recognised as a permanent state of affairs. It is unrealistic to expect a conflict-free situation.

Unfortunately, the situation in this country subsequently became even less conflict-free, indicating that neither a unitary nor a pluralistic frame of reference was adequate. The so-called 'radical' explains that this was because:

industrial society, while manifestly on one level a congeries of small special interest groups vying for scarce good, status, or influence, is more fundamentally characterised in terms of the over-arching exploitation of one class by another, of the propertyless by the propertied, of the less by the more powerful[55].

An alternative explanation is that formalisation of collective bargaining arrangements has formalised simply in turn the 'us and them' situation in British organisations, and strengthened the unions without dealing with deeper structural and cultural problems. A contrast is provided by both the north European and Japanese situations, where higher living standards have been achieved for both managers and workers with the active co-operation of the unions.

The industrial relations strategies and practices adopted by British management in recent years fall into five categories, according to Purcell and Sisson[56]. First, there are the 'traditionalists', who oppose trade unions. Secondly, there are the 'sophisticated paternalists' who spend considerable time and effort ensuring that individual aspirations are sufficiently well satisfied to make collective action seem inappropriate. Third, there are the 'sophisticated moderns' who encourage trade unions but within clearly defined limits in the expectation that the unions will co-operate in maintaining the status quo. The 'sophisticated moderns' fall into two groups: the 'constitutionalists', where relations are codified and managers manage according to the book; and the so-called 'consultators'; trade unions are recognised and collective bargaining well developed, but the emphasis is upon 'integrative' bargaining and the co-operative solution of problems following wide-ranging consultation.

This foray into contemporary industrial relations underlines the social context of industrial conflict. However, conflict and rejection of managerial control can also find expression in individual actions by employees alienated from both employers and trade unions. It is as well to remember that sickness and absenteeism costs British organisations far more than strikes and disputes, with well over three hundred million working days lost each year. In many cases, as Edwards and Scullion[57] put it, resentment against work and supervision surfaces in the form of absenteeism. The analysis and understanding of absenteeism is bound up with questions of job satisfaction and motivation, which takes us full circle back to the earlier chapters in this book. Absenteeism is a negative form of behaviour which the manager can understand and control only if he takes a wide-ranging behavioural science perspective, because a decision to go absent can be the outcome of personality, group pressures, defective organisation, bad supervision, incompetence, or quite simply, unsatisfying work. Unskilled workers go absent more frequently than skilled workers, and workers in the north of England go absent more frequently than workers in the south. It may be of some consolation to managers to know that in spite of the pressures they endure of internal politics and conflict they themselves are likely to have low levels of absenteeism because they find their work both interesting and challenging.

References

1 Dahl, R., 'The concept of power', *Behavioural Science,* 2, July, 1957.
2 Weber, M., *The Theory of Social and Economic Organisation,* The Free Press, 1947.
3 Bierstedt, R., 'An analysis of social power', *American Sociological Review,* 1950, p. 246.
4 Machiavelli, quoted by Jay, F. in *Management and Machiavelli,* Penguin, 1970.
5 Weber, M., *ibid.*
6 French, J. R. P. and Raven, B., 'The base of social power' in Cartwright, D. and Zander, A. (eds.), *Group Dynamics,* 3rd edn, Harper and Row, 1968.
7 Etzioni, A., *A comparative Analysis of Complex Organisations,* The Free Press, 1961.
8 Pelz, D., 'Influence: a key to effective leadership in the first line supervisor', *Personnel,* 1953.
9 Milgram, S., 'Behavioural study of obedience', *Abnormal Psychology Journal,* 1963.
10 Crozier, A., *The Bureaucratic Phenomenon,* Tavistock, 1964.
11 Perrow, C., 'Departmental power and perspective in industrial firms' in Zold, Mayer, N. (ed.), *Power in Organisations,* Vanderbilt University, 1970.
12 Burns, T. and Stalker, G. M., *Management of Innovation,* Tavistock, 1961.
13 Lawence, P. R. and Lorsch, J. W., *Organisation and Environment,* Harvard University Press, 1967.
14 Hickson, D., Hinings, C., Lee, C., Schneck, R. and Pennings, J., 'A strategic contingencies theory of intraorganisational power', *Administrative Sciences Quarterly,* 16, 1971.
15 Pettigrew, A., *The Politics of Organisational Decision-Making,* Tavistock, 1973.
16 Cyert, R. and Marsh, J., *A Behavioural Theory of the Firm,* Prentice Hall,

1963.

17 Normann, R., 'Organisational innovativeness: product variation and reorientation', *Administrative Science Quarterly,* **16**, no. 2, pp. 203–15, 1971.

18 Carter, E. C., 'The behavioural theory of the firm and top-level corporate decisions', *Administrative Science Quarterly,* **16**, no. 4, pp. 143–29, 1971.

19 Lindblom, C., 'The science of muddling through', *Public Administration Review,* **19**, 1954, pp. 79–88.

20 Pettigrew, A., 'The influence process between specialist and executives', *Personnel Review,* 1974.

21 Bronston, R. and Allen, R. W., 'Towards a definition of organisational politics', *Academy of Management Review,* **2**, 1977.

22 Hellriegel, D., Slocum, J. and Ward Woodman, R. W., *Organisational Behaviour,* 3rd edn, West Publishing, 1983, p. 440.

23 Zaleznik, A., 'Power and politics in organisational life', *Harvard Business Review,* May/June, 1970.

24 Gandz, J. and Murray, V. V., 'The experience of workplace politics', *Academy of Management Journal,* **23**, 1980.

25 Allen, R. W., Madison, D. L., Oorter, L. W., Renwicke, P. A. and Mayes, B. T., 'Organisational politics: tactics and characteristics in actors', *Californian Management Review,* **22**, 1979.

26 Mintzberg, H., *Power in and around Organisations,* Prentice-Hall, 1983.

27 Hirschman, A. E., Exit, voice and loyalty: Responses to decline in firms, organisations and states, Cambridge, Mass, Harvard University Press, 1970.

28 Legge, K., *Power Innovation and Problem Solving in Personnel Management,* McGraw Hill, 1978.

29 Pfeffer, J., *Organisation Design,* AHM Publishing Corporation, 1978.

30 Drucker, P., *Technology, Management and Society,* Heinemann, 1970.

31 Burnham, J., *The Managerial Revolution,* John Day, 1941.

32 Galbraith, J. K., *The Affluent Society,* Hamish Hamilton, 1958.

33 Florence, P. S., *Ownership Control and Success of Large Companies,* Sweet and Maxwell, 1961.

34 Nicholls, T., *Ownership, Control and Ideology,* Allen and Unwin, 1969.

35 Whitley, R. in Stanworth and Giddens (eds.), *Elites in Britain,* Cambridge University Press, 1974.

36 *The Times,* November 28th 1985, article, 'Small shareholders are selling their shares'.

37 *The Times,* October 9th 1985, article, 'Wealth and welfare'.

38 Dalton, M., *Men who Manage,* Wiley, 1959.

39 Kornhauser, W., *Scientists in Industry,* University of California Press, 1965.

40 Box, S. and Cotgrove, S., 'Scientific identity, occupational selection and role strain', *British Journal of Sociology,* March, 1966.

41 Hall, R. H., 'Professionalism and bureaucratisation', *American Sociological Review,* **33**, 1968.

42 Handy, C. B., *Understand Organisations,* Penguin, 1976.

43 Katz, D., 'Approaches to management Conflict' in Kahn and Boulding (eds.), *Power and Conflict in Organisation,* Basic Books, 1964.

44 Woodward, J., *Industrial Organisation, Theory and Practice,* Oxford

University Press, 1968.
45 Kuhn, J. W., *Bargaining in Grievance Settlement*, Columbia University, 1961.
46 Trist, E. L. and Bamforth, K. W., 'Social and psychological consequences of the longwall method of coal-getting', *Human Relations*, **4**, no. 1, 1951.
47 Wedderburn, D. and Crompton, R., *Workers' Attitudes and Technology*, Cambridge University Press, 1972.
48 Parker, S. R., 'Workplace industrial relations' in Warner, N. (ed.), *The Sociology of the Workplace*, Allen and Unwin, 1973.
49 Clegg, H. A., *The System of Industrial Relations in Great Britain*, Blackwell, 1972.
50 Sayless, L. R., *Behaviour of Industrial Work Groups*, Chapman and Hall, 1958.
51 Lupton, T., *On the Shop Floor*, Pergamon, 1963.
52 Roberts, B. C., review of *Working Order* by Eric Batstone (Blackwell, 1984), in *British Journal of Industrial Relations*, **23**, no. 2, July, 1985.
53 Fox, A., 'Research paper no. 3', Royal Commission on Trade Unions and Employers' Associations, HMSO, 1966.
54 Kesler, S. and Weekes, B. (eds.), *Conflict at Work*, British Broadcasting Corporation, 1971.
55 Fox, A., *Beyond Contract: Work, Power and Trust Relations*, Faber, 1974.
56 Purcell, J. and Sisson, K., in Bain, G. (ed.), *Strategy and Practice in the Management of Industrial Relations in Britain*, Blackwell, 1983.
57 Edwards, P. K. and Scullion, H., *The Social Organisation of Industrial Conflict*, Blackwell, 1982.

10
Changing organisations

The challenge of change

We are all influenced by 'the winds of change', and for many of us the pace of change appears to be quickening. Change has been vividly described by Alvin Toffler as 'a roaring current' that 'overturns institutions, shifts our values and shrivels our lives'[1]. The challenge of change to the manager is represented by the daunting task of creating and maintaining an efficient and adaptive organisation that can cope with the forces of change. This means that managers have to make changes within their own organisations in order to achieve appropriate levels of efficiency and adaptability. As the primary vehicle for the creation of change is people, behavioural scientists have been much concerned with internal change processes. In this chapter we shall look at the various theories and techniques that have contributed to organisational change, and at how the international recession that has persisted for over a decade has brought a challenge and a demand for organisation development.

Forces of change

The forces of change external to the organisation necessitating internal change derive from changes in the economy, technology, legislation and social values. Rosemary Stewart[2] listed the sources of major change affecting management as:

1 Innovations which lead to new products and new methods of manufacture
2 Shifts in market patterns as a result of innovations, of changes in consumer wants and of new methods of selling
3 Greater competition, especially as a result of lower tariffs
4 Changes in government regulations and taxation
5 New tools of management such as the computer
6 Changes in the background, training and occupation of those employed.

To this list may be added:

7 Changes in social values and in attitudes to work.

Resistance to change

Change is frequently resisted. Most of us look upon change with suspicion. Change may require personal readjustment, and this can sometimes prove painful. Paradoxically, we may look forward to change for its excitement and challenge, depending on our expectations about it. Change may be resisted by collective action, and economic and social history bears witness to numerous occasions when groups of work people have refused to adapt or co-operate. In contemporary society the newspapers, which have frequently castigated reluctance in other industries to operate new machinery or adopt new procedures, have been the centre of bitter rearguard action against automation of the newsprint industry. Sometimes workers' resistance to change appears to be irrational and damaging to their own long-term interests, but managers also earn their share of criticism for reluctance to change or for implementing change in an inconsiderate manner. There are some contemporary examples of major changes in the older industries of the UK which have taken place relatively smoothly, the docks industry being an example. There was a massive reduction in the numbers of dockers employed from the late 1960s to the late 1970s, and although some employers shed their dock labour force abruptly and cynically, the major reduction was through careful collaboration between employers and unions through the National Dock Labour Board, using voluntary redundancy agreements.

Group pressures and organisation structures

Individual perceptions of the likely effects of change are strongly influenced by group pressures. Once group norms have been established, particularly within a cohesive group, they are difficult to change. Resistance to change may be a characteristic of the nature of the organisation. Bureaucratic structures are notorious for their inability to adapt to change. Interdepartmental and vested interests conflict, and frequently lead to an escalation of internal politics.

Understanding change

It can be seen that organisational change is not only a matter of products, services, technology and finance. It is also a matter of human fears, perceptions, attitudes and motivations. To implement change successfully, the manager needs to understand and manage the social as well as the technical forces involved. Over the past fifty years, at first hesitantly, behavioural scientists have studied the processes of organisational change. The complex, dynamic, day-to-day life of modern organisations is a very difficult setting in which to attempt traditional experiments. One cannot easily isolate aspects or groups for study. Industrial relations or indeed ethics may prevent the experimental varying of conditions of work for some employees. New methods of investigation had to be developed, under the general title of 'action research'[3].

Action research

In pure research a theory or hypothesis is stated, an experiment is designed to test it, and the experiment is carried out exactly to plan, under controlled conditions with passive subjects, eliminating unwanted variables. Then the results are analysed to see if they uphold or disprove the theory. Action research begins with identifying a practical problem which seems to have theoretical implications: it involves practitioners seeking solutions and scientists in seeking to describe, understand and predict. It is a tentative, step-by-step process, where unexpected variables crop up, and results are continuously evaluated. In action research the roles of experimenter and practitioner are blended, which of course waters down the ideal rigour and objectivity of scientific enquiry. What action research gains is methodical insights into real events and, most important of all, turns the guinea-pigs into scientists. Action research involves managers and employees in monitoring, planning and testing their own activities. This active involvement of the participants is the hallmark of what has come to be known as organisation development (OD).

Organisation development: the 1940s and 1950s

The OD movement began with isolated efforts to apply behavioural science to the improvement of employee attitudes and job satisfaction. In the 1930s, the Hawthorne studies[4] had indicated the importance of work group attitudes and norms, and the potential benefits of better human relations at work. In the late 1940s Lewin's discovery of the practical benefits of feedback to community leaders about their group interaction paved the way for the use of T-group techniques in organisational team development[5]. Explorations of leadership and job satisfaction in the 1950s led to wide-scale attitude surveys such as those of the Michigan Survey Research Centre, which became the new tools for behavioural analysis in organisations. The survey feedback and discussion between different levels of employee that sometimes followed attitude surveys could be seen to contribute to attitude improvement and behaviour change.

In the UK the group dynamics approach and use of the psychoanaly-tic model was pursued by the Tavistock Institute of Human Relations. Some of their researchers went into industrial settings. In 1949 Elliot Jaques joined with Wilfred Brown, managing director of the Glacier Metal company, in an action research partnership which lasted many years and generated a number of books on company culture and communications[6]. They orginated the 'work discussion group' tech-nique still promoted by The Industrial Society, drawing attention to the shortcomings of organisational communication systems. Later, in the USA, Merton and Gouldner were to draw attention to the 'alienation' of workers in large organisations. Jaques and Brown also explored role conflict and role perceptions among managers.

Another venture by Tavistock personnel in the late 1940s was to have an even greater impact on OD. The work of Trist and Bamforth is described in Chapter Eight. They wished to study organisational change, and used Bamforth's coal industry connections to obtain access to Haighmoor colliery. Here the miners had rediscovered a traditional form of teamworking and were using new larger-scale technology in combination with small-scale human relations. Trist and Bamforth translated this formula for combining social and technologi-cal aspects of system design into a large-scale study in mines in the Midlands and Durham, showing benefits for morale, safety, flexibility and productivity. Their reports were set aside by the NCB and the NUM[7], but the work was saved from being just another case-study by the comprehensive theory of OD that Trist and others developed from this and later studies. It came to be known as the sociotechnical systems theory, and is a major theme in modern work design.

Organisation development: the 1960s

In the 1960s, OD became established in the USA as an identifiable set of values and techniques in business consultancy. Accounts of OD interventions appeared in the journals, and eminent authors set out a theoretical framework for the expanding range of techniques. OD came to be defined as planned, organisation-wide change, managed from the top of the organisation, using behavioural science (usually through an external catalyst or change-agent) in interventions into the organisation's systems and processes, aimed at increasing organi-sational health and efficiency[8].

Features of OD programmes were described by authors such as French & Bell:

1   Programmes aim to be 'normative-re-educative' and 'rational-empirical', based on the assumption that norms form the basis for

behaviour and change comes through a re-education process in which old norms are discarded and supplanted by new ones, and that people will change if and when they come to realise that change is advantageous to them. Thus the use of power and coercion are ruled out as vehicles for change.

2   A 'systems' approach should be adopted which appreciates the interrelatedness of organisational phenomena; one must aim to change systems, not just component parts.

3   Strong emphasis is placed on the value of data concerning human and social processes within the organisation and members of the organisation must learn how to collect and utilise such data for solving problems.

4   People learn best how to do things by doing them, and therefore participants are encouraged to learn about organisational dynamics by reflecting on their own experiences, aided by an expert 'change-agent'.

5   Both organisations and individuals need to manage their affairs against goals which are explicit, measurable and attainable.

6   Membership of normal organisational working groups should, as far as possible, be maintained within any learning programme, as this helps to ensure that effective team building takes place within the organisation[9].

Many OD initiatives taking place in the USA and the UK in the 1960s went unreported. This was partly due to the normal cloak of confidentiality in companies, but also partly due to the enthusiastic commitment to action, and endemic resistance to scientific evaluation that has characterised much human relations work. Interesting exceptions in the UK were Klein's[10] account of her experiences as a social scientist at Esso and Hill's[11] account of the major OD effort at Shell.

Organisation development: the 1970s

In the 1970s OD concepts and activities underwent much critical review. Some derided the missionary zeal of the early practitioners; Harvey[12] wrote amusingly of OD as a religious movement! Others, such as Mirvis and Berg[13] drew attention to OD failures that had gone unreported, and to the tendency of repeating faulty diagnoses and methods. As the international recession deepened and management fashions changed, the end of the 1970s seemed to bring the end of OD also, as if it had been just another fad.

In fact the critical reviews of OD in the 1970s served to strengthen and reformulate it, and its influence is now more pervasive than ever. Mirvis and Berg's book on *Failures in Organisation Development and Change* had the subtitle *Cases and Essays for Learning*. The points of challenge and change were:

1 The need for better organisation analysis
2 The need for better participation
3 The need for better methodology
4 The need for better evaluation
5 The need for a better conceptual framework

The need for better organisation analysis

Early OD work focused on human relationships in organisations, and on the aims of job satisfaction and self-actualisation emphasised by authors such as McGregor and Maslow. Early OD efforts tended to have ephemeral results because they changed perceptions, not structures and processes. Later writers such as Friedlander and Brown[14] called for a combination of technostructural and human-processual change efforts. Sociotechnical systems theory was at last making an impact.

To consider technostructural change one has to have a comprehensive system for analysing an organisation's size, shape, evolution and environment. Chapter Eight suggested the primary dimensions for analysing organisations. Is the environment stable, changing, complex, turbulent[15]? Is the organisation centralised or decentralised? These issues may be crucial in determining the best OD approach and, indeed, in determining whether any form of OD approach will succeed. The range of organisations in which OD had by now been tried ranged from industrial manufacturing and commercial organisations to service industries, and public institutions such as schools, colleges and hospitals. The need for OD to focus on general organisational effectiveness as well as human relations issues (i.e. develop business sense), meant that OD had to become multidisciplinary.

The systems model borrowed from the biological sciences (see Chapter Eight) has been a very useful perspective in OD (although writers such as Perrow point out its pernicious oversimplifications). Just as living organisms emerge from infancy, become mature, decline and die (the process of entropy), so one can note the life-stages of the organisation. Greiner[16] indicated the managerial crises that go with the stages of growth and development of an enterprise, and Sadler and Barry[17], in an early OD effort in the printing industry, record the growing pains of a family business as it expands and professionalises its management.

All organisations are moved to change in response to external pressures (reactive change) but for many the changes made are too little or too late. Successful organisations change in anticipation of external pressures and set out to modify their environments (proactive change). This approach emphasises that OD is a continuous activity of organisational renewal. Hedberg[18] wrote of the painful pattern of difficulties facing erstwhile successful organisations in the 1970s, which they must negotiate before emerging as 'self-designing' organisations, actively 'inventing tomorrow'. Typically, the successful organisation becomes complacent, coasting on its successes and not recognising danger signs in its environment. When things begin to go wrong they are interpreted as short-term problems. When the problems persist the organisation will 'do as before, only more' (repeating the formula of its earlier success). 'Riding the storm' involves balancing the books in the short term, activities such as research, development and training may be cut and valuable assets sold, thereby reducing the opportunity for long-term recovery. As short-term measures fail to halt the downward spiral, internal conflict escalates through scapegoating and empire-building, as rivals fight for shares of dwindling resource. By this stage an 'unlearning' phase should have begun. With luck, enlightened management, and possibly external help, the organisation will rethink its objectives and methods. Then the proactive phase of 'inventing tomorrow' and organisational redesign can begin. Knowing whether the organisation is ready for OD is the most crucial part of organisation analysis.

The need for better participation

The role of the OD consultant had been critically reviewed. Writers such as Tichy and Hornstein[19] began to provide a user's guide to consultants by classifying them according to personal characteristics and values, their ideas about change, their techniques and the settings in which they operated. The least approved consultants were those who operated under the 'medical' model, creating a certain mystique about their methods of diagnosis, with the organisation in the role of rather passive 'patient'. Also criticised were the consultants whose competence was limited to one or two techniques but who were ready to apply them to any problem regardless of its nature. Some early consultants seemed set on subverting management control, while others naively allowed themselves to be party to unethical uses by managers of techniques orginally designed to accomplish the opposite[20]. Very little attention had been paid to the ethics of OD, and authors such as Walton and Warwick[21] began to address the thorny issues of confidentialily, informed consent and coercion.

Three ways of meeting these difficulties emerged. The first was to incorporate the role of OD consultant increasingly within the organisation itself. With an increasing professionalisation of personnel management, the management of human resources acquired more status, and corporate policy-making increasingly involved those with behavioural science perspectives as well as manpower planning and management development skills. The role of training was expanded to include OD amongst its core competencies[22].

Second, the external consultant became less directive, and acted more as a specialist resource, helping the organisation to analyse its own activities by holding up a 'managerial mirror'. The same principles as those of the personal counsellor (see Chapter Five) were applied, with full participation by members of the organisation in data collection, analysis and choice of subsequent action. This principle was strongly endorsed by those who had continued and developed Jaques' social analysis methods in the UK[23]. The third development was in the choice of OD methods.

The need for better methodology

The 1960s generated a wide range of techniques that could be employed as part of an OD programme. These ranged from the managerial techniques of operational research, organisation and methods analysis, and Management by Objectives (MbO), to more overtly 'behavioural science' activities such as attitude surveys and work discussion groups, to the more individual and personal interactions of performance appraisal and counselling, TA and T-groups. Harrison suggested that these should not be viewed as competing ways of doing the same thing, but as a range of options to apply to different aspects of the organisation within overall strategies of change. Some are directed at individuals, some at groups, some at the whole organisation. A key point is that they can be classified according to the depth of individual emotional involvement required, the extent to which they touch on individual personality as opposed to external features of one's work.

The principle proposed by Harrison[24] was that OD methods should be chosen which operated at no deeper a level than that of the 'felt needs' of the client, the level at which the client felt comfortable. Although the consultant can anticipate deeper problems than those being revealed, the consultant should proceed at the pace of the client. This fits well with the reports of OD failure where the organisation culture is not ready for change.

Review of OD experiences led away from the idea of competing OD techniques to the idea of a spectrum of methods. Methods could be selected according to the contingencies of the situation, for example according to the evolving level of sophistication of the organisation. Methods could be integrated into a sequence of activities extended much further in time than early OD practitioners had allowed for. Often 'one off' interventions lasting a few weeks or months had failed in the long run, because it had not been realised that it can take ten years or more for the 'culture' of a large organisation to change. OD methods became integrated with day-to-day organisational activities such as review of work methods, training, communication systems and methods of reward and incentive. Regular attitude-surveys of employees began to replace crisis surveys.

The need for better evaluation

Evaluation in any field of organisational activity is contentious, and tends to be neglected for a number of reasons. In the training field, for instance, evaluation is often neglected because of urgent pressure for action, lack of time and of expertise in evaluation methods, availability of weak measures such as trainees' level of satisfaction and numbers trained, and last but not least the reluctance of trainers to have their efforts evaluated. Paradoxically, in spite of a common view of behavioural science as woolly and impractical, its very strength is its insistence on decent measurement and evaluation.

Evaluation is on the increase. In education and later in training (thanks particularly to the efforts of the Industrial Training Boards in the UK in the late 1960s), the need to set behavioural objectives as a first step in the instructional process became accepted. Evaluation came to be seen as a continuous activity commencing at the design stage, with feedback of interim evaluation acting as a servo-mechanism to keep the process on target. By the end of the 1970s there was a new insistence on quantifying the contribution of human resource management to corporate effectiveness[25].

Early OD efforts lacked rigorous evaluation for the same reasons as did training. The activity itself seemed to be its own justification, the practitioners were patently well-meaning, and there was no shortage of praise from participants. If the stated aims of an activity are weakly defined, evaluation becomes difficult, and if evaluation is left until the activity is over it becomes virtually impossible. As OD began to appear as a subject not just for consultancy but for business training and academic qualifications, the demand for better evaluation escalated. There had been some major studies such as the Michigan Inter-Company Longitudinal Study[26] covering twenty-three organisations in a comparative study of the effects of four categories of intervention method: Survey Feedback, Interpersonal Process Consultation, Task Process Consultation and Laboratory Training. Incidentally, Laboratory Training had rather poor results. Evaluation in such cases proved complex because of the difficulty of ensuring similar conditions across a number of organisations and consistency in the method of the OD practitioners involved.

Academics wished for a return to the clear evaluation standards of early studies such as that of Coch and French[27] in the late 1940s in the Harwood Manufacturing Corporation. This was a medium-sized factory producing pyjamas, which because of changes in style had to change its work methods from time to time. As the workers were paid piece-rate, their earnings were liable to suffer while they learned to cope with changed methods, and this in turn led to a degree of resistance to such innovations. In the experiment carried out in this plant, four groups of sewing machine operators were formed, matching each other in background and experience. One group formed the 'control' group and were changed to new jobs by normal factory procedures, which involved an explanation of why the changes were necessary, what the new job would be like, and what the new piece rates would be. A second group formed the first of the experimental groups. This group was given more information about changes than the control group, and was permitted to choose representatives to participate in the design of the new jobs, setting piece rates, and training procedures. The two remaining groups formed the second and third experimental groups. All members of these two groups participated directly in designing the job and setting piece rates. The results for the control group and experimental groups two and three are shown in Figure 10.1.

After the change, the control group dropped to an output of about 50 units per hour, a normal reaction in the circumstances. A number of

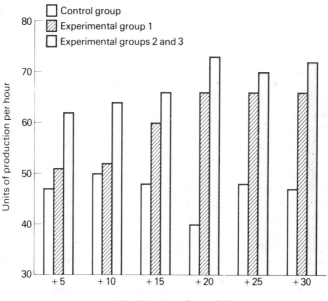

Fig. 10.1 Output in a garment manufacturing company under three systems of management (from data collected by Marrow, Coch and French)

workers in this group left the firm. Experimental group one dropped to about the same level, but soon began to improve, and ultimately reached an output of about 65 units per hour. Groups two and three, however, where all members participated in the new procedures, dropped hardly at all after the change, and thereafter showed a steady improvement which took them eventually to an output of 70 units per hour. Additionally, the labour turnover was low. Clear conclusions can be drawn from such evaluation, but in longer and more complex OD efforts evaluation is correspondingly more difficult.

The need for better concepts

Part of the difficulty of evaluating OD was its grounding in individual values. Tichy wrote: 'for example, Kurt Lewin's quest for scientific principles supporting democracy can be related to his escape from the totalitarian fascist Hitler regime'[28].' Early OD practitioners would assert that improving human relations at work is an end in itself, regardless of the increase in organisational effectiveness it might bring. In writing of OD as a religious movement, Harvey was pointing out a real dilemma. Managers had often indicated that they would be happy to accept the benefits of organisational flexibility and improved employee attitudes arising from OD provided they did not have to embrace the OD 'faith': the OD perspective on autonomy versus control and social responsibility versus profitability. In the 1970s this dilemma was partly solved by OD practitioners adopting a more managerial perspective on organisation structure, decision-making and goals. But a major event in expanding the concepts of OD and business came through the development of social values generally. In the UK a spate of employment legislation on equal opportunities, the right to redundancy compensation, and health and safety at work came into force. In other European countries the formalisation of worker participation went further. In the US the QWL (Quality of Working Life) movement began, and it was taken up energetically by major corporations such as General Motors.

The QWL movement had common origins with OD in the human relations movement. In the US it may also have derived impetus from social movements that were anti-war, pro-ecology and pro-civil rights. It adopted the aims of OD and the parallel development of job design and the work democracy movement in Europe, and these principles emerged:

1 Adequate and fair compensation
2 Safe and healthy work conditions
3 Immediate opportunity to use and develop human capacities
4 Future opportunity for continued growth and security

5 Social integration in the work organisation
6 Constitutionalism in the work organisation (equity, free speech etc.)
7 Work related to total life space (includes mental health concepts)
8 Social relevance of work life[29].

In addition, QWL has become synonymous with techniques of job enrichment, worker autonomy, job redesign and integrative industrial relations.

What seemed to be occurring at last was a direct treatment of the issues of power and conflict in organisations (see Chapter Nine), and the role of the organisation within the general social setting. This was the final tier in the conceptual structure of OD, which now consisted not of one unifying theory but a set of 'nested' theories encompassing individual, group, organisational and social change.

Organisation development: the 1980s

The 1960s' definition of OD could now be modified. OD is still seen as 'planned change' in the sense that OD activities should be preceded by analysis and should fit into an overall organisational strategy in which the desired form, style and performance to which the organisation is being moved should be clearly set out. Major corporations now define and redefine what their 'mission' is – their central reason for existence – and move from that to define strategy. Within the overall strategy, flexibility of methods, objectives and tasks is necessary. Studies of OD consultants in action have reported somewhat disapprovingly that they do not operate in a clearly planned sequence, but adapt to organisational variables, and that projects do not have clear starts and finishes[30]. Weisbord wrote in 1974 that there was 'a vast gap between OD as researched and written down, and OD as actually practised', and pointed out that 'OD – like the world – is nonlinear[31]'. Writing in 1984, Lovelady[32] repeats the point, and suggests a chain model of the change process.

The 1980s have brought better models of the change process itself. The chain model proposed by Lovelady includes an important link labelled 'approval in the power system', and Tichy's model of organisational change has three strands: technical (financial and business criteria), political (internal allocation of resources, decision-making power, and the conflict and bargaining they involve), and cultural (values, beliefs, attitudes, motivations). Any one strand may predominate in a particular organisation. Better analyses of change have enabled a shift of emphasis to be made in OD to the management of the change process itself, to the management of organisations in transition, and to the role of management in this process.

The 1960s definition of OD included 'organisation-wide'. This was reinforced by the use of the systems models. In practice, however, OD activities rarely involved all personnel in an organisation. Provided that the OD activity is part of an organisation-wide strategy of change, it may consist of 'local' interventions at different times, using different techniques, to meet different contingencies. The QWL movement has provided a workable organisation-wide OD framework for the 1980s.

The 1960s definition describes OD as 'managed from the top'. This still holds true, in that management commitment is vital to any planned change. The 1980s OD methods may involve employees from any level, whereas earlier OD efforts concentrated exclusively on senior and middle management. The impetus for OD has also become more diffuse, as it passes into the general armoury of good day-to-day management.

OD continues to 'use behavioural science' as in the 1960s definition but, as already outlined, has extended its concepts to deal with the tough issues of power, politics and conflict that are part of organisational life. Some writers have been somewhat disparaging of the way in which OD consultants have tended to get things done by developing relationships with 'gatekeepers' in organisations, and by tapping into the power systems. Yet many case-studies, such as Klein's account of work in Esso, demonstrate the need for the consultant to be clear about what power-bases and coalitions exist and the naivety of believing that an OD agent can operate independently, or be perceived to be operating independently. In fact, part of the OD activity is to make the processes of power and decision-making explicit to the participants.

OD continues to use behavioural science in the sense that evaluation of results is important, and that theoretical models continue to be tested. Consequently the academic perspective on OD continues to be critical, with obvious tensions between pure and applied research. Some authors re-analyse the material from earlier OD projects, suggesting that reported success was premature or over-optimistic. Blackler and Brown[34] wrote critically in 1981 of the OD effort in Shell a decade earlier, suggesting that there was some coercion or manipulation of participants, that there was covert resistance, that what were hailed as successes were short-lived, that the consultants wrongly claimed to be non-directive and that the employees were ultimately dissatisfied with their rewards. In spite of such complaints the Shell project was a major positive effort at clarifying organisational objectives, and the sociotechnical approach it adopted has formed a central theme in the corporation's OD efforts since.

The debate on whether there should be a single unifying theory underpinning OD continued, and looks likely to continue indefinitely, but at least a major integration of previously disparate theories has been achieved. In 1981 McLean wrote that 'now OD has shed the burden of being fashionable a major impediment to the development and credibility of the subject has been removed[35].'

Ethical issues in OD have still not been treated as fully as they deserve, and some authors bewail the departure from early OD values. Harrison[36] contends that 'OD is best regarded as a moral programme for organisational renewal' and writes of the need to 'reassert the radical potential of OD', suggesting that it has become a profiteer's tool for implementing change without dissent. OD is thus accused by some not of 'using behavioural science' but of 'abusing behavioural science'.

The 1960s definition of OD assumed that the behavioural science aspect would be applied by an external specialist, or catalyst, or change-agent. Although the use of an external consultant can be very valuable for assisting with major organisational reviews, the trend in the 1980s has been to embed OD more firmly in management and communication systems. Every manager has an OD obligation and some, particularly in personnel management and corporate planning, are given specific OD responsibilities. The image of the exotic consultant who could effect miracle cures by revolutionary methods in a brief intervention has disappeared.

OD methods in the 1980s

Organisational diagnosis

A multitude of OD methods have been developed and only a representative selection can be mentioned here. They fall into categories: those aimed at organisational diagnosis; those aimed at teams and those aimed at individuals. A common mistake is to assume that only the challenging experimental methods such as T-groups and Transactional Analysis qualify as OD methods. In fact the apparently routine activities of work meetings, employee appraisal, and company newsletters can form part of an OD strategy.

Organisational diagnosis of some kind should be the first step in an OD strategy. It may be done at a time of crisis, but is increasingly becoming a routine. Typically it uses attitude survey methods of assessing the organisation's culture and climate. There is debate about whether the term 'climate' is necessary, since it seems to be synonymous with 'levels of job satisfaction', but even though it is not a precise concept it is a useful everyday term. Organisation culture may be analysed in terms of:

structure
individual responsibility
rewards

risks and risk taking
warmth and support
tolerance and conflict.[37]

These factors can be assessed subjectively by a consultant on the basis of interviews and discussions, and analysis of organisation charts and management methods. Equally important is the investigation of how organisation members perceive and respond to those organisational features assumed to influence motivation and behaviour. The Litwin and Stringer Organisational Climate Questionnaire[38] measures six organisational factors:

1 General attitude towards other people in the organisation
2 General attitude towards management and/or the organisation
3 Policy and promotion clarity
4 Job pressure and standards
5 Openness of upward communication
6 Risk in decision-making.

The Cornell Job Descriptive Index (JDI) is an example of a questionnaire which has been used to measure job satisfaction in a wide range of jobs and job-levels. It focusses on five aspects of the work situation: the work itself, supervision, co-workers, pay and promotion. It is short and simple, asking the respondent to answer 'yes' or 'no' to a series of adjectives describing the various job aspects. This is an easier task for the lower-level worker than trying to describe internal feelings[39]. Measurement of attitudes on specific aspects in a particular organisation will require the development of tailor-made attitude surveys, which is a rather specialised task requiring some expertise[40]. In Chapter Three the use of repertory grid analysis to discover individual values was described. It can also be used to discover the 'implicit management theory' of individual executives, what values they hold about the organisation, leadership style and so on. When carried out across a range of executives, it gives a good insight into the organisation's management culture. OD could be described as 'creating culture'.

Chapter Four included a description of the job characteristics model of work motivation. This work generated a set of questionnaires which measure the characteristics of the job and its motivating potential, the current levels of motivation, satisfaction and work performance of employees on the job, and the level of growth need of present employees. This last element provides a crucial indicator of the readiness for change of present employees, which should be taken into account before any job redesign takes place[41]. This makes the Job Diagnostic Survey a very useful instrument indeed. Organisational analysis by the various means suggested will indicate to the OD strategist whether or not the organisation is likely to take part in innovation. Key indicators will be the style of leadership, and the extent to which the organisation values diversity and creativity[42].

Group techniques

The outcome of organisation analysis may be used in OD methods aimed at groups within the organisation. Attitude survey material may be fed back to key groups of managers, or released downwards to all employees through a 'cascade' of meetings at different levels. Research on the effectiveness of survey feedback suggests that it should be participative, that the communicators should be effective, that the issues should be related to the interests of those involved, and that face-to-face is better than written feedback (although badly handled verbal feedback may produce worse results than no feedback at all)[43].

As discussed in Chapter Six, groups exert important influences over their members. Group cohesion and normative influence can be an important factor in productivity and efficiency, but can work for or against. Janis[44] has written of 'groupthink', a symptom to be found particularly where there is conflict or competition between groups. Group pressures towards conformity and consensus result in:

1 Seeing and magnifying the weaknesses of the opposition and blocking any perception of their strengths
2 Seeing and magnifying the strengths of one's own group and blocking any perception of one's weaknesses
3 Suppressing dissent within the group, creating a spurious sense of unanimity
4 Reducing communication with the outgroup, which facilitates the stereotyping arising from 1
5 Developing a sense of invulnerability.

Conflict between groups or departments in organisations arises partly from the group loyalty that naturally develops, and partly from organisation structure and aims. Feedback of attitude survey data can be a useful OD strategy for promoting inter-group collaboration. Beckhard[45] suggests confrontation meetings where urgency dictates immediate intervention. Conflict issues are openly confronted in a constructive rather than destructive way. The groups or departments can be asked to complete questionnaires on how they see the other group, how they think the other group sees them, how they think the other group see themselves, how they think the other group thinks they see themselves. In passing each party's perceptions to the other groups, major misjudgements, for example that the other party's view of one is not as negative as one had assumed, can be instantly revealed.

In a constructive way each group can be asked to suggest what behaviours of the other parties make the group's work more difficult, what behaviours they would like the opposition to do less of and what helpful behaviours they would like them to increase. This should lead to discussion of methods and systems of achieving improvements, and commitment to change.

The general term 'industrial relations' includes a range of conflict types, some of which are amenable to group-level interventions of an OD nature. Distributive bargaining, for example on pay, is inherently conflictful, but unnecessary conflict often arises over issues, such as technological innovation, in which an integrative ('win/win') bargaining mode is possible. An OD perspective on industrial relations has been suggested by authors such as Molander[46], and put into practice by Blake and Mouton[47] in the USA and Warr *et al.*[48] in the UK steel industry. Just as role-play and simulation can develop individual skills, they can be used by teams to develop integrative bargaining through simulating forthcoming negotiations.

A group technique aimed at shop floor level, which has expanded rapidly in the UK in the 1980s after American successes, is the Quality Circle (QC). The first QCs were formally recorded in Japan in 1962[49], and a rapid expansion followed. The original aims were to improve quality standards by improving the leadership ability of supervisors, encouraging self-development, increasing workers' morale, creating an environment in which everyone was conscious of quality and the need for its improvement, and by acting as a nucleus for company-wide control at the workshop level. Like many other major techniques, QCs had their origin in behavioural science theory, showed good results when first applied, and were then widely applied without proper evaluation. Revans' writings and experiments with small group development in the UK are credited as an important theoretical source for the Japanese development of QCs. Later usage has tended to neglect behavioural outcomes in favour of the financial advantages that readily result. Consequently there have been QC failures both at introduction and following initial success. In the USA the first queries about the aims and results of QCs by writers such as Rafaeli[50] seemed fussy in the face of the huge popularity which QCs enjoyed. In the UK, Dale and Ball recorded the difficulties and failures experienced with QCs as well as the successes, so that now a more balanced perspective on the QC method exists[51].

Quality Circles consist of from four or five to about eighteen volunteers at most. The members come from the same work area of the organisation and meet regularly in company time, perhaps weekly or fortnightly for an hour or two. Leader and members are trained in participative problem-solving, and focus on the work problems and opportunities for improvement in their own area. The leader of the circle is often the supervisor. The leader in turn is helped and supported by a facilitator who links with a central steering committee and may devote his or her time completely to the QC programme. Major savings have been effected by QC activity, although companies typically put improved morale high on their list of intended benefits. The problems which arise are:

1 obstruction from different levels of management who see QCs undermining their authority
2 obstruction from unions who see QCs usurping their role as communicators and negotiators
3 disenchantment from members who do not directly gain the financial benefit arising from their suggestions
4 disenchantment from members who feel obstructed by management from discussing 'the real issues' e.g. pay and promotion.

A great deal rests upon the abilities of the QC facilitators, who have the role of internal OD consultant to play, and upon the wholehearted support of all levels of management[52]. The mainspring of QC effectiveness is in the powerful commitment to change which is engendered in the individuals who take part in the group discussion and decision, as discussed in Chapter Six.

Individual techniques

Chapter Five mentions various methods of developing the individual's attitudes and interpersonal skills. The leadership and team-building efforts mentioned in Chapter Six are assisted by diagnostic questionnaires for the individual, such as Mumma's *Team-Work and Team-Roles Inventory*[53] and the *Myers-Briggs Type Indicator*[54]. OD techniques of process observation and process consultation enable individuals to obtain feedback from a consultant on the effectiveness of their contribution to teamwork. By these and other means the individual can begin to rethink his or her behaviour and attitudes. A major trend in the 1980s in which OD and training converge is that of self-managed learning, continuous learning and open learning. The new emphasis is on learning how to learn.

The traditional approach in education and training has been to teach the principles or concepts first, then encourage practice for skill development. A new model – practice first and concepts later – arose from work by Kolb and others. Kolb[55] suggested a sequence of experience, reflection, conceptualisation and experiment, which fits with practical methods such as 'versatility training' and 'mentoring'. The former was developed experimentally by the Industrial Training Research Unit at Cambridge in response to the burden of continually retraining factory workers in the manufacture of new products. By mobilising the trainee's ability for 'discovery' learning and developing skills of self-monitoring, a flexible and well-motivated workforce can be created[56]. 'Mentoring' uses social learning theory, the subtle process whereby we learn from others' behaviour, but with review and analysis aided by an experienced mentor who might be a manager or consultant, or both[57]. The skills of getting feedback and guidance from others, as an individual seeking self-development, are explored by Stuart[58] in terms of being able to get support and encouragement from others, being able to express one's thoughts and feelings and share ideas, seeking objective criticism from others, learning from others' experiences, and so on. Developing as a manager involves not just being able to do the right thing instinctively or imitatively, but being able to communicate and discuss it, and having a model or theory in one's head which enables one to fit particular events into a broader context. Otherwise one can be said only to have developed for a specific job in a specific setting[59].

Integrated systems

A number of packages of organisation development incorporate methods of individual, group and organisation-wide change. The Grid approach of Blake and Mouton[60] aimed at developing 'corporate excellence' is perhaps the best known. Its full implementation consists of six phases:

Phase 1   The Grid Seminar helps individual managers to analyse their own style of leadership on the dimensions of concern for production and concern for people, in relation to the ideal style
Phase 2   The Teamwork Development phase consists of work teams analysing their performance and planning improvements
Phase 3   In Intergroup Development, managers of groups collaborate in analysing levels of co-operation between their groups
Phase 4   Management formulate their objectives for the ideal organisation including financial, product and structure aspects
Phase 5   Management plan the implementation of their strategy for the ideal organisation
Phase 6   Management review progress through Grid development, and stabilise the change processes.

Job design or redesign may be an organisation-wide process affecting individuals and work groups in various ways, and may result from adopting QWL principles. It may involve the integration of job enrichment, flexible work schedules, and participative communication and decision-making. Computerisation has mechanised communication in organisations, enabling easy dissemination of information to employees, or the opposite, rigid centralisation of data resulting in more monitoring and direction of individuals. Wainwright[61] discusses the scope of sociotechnical systems design in office automation, and writers such as Mumford and Hedberg have analysed the options in design of computerised data systems for inclusion or exclusion of employees and their representatives. Indeed, the trend towards distance workers, employees who work at home by electronic links with the company premises, heralds a revolutionary new concept of the organisation[62].

Culture and organisational change

Reference has been made on a number of occasions to the relevance of culture to organisation development. There has been a recent upsurge of interest in the relationship between culture and organisational success or 'excellence'. Top management is now being urged to treat culture as being a consideration every bit as important as structure or strategy.

Culture is a concept rooted in sociology and social anthropology, where it is a key term in explaining the existence and nature of social order. This approach to culture is typified by Stephen Cotgrove as 'the shared norms and values of a social system (which) are a most important aspect of a society. Shared norms, values and beliefs are referred to as the culture of a society'[63]. Sociologists have traditionally concerned themselves with society and social institutions but behavioural scientists have recently applied this concept to work organisations in the context of corporate strategy and organisational change.

But before looking at the culture of organisations in more detail, it is important to note another use of the concept of culture which is relevant to the human problems of organisations, particularly multinational organisations. This is concerned with an examination of the significance of national culture in modifying the behaviour of employees and the effectiveness of management techniques and practices. Practices which are effective in the United States may not be as effective in Europe, and Japanese management methods may have to be modified when applied in Asia. Furthermore employees who are sent overseas by their companies as expatriates may suffer initially from so called 'culture shock'. Organisations which are aware of this problem are careful in their selection of staff to serve overseas, and arrange for appropriate training and briefing prior to departure. One of the most useful and perceptive studies in this area is provided by Gert Hofstede. He carried out research within a large high-technology multinational operating in forty countries in which he concentrated on the attitudes of staff to leadership style and hierarchy within the company. He found significant differences between the various cultures in these respects in spite of common products and company philosophy. Managers in 'Latin' Europe for example, differed markedly from managers in 'Germanic' Europe, with the former preferring a more hierarchical structure of authority and a more authoritarian style of management[64].

Recently greater interest however has been shown in organisational rather than social culture. Precise definition and measurement is of course difficult, and definitions have tended to take a pragmatic turn. Thus Andrew Pettigrew sees culture as '. . . the source of a family of concepts – symbol, language, ideology, belief, ritual and myth[65], and again '. . . as a system of publicly accepted meanings'. Ed Schein describes the essence of culture as '. . . that set of basic assumptions which has worked well enough to be considered valid, and therefore to be taught to new members as a requirement for membership[66]. Ouichi and Johnson try to capture it in the phrase 'How things are done around here'[67]. Peters and Waterman prefer to place their emphasis on 'shared values', while Charles Handy reminds us that each culture makes different assumptions about the following aspects of work[69].

the relationship of the individual to the organisation
the motivation of individuals
the job of leader
the priorities at work
the sources of influence

Organisational culture then is to do with the manner in which behaviour at work is influenced and constrained by prevailing customs and norms, which are in turn the outcome of the relationship between the expectations and value systems of employees and those of their leaders.

The importance of values, and in particular, the extent to which those values are shared, are stressed by Peters and Waterman in consequence of their study of 'excellent' American organisations. This leads them to advocate the model illustrated below, adapted from one used by McKinsey consultants in the United States[68]. They are consequently led to say to professional managers, 'all that stuff you have been dismissing for so long as intractable, irrational, intuitive, informal organisation can be managed'.

Many senior managers probably have an intuitive feeling for the importance of culture in promoting or hindering success. But promoting cultural change in a desired direction can present formidable difficulties, as was indicated earlier in this chapter. Attitudes to work are influenced by powerful and deep rooted social forces, outlined previously in Chapters Two and Three. Michael Cross reminds us that: 'there are a number of points which many companies fail to appreciate when introducing change'[70]. He pinpoints the following faults:

1   a willingness to base actions upon perceptions of reality, and not on

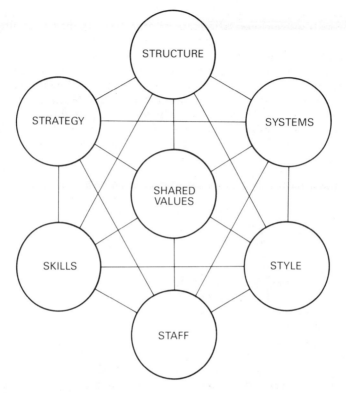

Fig. 10.2 McKinsey 7–S framework C

    what actually happens
2 an underestimation of the significance of changes in the eyes of those affected
3 a failure to provide sufficient resources
4 an expectation that the society at the workplace can change in months rather than years
5 a tendency to manage changes as a series of events rather than in an integrated and parallel fashion, and
6 an underestimation of the talents of employees in circumscribed jobs

    Turning from the 'don'ts' to the 'dos', Terence Deal and Allan Kennedy recommend the following procedures, based on experience in the United States[71]:

1 position a 'hero' in charge of the process (i.e. an outstanding manager)

2   recognise a real threat from outside (the greater the perceived threat to the organisation, the greater the chance that the change programmes will succeed)
3   make transition rituals the pivotal elements of change ('mourn' the passing of the old ways while encouraging new values and relationships)
4   provide training in new values and behaviour patterns
5   bring in outside 'shamans' (i.e. outsiders who can bring their own 'magic' and help to defuse conflict)
6   build tangible symbols of the new directions (which act like road signs)
7   insist on the importance of security in times of transition (security dispels resistance to change)

Deal and Kennedy warn that this costs a lot of money. For example, they estimate that for AT&T to have adapted its culture to deregulation would have cost at the time between one and half and three billion dollars. But the alternative cost of not changing might well be total failure.

An example of successful cultural change in a British company is provided by the London Life insurance company. As described by its chief executive, this involved in the first instance the production of a corporate plan that included a clear mission statement, followed by the development of better budgets, sales plans, and company structure[72]. The chief executive set a personal lead in improving communications by practising 'management by walking about'. A major training and development plan for managers was launched with the label 'Corporate Training and Development'. The management team collectively analysed the current corporate culture and identified what changes needed to be made, overcoming an initial reluctance to discuss unfamiliar concepts such as culture, values, and beliefs. Success was attained and the interaction of the development plan and the new shared values led to a desire for fulfilment challenge and excellence. However, the verdict was that the process of change is slow and requires patience and persistence.

References

1   Toffler, A., Future Shock, Pan, 1971.
2   Stewart, R., *The Reality of Management,* Heinemann, 1963.
3   Clark, P. A., *Action Research and Organisational Change,* Harper Row, 1972.
4   See Chapter Six.
5   Lewin, K., *Field Theory and Social Science,* Harper Row, 1951.
6   Jaques, E., *The Changing Culture of a Factory,* Tavistock, 1951; Brown, W., *Exploration in Management,* Heinemann Educational Books, 1960.
7   Trist, E., (1981) 'The evolution of sociotechnical systems', Ontario

Quality of Working Life Centre, Paper No. 2, 1981; Miller, E., 'Sociotechnical systems in weaving 1953–70: a follow-up study', *Human Relations,* **28**, 1975, pp. 348–86.

8   Beckhard, R., *Organisation Development: strategies and models,* Addison Wesley, 1969.

9   French, W. L. and Bell, C. H., *Organisation Development: behavioural science interventions for organisation improvement,* Englewood Cliffs' Prentice Hall, 1973.

10   Klein, L., *A Social Scientist in Industry,* Gower Press, 1976.

11   Hill, C. P., *Towards a New Philosophy of Management,* Gower Press, 1971.

12   Harvey, J. B., Organisation development as a religious movement', *Training and Development Journal,* **28**, no. 3, 1974, pp. 24–27.

13   Mirvis, P. M. and Berg, D. N. (eds.), *Failures in Organisation Development and Change,* John Wiley and Sons, 1977.

14   Friedlander, F. and Brown, L. D., 'Organisation Development', *Annual Review of Psychology,* **25**, 1974, pp. 313–41.

15   Emergy, F. E. and Trist, E. L., 'The Causal Texture of Organisational Environments', *Human Relations,* **18**, no. 1, 1965, 21–31.

16   Greiner, L. E., 'Patterns of organisational change', *Harvard Business Review,* **45**, 1967, pp. 119–30.

17   Sadler, P. B. and Barry, B., 'Action research in a small firm', *Journal of Management Studies,* October, 1968, pp. 316–37; *Organisation Development: case studies in the printing industry,* Longman, 1970.

18   Hedberg, B., Nystrom, P. C. and Starbuck, W. H., 'Camping on seesaws: prescriptions for a self-designing organisation', *Administrative Science Quarterly,* **21**, 1976, pp. 41–65.

19   Tichy, N. M. and Hornstein, H. A., 'Stand when your number is called: an empirical attempt to classify types of social change agents', *Human Relations,* **29**, no. 10, 1976, pp. 945–67.

20   Burke, W. W., *Current Issues and Strategies in Organisation Development,* Human Sciences Press, 1977.

21   Walton, R. E. and Warwick, D. P., 'The ethics of organisation development', *Journal of Applied Behavioural Science,* **9**, no. 6, 1973, pp. 681–98.

22   Training of Trainers Committee, 'Report No. 2', Manpower Services Commission, 1980.

23   Rowbottom, R., *Social Analysis,* Heinemann, 1977.

24   Harrison, R., 'Choosing the depth of organisational intervention', *Journal of Applied Behavioural Science,* **6**, no. 2, 1970, pp. 181–202.

25   Porras, J. I. and Berg, P. O., (1978), 'Evaluation methodology in OD: an analysis and a critique', *Journal of Applied Behavioural Science,* **14**, no. 2, 1978; Phillips, J., *Handbook of Training Evaluation and Measurement Methods,* Gulf, 1983.

26   Bowers, D., 'OD techniques and their results in 23 organisations: the Michigan ICL study', *Journal of Applied Behavioural Science,* **9**, 1973, pp. 21–43.

27   Coch, L. and French, J. R. P., 'Overcoming resistance to change', *Human Relations,* **1**, 1948, pp. 512–32.

28   Tqchy, N. M., *Managing Strategic Change: technical, political and cultural dynamics,* John Wiley & Sons, 1983.

29 Walton, R. E., 'Quality of working life: what is it?', *Sloan Management Review,* **15**, no. 1, 1973, pp. 11–21.

30 Lovelady, L., 'Evaluation of planned organisational change', *Personnel Review,* **9**, no. 4, 1980, pp. 5–14.

31 Weisbord, M. R., 'The Gap between OD Practice and Theory', *Journal of Applied Behavioural Science,* **10**, no. 4, 1974.

32 Lovelady, L., 'The process of organisation development: a reformulated model of the change process', *Personnel Review,* **13**, no. 2, 1984, pp. 2–12.

34 Blackler, F. H. M. and Brown, C. A., 'A new philosophy of management: Shell revisited', *Personnel Review,* **10**, no. 1, 1981, pp. 15–21.

35 McLean, A., 'Organisation development: a case of the emperor's new clothes?', *Personnel Review,* **10**, no. 1, 1981, pp. 3–14.

36 Harrison, R., 'Reasserting the radical potential of OD', *Personnel Review,* **13**, no. 2, 1984, pp. 12–18.

37 Campbell, J. P. *et al., Managerial Behaviour, Performance and Effectiveness,* McGraw Hill, 1970.

38 Litwin, G. H. and Stringer, R. Jnr., *Motivation and Organisational Climate,* Harvard University Press, 1968.

39 Smith, P. C., Kendall, L. M. and Hulin, C. L., *Measurement of Satisfaction in Work and Retirement,* Rand McNally, 1969.

40 Oppenheim, A. N., *Questionnaire Design and Attitude Measurement,* Heinemann, 1966.

41 Hackman, J. R. and Oldham, G. R., 'Development of the Job Diagnostic Survey', *Journal of Applied Psychology,* **60**, no. 2, 1975, pp. 159–70.

42 Siegel, S. and Kaemmerer, W., 'Measuring the perceived support for innovation in organisations', *Journal of Applied Psychology,* **63**, no. 5, 1978, pp. 553–62.

43 Klein, S. M. *et al.,* 'Employee reactions to attitude survey feedback', *Administrative Science Quarterly,* **16**, 1971, pp. 497–513.

44 Janis, I. L., *Victims of Groupthink,* Houghton Mifflin, 1972; Janis, I. L. and Mann, L., *Decision-making: a psychological analysis of conflict, choice and commitment,* The Free Press, 1977.

45 Beckhard, R., 'The confrontation meeting', *Harvard Business Review,* **45**, 1967, pp. 149–55.

46 Molander, C., (1973) 'Organisation development and industrial relations', *Personnel Review,* **2**, no. 1, 1973.

47 Blake, R. R., Shepard, H. A. and Mouton, J. S., *Managing Intergroup Conflict in Industry,* Gulf, 1964; Blake, R. R. and Mouton, J. S., *The Managerial Grid III,* Gulf, 1984.

48 Warr, P., Fineman, S., Nicholson, N. and Payne, R., *Developing Employee Relations,* Saxon, 1978.

49 Sugimoto, R., reported in Dale and Barlow (see n. 52).

50 Rafaeli, A., 'Quality circles and employee attitudes', *Personnel Psychology,* **38**, no. 3, 1985.

51 Dale, B. G. and Ball, T. S., 'A study of quality circles in UK manufacturing organisations', Occasional Paper 8306, UMIST, 1983.

52 Dale, B. G. and Barlow, E., 'Facilitator viewpoints on specific aspects of quality circles programmes', *Personnel Review,* **13**, no. 4, 1984.

53 Mumma, F., *Team-work and Team-roles Inventory,* Organisation Design and Development Inc., 1984.

54 Myers, D. B. and Briggs, K. C., *Myers-Briggs Type Indicator,* Educational Testing Service, 1962.

55 Kolb, D., *Experimental Learning,* Prentice Hall, 1984; Pedler, M., *Action Learning in Practice,* Gower Press, 1984.

56 Industrial Training Research Unit, *Versatility at Work,* 1974.

57 Mumford, A., 'What's new in management development?', *Personnel Management,* May, 1985, pp. 30–32.

58 Stuart, R., 'Using others to learn', *Personnel Review,* **13**, no. 4, 1984, pp. 13–19.

59 Davies, J., 'An evaluation framework for management education', *Industrial Training International,* **11**, no. 10, 1976.

60 Blake, R. and Mouton, J., *The Managerial Grid,* Gulf (1964).
   Blake, R., *The New Managerial Grid,* Gulf (1978).

61 Wainwright, J., 'Office Automation – its design, implementation and impact', *Personnel Review,* **13**, no. 1, pp. 2–10, 1984.

62 Hedberg, B., 'Computer systems to support industrial democracy' in *Human Choice and Computers* (eds) Mumford, G. and Sackman, H., North Holland, 1975.
   Hedberg, B. and Mehlman, M., 'Computer power to the people', *Nordata* **81**, Arbetslivcentrum, Stockholm.

63 Cotgrove, S., *The Science of Society,* George Allen and Unwin, 4th edn, 1978, pp. 21–23.

64 Hofstede, G., 'Hierarchical power distance in forty countries' in *Organisations Alike and Unalike,* Edited by Lammers, C. J. and Hickson, D. J. (eds.), Routledge and Kegan Paul, 1979.

65 Pettigrew, A., 'On Studying Organisational Cultures', *Administrative Science Quarterly,* **24**, 1979.

66 Schein, E., 'Corporate Culture' in *P.A. Journal for Management,* P.A. Consultants, London **1**, no. 1, 1984.

67 Ouichi, W. G. and Johnson, J. B., 'Types of organisational control and their relationship to emotional well-being', *Administrative Science Quarterly,* **23**, pp. 292–317, 1978.

68 Peters, T. J. and Waterman, R. H., *In Search of Excellence,* Harper and Row, 1982.

69 Handly, C. B., 'So you want to change your organisation? Then first identify its culture', *Management Education and Development,* **7**, 1976.

70 Cross, M., letter in *The Financial Times,* October 31st, 1984.

71 Deal, R. E. and Kennedy, A. A., *Corporate Cultures,* Addison Wesley, 1982.

72 Thompson-McCausland, B. and Biddle, D., 'Change, Business Performance and Values', Gresham College, London, 1985.

11

The small firm – a neglected area of management

The overwhelming mass of literature in the field of management is directed towards the larger firm. This is perhaps not surprising since the bulk of managers and employees work for large firms. However, small firms do exist in our economy and perform a vital and indispensable role and, as such warrant more attention in a book of this kind than they normally receive. Some of the material presented in earlier chapters, for example on leadership, power, groups and interpersonal communications, does have relevance to the problems of the smaller firm but it has, almost without exception, been developed essentially with the larger firm in mind. This being so, it is worthwhile re-examining these issues with the small firm specifically in focus.

The reasons for the previous neglect of the small firm are not difficult to pinpoint. The post-war boom and the spate of take-overs and mergers which took place during the 1950s and 1960s led to the small firm being regarded as a hangover from the industrial revolution doomed to rapid extinction in an economy dominated by large-scale public and private enterprise. It was widely considered that the age of specialisation and mass production, with its associated economies of scale, spelled certain death for the smaller business. Another reason for the neglect of the small firm stems from the difficulties of access to such firms experienced by both researchers and advisers. Because the small businessman often tends to talk a different language from academics and consultant advisers, and sometimes feels that his business methods may attract criticism and even ridicule if exposed to critical examination, he has tended to maintain a distance from them. In addition, pressure of work has usually kept small firm managers from participation in formal management training courses and so, once again, the two worlds have remained apart.

The importance of the small firm to the economy

For many, one of the most surprising changes in the 1970s and 1980s has been the revival of the small enterprise. In 1971, the *Bolton*

Report[1] on the small firm estimated that there were about 1.25 million small enterprises in the UK, between them employing around 6 million people, or about a quarter of the labour force. But the report also emphasised that the decline in the importance of such enterprises was well-established in Britain and in most other developed countries: 'we have found it very difficult to identify any factors working strongly in favour of the small firm[2].'

In fact, it now seems that the reversal of this decline had already begun before the report was published. For example, in manufacturing, there were 71,400 small enterprises in 1971 (an increase of over 5,000 since the mid-1960s) but by 1980 this figure had risen to 87,400, and it has continued to rise since[3]. Data for other sectors of the economy is rather harder to come by but many would argue that, apart from areas such as retailing, where the decline has continued, there has been an expansion in small enterprises, particularly in the service sector, a sector which is assuming greater economic importance as primary and manufacturing industry declines.

In addition, there have been notable increases in other forms of small enterprise such as franchises and producer co-operatives. Most people are familiar with franchised outlets in the fast food sector but this business form now extends into areas ranging from driving schools to cosmetics and from car tuning to instant printing. Essentially, the franchise relationship involves a 'host' company (the franchisor) promoting a large number of small satellite enterprises (franchises owned by franchisees). The latter operate legally independent businesses under the franchisor's trade name and produce and/or market goods or services in a manner clearly specified by the franchisor.

The British Franchise Association, to which most of the major franchisors in Britain belong, claimed that its members had over 4,000 outlets in operation by the end of 1982 and that expansion was occurring at around 10 per cent a year[4]. Others have argued that similar forms of business such as retail petrol outlets franchised to independent owners by oil companies, franchised car dealerships, wholesale-retail franchises in food retailing and tenanted public houses should also be included in any assessment of this form of small business[5]. They have also suggested why further expansion of this form can be expected in the future[6].

Producer co-operatives were relatively rare in Britain in the early 1970s, though they have been around for a long time[7]. These are enterprises owned and controlled by those who work in them, and most are small. In 1971 it was estimated that there were only 35 producer co-operatives in Britain[8], but since then the number has increased to well over 500 and may be even as high as 900[9]. Depite popular belief to the contrary, their survival rate appears to be at least as good as that of similar conventional small businesses[10]. Most are in retailing, crafts or small-scale manufacturing.

The above concentrates on *legitimate* small enterprises, but in the 1970s there was also a substantial expansion in *illegitimate* small enterprises, or the 'black economy'. The major factor inducing this expansion was undoubtedly the introduction of VAT in 1973, which taxed a whole range of hitherto untaxed services and activities and promoted wholesale evasion. Of course, no-one can be sure just how far the 'black economy' extends. One estimate[11] suggested that it might be worth 15 per cent of the national income, but a more recent estimate by the Inland Revenue[12] was that it was equal to 6–8 per cent of the gross domestic product or about £16 billion per year.

Interestingly, the revival of the small enterprise has not been confined to Britain. Surveys of small enterprises in other advanced industrial societies show that this upturn is widespread internationally and, moreover, that Britain is something of an 'odd man out' since it has the smallest small firm sector of any of the advanced industrial societies[13]. One view frequently reiterated in the past was that where an economy had a high proportion of small firms it was likely to be 'backward' but, in fact, international comparisons offer virtually no support for this notion. Japan, for example, probably economically the most successful industrial society in the last twenty years, has one of the largest small firm sectors of any industrial society[14].

What is a small firm?

All the above presupposes an agreed definition of the small firm which, in fact, does not exist. The Bolton Committee[15] saw the small firm as a socio-economic unit with the following characteristics.

1   Economically, a small firm is one that has a relatively small share of its market.
2   Managerially, the small firm is administered by its owners or part-owners in a personalised way, rather than through the medium of a formalised management structure.
3   Finally, it is independent in the sense that it does not form part of a larger enterprise and owner-managers are free from outside control in taking their principal decisions.

This definition can be criticised on several grouds. Some small firms, for instance, have quite large shares of their often specialised markets. However, a practical drawback here is the lack of available data on ownership, management structures and market shares of firms, which rules out the application of this definition. Instead, for the manufacturing industry, for example, the Committee was forced to adopt the less satisfactory statistical definition of '200 employees or less'.

No one simple definition of size fits all instances. Even a definition of size, in terms of numbers employed, leaves us with problems. For instance, a car firm employing a thousand personnel would be considered 'small' in the context of its industry. On the other hand, in the printing industry (the national newspaper sector apart) a firm employing 200 personnel would be considered by many to be medium-sized or even large. However, in any examination of the social character and social dynamics of the small firm, a definition of size in terms of numbers employed is, overall, usually the most appropriate. The Bolton Committee's definition of '200 employees or less' may be erring on the large side given that subsequent research suggests that many of the small firm's special characteristics are likely to have disappeared or become markedly modified by the time work force size approaches 200. However, it is broadly acceptable as a starting point for discussion.

Outside the manufacturing industry, the Bolton Committee used alternative definitions of a small firm. Sometimes these were still expressed in terms of numbers employed (e.g. 25 employees or less for the construction industry) but in other instances alternative bases were used (e.g. sales turnover for the retail and wholesale trades, and number of vehicles for the road transport industry).

Since the Bolton Committee deliberated, this definitional problem has remained. Most researchers and policy-makers continue to adopt arbitrary numerical definitions or have updated the Bolton Committee's definitions based on turnover to allow for inflation. However, provided that definitions are clear and not widely inconsistent with each other, discussion and analysis of enterprise can continue on a sensible basis. The more important problem is the lack of accurate and comprehensive data at the official level on the small firm population in Britain which means that most of the figures in the previous section are subject to a range of error and should be treated with caution.

The owner-manager and the self-employed

Those who set up, purchase or inherit a small enterprise have taken on one of the most distinctive of all occupational roles in industrial society. Given that, by definition, the enterprise in question is small, their psychological make-up and world view is likely to have an enormous impact on its aims and goals and especially on social relations within the enterprise as well as with outsiders such as customers.

Owner-managers own and operate a small enterprise that employs others, even if on only a part-time basis. The self-employed, on the other hand, are rather more difficult to define. Many professionals, for example, solicitors, accountants and architects, are self-employed but, for our purposes, the self-employed are those without a professional or equivalent qualification who operate an enterprise employing no others[16]. Plumbers, window clearners, car mechanics and contract workers in the contruction industry, often work on the basis of a 'one-person business'.

Interestingly, and contrary to the expectations of many, the numbers of small business owners and self-employed people has recently been rising sharply. The Manpower Services Commission[17] reported that in 1984 there were amost 2.5 million, of whom 551,000 were women, indicating an increase of nearly a third since 1979. This could not be accounted for simply by the 8 per cent fall in the number of employees in employment in this period[18]. Nearly 40 per cent of the 2.5 million are owner-managers as defined above and around 400,000 are professionals rather than self-employed according to our definition[19]. Overall, something under 10 per cent of the labour force are owner-managers or self-employed in terms of the labels used here. A further point to emphasise strongly is that the small enterprise is represented in almost every area of the economy, so the experiences of those who run such enterprises vary enormously. In turn, this means that it is easy to over-generalise about the psychological make-up and world views of owner-managers and self-employed. The owner of a corner shop may have little in common with the owner-director of a quality printing firm and such differences may be widened still further if they are of different genders or ethnic backgrounds[20].

Moreover, researchers have given very unequal attention to owner-managers and the self-employed. The latter, in fact, have hardly been researched at all and while a lot is known about owner-managers in manufacturing and retailing, owner-managers in other areas of the economy remain neglected. Most of what is written below refers to owner-managers in manufacturing and it should not be assumed that in terms of managerial style, organisational framework and employer-employee relations, the available findings apply equally to all small enterprises.

Nevertheless, it is still possible to offer at least a broad indication of the key psychological attributes which have now been reported in a large number of studies. Indeed, researchers for the Bolton Committee offered a psychological picture of the owner-manager which subsequent researchers have only refined. They described small firm owner-managers as different in temperament and character from their counterparts in larger enterprises. They described the underlying motivation in terms of a need to 'attain and preserve independence':

This need for 'independence' sums up a wide range of highly personal gratifications provided by working for oneself and not for anybody else. It embraced many important satisfactions which running a small business provides – the personal supervision and control of staff, direct contact with customers, the opportunity to develop one's own ideas, a strong feeling of personal challenge and an almost egotistical sense of personal achievement and pride –psychological satisfactions which appeared to be much more powerful motivators than money or the possibility of large financial gains[21]

Further, Golby and Johns claimed that this desire for independence acted as a strong influence in determining the guiding strategies and policies of small firm managements.

The powerful underlying need to maintain and preserve independence and the strong feelings of personal satisfaction derived from one's own achievement go a long way to explaining the attitudes to outside help and assistance. Government assistance was seen as leading to Government intervention; using more sophisticated financial assistance than that provided by the local bank manager would lead to a loss of independence because the assistance would want some measure of control over the firm. Having rejected 'the boss', respondents didn't want to suffer the paternalism of Government or anyone else for that matter.

Because the sense of satisfaction derived from personal achievement was so important, many of these respondents appeared almost to turn a deaf ear to any outside source of advice or help. They neither knew nor wished to know about it[22].

It should not be surprising, therefore, that the managerial style of many owner-managers is highly centralised, with a lack of well-defined authority for those holding employee roles. There is often little forward planning and little precise distinction of managerial functions. Thus, since the owner-manager retains responsibility for most major functions – production, personnel, marketing, financial control – these tend to blur into each other or some tend to get neglected, except where a crisis in relation to that function arises. On the whole, production tends to get due or more than due attention while the other functions are more likely to be under-emphasised[23].

Organisationally, the small enterprise is unlikely to resemble the hierarchically well-defined pyramid of the text book large enterprise. Some observers have instead likened the small firm to a spider's web with the owner-manager at the centre controlling virtually every aspect of the organisation. In turn, the small business organisation lacks the predictability and orderliness of the large-scale bureaucratic enterprise for all those involved. While this informal environment may offer a stimulating, exciting and interesting experience for all those involved, it can also sometimes mean uncertainty and frustration, especially for those not in the confidence of the owner-manager.

It is worth stressing again here the dangers of over-generalisation inherent in discussing anything as variable as the small enterprise. Goffee and Scase[24], for example, in a study of small businesses in the building industry, reported that one managerial style they encountered frequently was what might be termed 'fraternalism'. A craftsman owner-manager worked alongside his employee craftsmen rather as a first among equals. He was highly dependent on their skills and commitment and tended to reserve overtly managerial activities for times when he was away from his employees or for evenings and weekends.

The same authors, in a rare study of women small business owners in Britain (*not* in the building industry), have noted how gender characteristics are incorporated into female owners' managerial styles and organisational structures[25]. Equally, ethnicity has links with owner-manager and organisational forms[26]. However, it is fair to say that both sets of authors also emphasise the wide range of similarities between women and ethnic owner-managers and their white male counterparts.

Employment in the small enterprise

In the previous section several points implied that employment and employer-employees relations in the small enterprise might also have distinct features ensuring that they do not simply replicate in miniature those found in the large enterprise. On the whole, this aspect of the small enterprise has been very much neglected in the past and much popular discussion of the role of the small firm in helping to stimulate the economy continues to imply that the owner-manager is the only person involved in the enterprise.

Small firm employee-employer relations do offer a markedly different profile to those associated with the large firm, even in the same industry or community. The bases of these differences have their origins in the operation of the labour market itself. In the 1970s, economists and others[27] developed theories of the labour market that suggested that large enterprises had particular preferences for certain types of employee – well-qualified, experienced, married rather than single, with stable work histories and, where appropriate, membership of a trade union or professional association. For these kinds of employees, the firms were prepared not only to pay well but also to offer a wide range of fringe benefits and opportunities for career advancement within the enterprise. The small enterprise, on the other hand, was more likely to recruit younger, less well-qualified and less experienced employees, often with unstable work histories. This was partly because smaller firms could not match the reward packages of the large firm. Most were unable to offer such good fringe benefits because they could not afford to and, because of their small size, were unable to offer many internal career opportunities. Also, small firm recruiting practices resulted from distinctive employer preferences. Large firms used bureaucratic recruiting procedures emphasising credentials and hard evidence of previous achievement, while the small enterprise owner was more willing to back his or her personal judgement of a job applicant and to attach less importance to paper qualifications. The small firm owner, in other words, wanted someone who 'fitted in', since a wrong choice of employee would potentially be much more disruptive than for a large firm. Trade union members, for instance, were often rejected because of the owner-manager's dislike of unions and fear of their impact should the firm become unionised.

However, 'dual' or 'segmented' labour market theories of the above kind have come under stringent criticism of late[28]. The simple division of small and large firms into separate 'primary' and 'secondary' labour markets has been questioned on the grounds that there is no clear correspondence between size of economic unit and the labour market in which it operates. In a recession or period of massive economic reconstruction, for instance, large firms may be unwilling or unable to offer high stable rewards, security and internal career mobility to their employees. Successful high technology small firms, on the other hand, growing rapidly and needing the cream of scarce specialised skills, may well adopt what were previously seen as 'primary' labour market strategies. Nevertheless, marked labour market differences between small and large firms are likely to remain, even if their exact empirical configurations need more careful tracing.

Employees also have preferences. One early piece of research[29] suggested that employees might well 'self-select' themselves into enterprises of differing size depending on the long-term work orientations they developed as their work experience increased. Some workers would develop an *economistic-instrumental orientation*, which combines a desire for high economic rewards with a relative indifference to intrinsic rewards such as job satisfaction and a friendly workplace.

Workers with this orientation would prefer large firm employment since, on the whole, they offer better material rewards than the small firm. Other workers developed a *non-economistic-expressive orientation*, which combines a relatively low desire for economic rewards with a strong desire for a varied and interesting job, friendly workmates and close relations with the boss. Workers with the latter orientation would be more likely to opt for a small firm since it would be much more likely to offer a congenial environment for this orientation.

Despite the plausibility of this thesis, later researchers have been critical. Firstly, little evidence has been found that small firm employees develop a single overall orientation that influences their job seeking[30]. Instead, as for most workers, finding a job is argued to be rather less a matter of choice or rational decision-making than the result of the host of influences discussed above which constitute the labour market and over which the employee has little control[31]. This counter-argument is further strengthened when it is remembered that since the original thesis was published, unemployment has risen to a high level, drastically reducing the importance of individual choice in occupational placement.

It has also been suggested that certain kinds of employee, for example those who are highly qualified (such as professional workers), will also be reluctant to work in smaller firms. Small firms owner-managers are often unable to offer the salaries or career opportunities that such employees may command elsewhere in the labour market. Highly qualified workers may also feel that experience gained with a household name in industry or commerce will carry more weight later when they present themselves to other employers, than if they have worked only for small, less well-known, firms.

Unfortunately, there is relatively little evidence to indicate the strength of the above suggestions. However, that which is available does seem to support them broadly. One study[32] reports that almost half of the small- and medium-sized enterprises in the research sample employed no professionally qualified staff at all. Some respondents also indicated that they were reluctant to encourage managerial staff to develop their skills for fear they would leave and start on their own, thus becoming competitors.

Others have argued that owner-managers hiring professionals or highly qualified personnel for the first time are often reluctant to delegate full authority and responsibility to newcomers. Having previously been responsible for tasks themselves, they find it difficult to abandon them to others. Equally, new entrants often feel they must demonstrate their expertise by reorganising the area of the organisation for which they have assumed responsibility: the owner-manager may well take this as implicit criticism of his or her previous efforts, leading to friction with the new employee[33].

Industrial relations

Two stereotypes have dominated views of industrial relations in the small enterprise[34]. First is the small firm as a sweatshop in which a grasping, exploitative employer pays low wages for long hours, replacing any worker who, for any reason, objects to the wages and conditions offered or cannot meet the production targets demanded. This stereotype has been associated particularly with certain industries, such as clothes manufacturing. The second stereotype is the happy, harmonious small firm, virtually free of industrial conflict.

Everyone in the firm relates in a friendly way to everyone else, the owner-manager knows every employee personally and takes a close personal interest in their welfare, in and outside the firm. Of late, this second stereotype has received much the greater emphasis in the media and in politicians' speeches. The *Bolton Report* also adopted this view[35].

Advocates of the second stereotype often point to the lack of strikes, or other overt forms of industrial conflict, and to low levels of unionisation in small firms as evidence of the small firm's superiority over the large in employer-employee relations. This evidence appears incontrovertible. An establishment with over 1,000 full-time employees, for example, has been shown by one recent study to be almost six times as likely to have experienced industrial action as one employing between 25 and 49, and almost forty times more likely than an establishment with under 10 employees[36]. Trade union membership has also been shown to be correlated closely with size, with small enterprises much less likely to be unionised[37].

However, some observers have argued that data on small firm dispute levels and union membership are not such solid evidence for the thesis that employer-employee relations in the small firm are conflict-free. Statistical correlation should not be confused with causality, and investigation of the reasons for these differences might well suggest alternative interpretations. In fact, there is now a substantial body of research and theory pointing towards a rather different picture of small firm industrial relations than is suggested by either of the above stereotypes.

First of all, the use of statistics relating to strikes or other overt forms of industrial conflict as a measure of overall levels of conflict in the enterprise suffers from several drawbacks. Strikes or other collective expressions of worker protest represent only some of the forms such conflict may take and, indeed, may be relatively infrequent overall, compared to *individual* expressions of worker disagreement with management. For example, labour turnover is probably a much more common expression of conflict, particularly in industries or firms with low levels of unionisation[38].

When an employee is seriously at odds with his or her employer, staying on may be very difficult. The employee may leave or the employer may decide that somebody else would be better in the job. In a unionised firm, the employee may turn to a shop steward or other union official to negotiate on his or her behalf or to provide support in a dispute with management, but where there is no union this option is not open; neither is a one-person stike likely to be very effective. A study of turnover rates in small and large firms in the same industries provides evidence that turnover is substantially higher in small firms[39].

Small firms are environments in which people are likely to interact closely on a face-to-face basis, creating opportunities for friendly relations and strong personal links. Equally, the same conditions also offer greater opportunities for interpersonal conflict: in a large enterprise those who don't hit it off can more easily avoid each other because departments or sections are bigger. Alternatively, they may get transferred to another part of the firm so that contact is minimised. In a small enterprise these solutions are less readily available and, again, leaving the firm may be the only real alternative for one or other of those involved.

What is also often forgotten is that the small enterprise is part of the wider environment of a market-dominated, free enterprise society. Owner-managers must respond to the pressures of the market in order to survive. Indeed, the small enterprise is much more subject to these pressures than the typical large firm, which can more easily insulate itself from, or even control, these external forces. Profit and loss considerations, the preservation of the owner-manager's investment and the minimisation of costs (of which labour costs are a major element) must ultimately override any personal social relations if the firm is to survive successfully.

Research evidence shows that employees are aware of these economic realities. For instance, in several studies workers have been asked whether they see the firm as a football team with everybody working together for the common good or whether they see workers and management as being on different sides. Samples of small firm employees, contrary to the expectations of some, have been reported as being no more likely to opt for a team work view when compared with workers doing similar jobs in large firms[40].

This raises the further question of why, if the above is true, do small firm employees not join trade unions to the same extent as workers in large firms? One answer to this question is that unions themselves may be more reluctant to recruit small firm employees. The cost per capita of recruiting in small firms is substantially higher than in large firms. At best, each firm yields a handful of subscriptions and the cost of maintaining any membership gain may be high if, as argued above, labour turnover is higher in small firms.

Moreover, small firms employers are, by and large, unwilling to concede recognition to unions and will often go to considerable lengths to prevent a union successfully organising their employees[41]. Changes in trade union legislation in the 1980s have reinforced employer resistance by making it more difficult to insist on recognition. So, faced with the likelihood of stiff opposition from owner-managers, trade unions have a further reason for not embarking on a small firm recruitment campaign.

Small firm employees themselves do no appear to be anti-trade union despite their lower propensity to be union members. Research indicates that, like most British workers, small firm employees are not especially 'ideological' about trade unions, one way or the other. For instance, one study[42] found that, although the majority of non-trade union members did not think it would be a good idea if their present firm became unionised, many would join if this occurred. In fact, only a minority – just over 15 per cent – disapproved of unions as such.

Those who were union members were more favourable to unions, and the implication of the findings might be that if more small firm employees had the opportunity to become union members they would do so. The main reasons for lower levels of membership in small enterprises were the difficulties involved in becoming a member and the lack of awareness of the benefits of membership. The latter may well tend to operate as a self-fulfilling prophecy: a lack of direct experience of the benefits of union membership makes it less likely that small firm employees will join unions, which in turn makes it less likely that this direct experience will ever be gained.

Rather than the two stereotypes of small firm industrial relations – the small enterprise as a sweatshop or as happy, harmonious and conflict-free – the reality is shown to be more complex and unlikely to approximate to either. Of course, there are sweatshops among small firms but the limitations of the managerial strategies they embody are obvious. Employee goodwill – commitment, ingenuity and energy – are valuable assets to any enterprise and are much less likely to prevail in a sweatshop. Sweatshop firms and industries tend to acquire a seedy, unsavoury reputation in the wider community, unlikely to lead to high status and recognition of those who own them. Equally, some small enterprises do generate exceptionally good relations between those involved but, as noted earlier, the wider environment is likely to put a severe strain on maintaining such highly positive relations.

The small firm and growth

In the literature on small firms, a great deal of attention is given to analysing growth. Small enterprises are seen as the seed corn of the economy, providing the important firms of tomorrow, medium and large, who will replace present firms unable to survive. Texts sometimes offer lists of the largest and most successful enterprises of forty or fifty years ago to point out how many have disappeared, to be replaced by new firms which were either small or not even in existence when the original firms dominated the economy.

Currently, with massive economic restructuring and an exceptionally high rate of technological innovation, even more importance is placed on the role new small firms can play. Yet the processes that bring about this economic rejuvenation are not well understood and there is a good deal of controversy about just what contribution the small firm will make. More fundamentally, how and why small firms grow is not fully understood.

A survey of the literature[43] reveals a number of contributions to understanding small firm growth with certain similarities between the various approaches. Without commenting on each in detail, and at the risk of some oversimplification, it can be argued that they reveal two basic themes. The dominant theme is that of a 'stage' model where the firm is seen as passing through a sequence of stages of growth. The number of stages varies from writer to writer but typically there are three or four. Stage models, regardless of the number of stages offered, have certain similarities. The initial stage, as might be expected, stresses the individual entrepreneur(s) with an idea for a product or service setting up an economic unit to produce the item in question. The next stage (or sometimes the next but one), is usually concerned with the division of managerial tasks. As the entrepreneur or founding partners of the firm can no longer exercise total managerial control over the enterprise, non-owner managers are recruited, usually because they possess skills not possessed by the founder(s).

The remaining stages tend to concentrate on organisational maturity and stability. The small firm becomes more bureaucratic and rationalised in its organisation and takes on the character of a large company. It evolves a board of directors who are essentially managers rather than entrepreneurs and exploits a wide range of management, production and marketing techniques. There is also an acceptance that it must develop systematic working relations with other organisations in society such as outside pressure groups, government departments, trade unions and the media.

The other theme present in theorising on growth in the small firm is the so-called 's-curve hypothesis'[44], which can, in effect, be seen as a special case of the stage theory. This suggests that the small firm will have a short formative period followed by a period of rapid growth, perhaps reaching an exponential rate before tailing off. The thinking behind this is that after the entrepreneur(s) have developed an idea for a product or service, there is an initial establishing period for the firm which ends with the clear demonstration of market advantage. This leads to a high rate of profit re-investment to exploit further the advantage, plus an injection of outside capital attracted by the firm's performance in the establishing period. This investment fuels the high rate of growth in the next period of the firm's history.

Exceptional growth, however, tails off as competition is offered by other firms who become aware of the market opportunities. This is reinforced by a lowering of investment levels in the firm, due to profit-taking by the owner-managers, and a decline in the firm's attraction as an investment due to increased competition as well as other possible changes such as market saturation. In order to survive and stabilise as an economic entity, the firm, now relatively large, begins to behave in ways typical of other firms in its sector of the economy. Investment is restricted to conventional levels and tied to a product mix which appears to offer an approximation to the average rate of return in the relevant area of the economy.

The three broad phases delineated in this theory – formation followed by a high rate of growth and then a stabilising phase – explain how the 's-curve hypothesis' gets its name. It will also be apparent from the aspects most discussed that this model is one primarily developed by economists rather than organisation theorists. Nevertheless, it would not be difficult to fit this model into most of the stage models discussed above.

All these various approaches to growth contain a considerable element of truth, but this is often superficial. For instance, for stage models to define a first stage in terms of an individual or small group deciding that they can, by setting up for themselves in business, exploit a market for a product or service, is to say very little beyond defining the coming into existence of a new independent economic entity.

Another curious aspect of both the stage and 's-curve' models of growth is an implied ignorance of the size distribution of firms in our economy discussed earlier. Census of Production data reveal that this size distribution is highly skewed, with over 95 per cent of manufacturing firms employing less than 200 people and the typical firm, in a statistical sense, employing less than 30. The remaining 5 per cent or so of firms employ about two-thirds of the labour force in the manufacturing industry. To put it more simply, there is a great number of very small firms and a mere handful of large ones. This characterisation of the manufacturing sector (which is broadly repeated in many other areas of the economy), has two important consequences for most stage models of growth in the small firm.

First, most firms will *not* grow to any considerable size in terms of the number of people employed (which we may assume is broadly correlated with several other dimensions of growth) and that, in practice, growth of any significant proportion is a rather *exceptional* process. This point is reinforced by data which shows that there is a high failure rate among small firms, especially in the years immediately following formation[45]. In other words, existing theories of small firm growth fail to discuss, let alone account for, the rarity of the process they purport to explain.

Second, an inspection of the implied characteristics of the organisational and managerial structure of the firm, contained within the later stages in most of the models, indicates that the authors are discussing a firm which has long since entered the 6 per cent of large firms in our economy. In short, most of these theories are weakened by attempting to explain too much. Instead of concentrating on growth in the *small* firm, a good deal of the theoretical effort is devoted to the growth processes of firms which are, by reference to the actual size distribution of firms, among the largest in the economy.

The major problem with these approaches to small firm growth, however, is their neglect of motivational influences. The central figure in the small enterprise is the owner-manager, and the question to be asked is whether owner-managers *want* growth. A number of researchers have expressed doubts on this. Golby and Johns, for example, whose research for the Bolton Committee was quoted earlier, reported that their sample of small business owners was:

> roughly divided on this question [the amount of growth thought desirable]. Rather more argued that expansion was desirable than backed the maintenance of the status quo. But it was noticeable that they often tended to express their views in a somewhat generalised way, as if they were playing lip service to an absolute abstract ideal of growth[46].

Why should this reluctance to grow be so common, particularly in a society which is so growth-minded and where economic success is so often equated with developing a small firm into a large one? There are several possible reasons, which can be derived from an examination of those who found, buy or inherit a small enterprise. For instance, the main 'feeder' groups for supplying new small business owners are, firstly, the children of those who operate or have at some time operated a small business themselves, and then the skilled manual and supervisory groups and the lower middle class. People who set up on their own are often not particularly well educated[47]: indeed, some writers have suggested that small business ownership may be an occupational alternative for able people who, for all kinds of reasons, do not succeed in the conventional educational system[48].

For people from the above backgrounds, a rapidly growing business may well be perceived as a danger – an emerging situation over which they are losing control. As a firm grows bigger it requires increasingly sophisticated management using special skills, which often only a team of trained managers can provide. In other words, the demands of the growing enterprise can quickly outstrip the managerial expertise of the founder owner-managers, perhaps leading to a loss of control of the business. Of course, some owner-managers can adapt to match the expanding needs of the enterprise but, for many others, coping with long hours, the demand for quick decision-making and all the other needs of a rapidly growing business, there is often little time left for personal growth and development.

Equally, as was stressed at the beginning of the chapter, one major motivation for entry into small business ownership is a strong need for autonomy and independence. Again, such needs may be threatened by any sizeable growth of the enterprise. The very means by which these motivational needs are served – the economic enterprise created by the owner-manager – threatens to destroy their satisfaction as it grows. The need to build a management team, to delegate, to create complex administrative systems and formal channels of communication, to cope with external investors and so on, all restrict independence and autonomy[49].

These considerations may not apply with anything like the same force to the person who *inherits* a small enterprise. The latter may have received a business or professional education so that they are motivationally prepared and mentally equipped to shift the business into a high growth mode. Their needs for autonomy and independence may not be as developed as those of their parents, particularly where parental motivation towards business ownership arose out of deprivations in early life. On the other hand, some who inherit membership of the small business owning stratum also inherit a suspicion of growth and its risks: there will, as usual, be substantial variation in owner-manager responses rather than one simple identifiable one.

Many small firms are not really in a position to grow very large in any case since they occupy niches in the economy where few firms can grow. For instance, the building and construction industry, retailing, and hotel and catering industries are basically small firm industries, despite the handful of giant enterprises to be found in each. Even if a high proportion of small enterprise owner-managers in these industries were very growth-minded, the opportunities for growth would be restricted by the basic characteristics of the industries themselves. Again, this is not to say that no determined, ambitious and able small business owner could not possibly succeed in building an empire – the dangers of over-generalisation always have to be resisted – but to recognise that in many of these industries where entry is relatively cheap for the newcomer, changing from a minnow to a whale may be very difficult.

The growth process of the small firm is, therefore, likely to be a good deal less common than might be first supposed. Nor does the process have to be very common if the present size distribution of enterprises in most industrial societies is to continue. Most new enterprises will either fail or grow to only a very modest size, employing only a handful of people even when they survive for a long period. A few, on the other hand, do grow to become medium-sized and even fewer become the new giant enterprises of tomorrow.

The future of the small firm in industrial society

The 1980s have emerged as the decade of small enterprise: politicians and the media extol the merits of self-employment and the small firm as a vehicle for self-fulfilment, economic rejuvenation, employment generation and as a conflict-free work environment. Governments back their words with a range of financial and other forms of official encouragement, educationalists and academics put together training courses and the mass media offers example after example of those who have succeeded. All this represents a sharp reversal of views compared to those of only twenty years ago and of the pessimism of much of the *Bolton Report* of 1971, which saw a steady decline in the importance of the small firm in Britain and other industrial societies. There is, however, a danger that the importance of the small enterprise is now being oversold. Small enterprise is important – indeed, no industrial society could function effectively economically without its small business sector – but it co-exists with other forms of enterprise whose importance is also not diminishing.

All industrial societies are composed of three sub-economies – the large enterprise sector, the public or state sector and the small firm sector. The large enterprise sub-economy is not shrinking; if anything, the reverse is occurring. Economic concentration has proceeded further in Britain than in most other industrial societies (which is another way of saying that Britain has the smallest small firm sector of any of these societies) and shows little indication of halting[50]. In fact, there are indications that a 'merger fever' of the kind seen in Britain in the 1960s may emerge again in the late 1980s. Many of these large enterprises are transnationals who operate in a world rather than a national economy.

The state or public sector is a major supplier of goods and especially services as well as a major employer. Health and welfare, education, defence and the maintenance of law and order consume huge amounts of resources which are converted in a wide range of provisions reaching virtually every member of society at some time. Despite recent government attempts to 'roll back the frontiers of the state' and privatise many public services, in practice the reversal has not been very great. About a third of the national labour force work for government or other public sector organisations and, while some have been switched to the private sector by privatisation, other areas of public sector employment have increased.

The small enterprise economy relates to the large firm and public sector sub-economies in a variety of ways. Some small firms have little to do with either, but most have rather closer links. For instance, in retailing it has been argued that the major overall pattern emerging in Britain is one where large retailers are dominating in the high streets and especially through out-of-town hypermarkets, while small retail outlets provide customers with the means to top up on items they have forgotten or run out of before their next visit to a big retail outlet.

Small outlets also cater for those unable to get to the big outlets and those who want specialist goods or services that the bigger outlets are not interested in providing[51].

Other links between small and large firms have developed in industries such as textiles, where retail outlets, especially large high street stores, have built up strong links with a host of small suppliers, particularly of fashion clothes. The large stores depend on the small suppliers to respond rapidly to changes in fashion – something they would find difficult if they attempted to mass produce in wholly-owned large factories – and, in turn, the small suppliers depend on the large stores for a steady stream of orders[52]. Some industrial societies such as Japan show this form of link as a central feature of their economy for a wide range of production[53].

Even more complex interrelations have been reported in some of the new high-technology industries. Here a complex industry-product cycle may develop in which initial innovation occurs in large firm Research and Development departments but small firms often pioneer its application in the market. In this they may be encouraged by large enterprises, which may themselves later enter the resulting new markets while the small firms come to occupy small niches or move on again. These links between small and large firms may well vary in different industrial societies, but the main point is that they offer distinct and different roles to the small and the large in the various stages of the product-industry life cycle[54].

The restructuring of the economies of advanced industrial societies now taking place will almost certainly mean more opportunities for the small firm even if opportunities in some other sectors disappear. But any upsurge in small enterprise will only occur in the mixed economy described above. Small firms, as opportunities for self-fulfilment for those who go into business for themselves, as contributors to job generation and to innovation, will play a role in economic change rather than constitute the main means by which it occurs.

Conclusions

The behavioural science view of the small enterprise presented in this chapter provides some important lessons for management practice in relation to the small firm. It illustrates how careful work by researchers and theorists from the main behavioural science disciplines – economics, social psychology, psychology and sociology – can unveil the motivational, organisational and wider economic setting of the small business. Such a research-based picture replaces the previous stereotypes, half-truths, guesses and exaggerations of many of the superficial accounts of the small enterprise offered in the mass media and elsewhere.

The implications for management practice are also clear. As small business and self-employment have re-assumed importance, there has been a rush to fill the vacuum in small enterprise education and training. Today there is hardly a university, polytechnic or college without some form of small business training for those who want to start up on their own or who already run a small enterprise. Many conventional undergraduate and postgraduate business degrees and diplomas also now offer a small business option or include reference to the small business sector.

Yet much of this educational and training effort is constructed on the assumption – usually not made explicit – that small firms are simply scaled down versions of large firms or that small firms should be pushed into becoming micro-copies of the large firm. The techniques and skills offered are frequently adapted versions of those originally devised for the large enterprise. What this chapter shows is that these assumptions are highly questionable. What is needed is not a 'top-down' approach to management practice in the small firm but a 'bottom-up' approach based on the experience of real managers in real small firms. Their problems, their abilities, their goals and their situations are different from those of their large firm counterparts and require an approach to management practice tailored to their needs.

References

1 *Small Firms*, Report of the Committee of Inquiry on Small Firms, Cmnd 4811, HMSO, November 1971, usually known as 'The Bolton Report' after the chairman of the committee, John Bolton.
2 *Ibid.*, p. 75.
3 Interim Report of the Committee to Review the Functioning of Financial Institutions, Cmnd 7503, HMSO, 1979 and Reports of the Censuses of Production for various years, all HMSO.
4 Churchill, D., 'Franchising: Rewards and Independence', *The Financial Times,* October 28th, 1982.

5 Curran, J. and Stanworth, J., 'Small business research in Britain' in Levicki, C. (ed.), *Small Business, Theory and Policy,* Croom Helm, 1984, especially pp. 131–32.
6 Curran, J. and Stanworth, J., 'Franchising in the modern economy – towards a theoretical understanding', *International Small Business Journal,* **2**, no. 1, 1983, pp. 8–26.
7 Thornley, J., *Workers' Co-operatives: Jobs and Dreams,* Heinemann, 1981.
8 Chaplin, P., 'Co-operatives in contemporary Britain' in Stanworth, J. *et al.* (eds.), *Perspectives on a Decade of Small Business Research,* Gower, 1982.
9 Mason, C. M. and Harrison, R. T., 'The geography of small firms in the UK: towards a research agenda', *Progress in Human Geography,* **9**, no. 1,

1985, pp. 3–37.

10 Cornforth, C., 'Some factors affecting the success or failure of worker co-operatives: a review of empirical research in the UK', *Economic and Industrial Democracy,* **4**, no. 2, 1983, pp. 163–90.

11 Feige, E. L. and McGee, R. T., 'Tax revenue losses and the unobserved economy in the UK', *Journal of Economic Affairs,* **2**, no. 3, 1982. There is also sometimes a certain vagueness as to what is meant by the phrase 'the black economy'. For our purposes it is the production of goods and services for cash where these activities are deliberately hidden from official notice in order to avoid the payment of tax or other dues to the state.

12 BBC Radio 4, *In Business,* broadcast October 30th, 1985.

13 Bannock, G., *The Economics of Small Firms,* Blackwell, 1981, especially Chapter Four, and Storey, D. (ed.), *The Small Firm, an International Survey,* Croom Helm, 1983.

14 Anthony, D., 'Japan' in Storey, *ibid.*

15 'The Bolton Report', *op. cit.,* pp. 1–2.

16 This is not, of course, to dismiss professionals as an unimportant occupational category – they are given due attention in several places elsewhere in this book – but merely to recognise that they may have little in common with the corner shop owner, garage owner, plumber or window cleaner and are, hence, more properly treated as a separate, distinct category.

17 Manpower Services Commission, 'Special Feature Self-Employment', *Labour Market Quarterly Report GB,* February, 1985, p. 5.

18 Ibid.

19 *Ibid.* Again, however, while the increase in the number of self-employed seems established, the numbers themselves should be treated with some caution.

20 Ethnic small business owners, particularly those from the Asian community, have received a great deal of attention from the media of late, but academic observers have argued that self-employment is very much a minority occupation even among Asian sub-groups. Among Afro-Carribbeans the likelihood of going into business for themselves is markedly lower than in the population as a whole. See Jones, R. and McEvoy, D., 'Ethnic enterprise: the popular image' in Curran, J. *et al.* (eds.), *The Survival of the Small Firm,* Gower, 1986, Vol. 1; Brooks, A., 'Black business in Lambeth: obstacles to expansion', *New Community,* **11**, 1983–84, pp. 42–54; Wilson, P. and Stanworth, J., *Black Business in Brent,* Small Business Research Trust, 1985.

21 Golby, C. W. and Johns, G., 'Attitudes and motivation', *Committee of Inquiry on Small Firms, Research Report No. 7,* HMSO, 1971, p. 5.

22 *Ibid.,* p. 5. For a recent survey of the literature on psychological and sociological characteristics of owner-managers see, Chell, E., 'The entrepreneurial personality: a few ghosts laid to rest?', *International Small Business Journal,* **3**, no. 3, 1985.

23 Gill, J., *Factors Affecting the Survival and Growth of the Smaller Company,* Gower, 1985, provides some graphic accounts bearing out these generalisations. See also Scase, R. and Goffee, R., *The Real World of the Small Business Owner,* Croom Helm, 1980, especially Chapters Five to Seven.

24   Goffee, R. and Scase, R., ' "Fraternalism" and "paternalism" as employer strategies in small firms' in Day, G. (ed.), *Diversity and Decomposition in the Labour Market,* Gower, 1982; 'Proprietorial control in family firms: some functions of quasi-organic management systems', *Journal of Management Studies,* **24**, no. 1, 1984.

25   Goffee, R. and Scase, R., *Women in Charge,* Allen and Unwin, 1985.

26   Jones and McEvoy, *op. cit.*

27   See e.g. Blackburn, R. and Mann, M., *The Working Class in the Labour Market,* Macmillan, 1979; Curran, J. and Stanworth, J., 'Self-selection and the small firm worker – a critique and an alternative view', *Sociology,* **13**, no. 3, 1979, pp. 427–44; Kreckel, R., 'Unequal opportunity and labour market segmentation', *Sociology,* **14**, no. 4, 1980, pp. 525–50.

28   See, e.g., Barron, J. and Bielby, W. T., 'The organisation of work in a segmented economy', *American Sociological Review,* **49**, June, 1984, pp. 335–48; Granovetter, M., 'Small is bountiful: labour markets and establishment size', *American Sociological Review,* **49**, June, 1984, pp. 323–34.

29   Ingham, G. K., *Size of Industrial Organisation and Worker Behaviour,* Cambridge University Press, 1970.

30   Curran, J. and Stanworth, J., 'Self-selection and the small firm worker – a critique and an alternative view', *Sociology,* **13**, no. 3, 1979, 427–44.

31   For further support, see Blackburn, R. and Mann, M., *The Working Class in the Labour Market,* Macmillan, 1979, and Edwards, P. K. and Scullion, H., *The Social Organisation of Industrial Conflict,* Blackwell, 1982, Chapter Three.

32   Watkins, D. S., 'Development, training and education for the small firm: a European perspective', *European Small Business Journal,* no. 3, 1983, pp. 29–44, especially pp. 33–34.

33   For some empirical examples of these problems, see Stanworth, J. and Curran, J., *Management Motivation in the Smaller Business,* Gower, 1973, Chapter Eight.

34   See Rainnie, A. and Scott, M. G., 'Industrial relations and the small firm' in Curran, J., *et al.* (eds.), *The Survival of the Small Firm,* Gower, 1986, Vol. 2.

35   'The Bolton Report', *op. cit.,* especially pp. 20–21.

36   Daniel, W. W. and Millward, W., *Workplace Industrial Relations in Britain,* Heinemann, 1983.

37   *Ibid.* and Bain, G. S. and Price, R., 'Union growth: dimensions, determinants and destiny' in Bain, G. S. (ed.), *Industrial Relations in Britain,* Blackwell, 1983.

38   Edwards, P. K. and Scullion, H., *op. cit.,* Chapter Three.

39   Curran, J. and Stanworth, J., 'Self-selection and the small firm worker – a critique and an alternative view', *Sociology,* **13**, no. 3, 1979, pp. 427–44.

40   Curran, J. and Stanworth, J., 'Worker involvement and social relations in the small firm', *Sociological Review,* **27**, no. 2, 1979, pp. 317–42, and Batsone, E. V., *Aspects of Stratification in a Community Context: A Study of Class Attitudes and the Size Effect,* Ph.D. thesis, University of Wales, 1969.

41   Two spectacular examples of employer resistance to trade unions were the Grunwick dispute in 1976 (see Rogally, J., *Grunwick,* Penguin, 1977) and, more recently, the disputes between Mr Eddie Shah and the

National Graphical Association.

42 Curran, J. and Stanworth, J., 'Size of workplace and attitudes to industrial relations in the printing and electronics industries', *British Journal of Industrial Relations,* **19**, no. 1, 1981, pp. 14–25. See also Rainnie, A., 'Is small beautiful? Industrial relations in small clothing firms', *Sociology,* **19**, no. 2, 1985, pp. 213–24 and, for an even more revealing study of the complexity of these issues, Stephenson, G., *et al.,* 'Size of organisation, attitudes to work and job satisfaction', *Industrial Relations Journal,* **14**, no. 2, 1983, pp. 28–40.

43 Among the best known historical examples are: Schumpeter, J. A., *The Theory of Economic Development,* Harvard University Press, 1934; Penrose, E., *The Theory of the Growth of the Firm,* Blackwell, 1957; Steinmetz, L. L., 'Critical stages of small business growth', *Business Horizons,* February, 1969, pp. 29–34. A more recent version is Churchill, N. C. and Lewis, V. L., 'The five stages of small business growth', *Harvard Business Review,* **61**, no. 3, 1983, pp. 30–50.

44 Mueller, D. C., 'A life cycle theory of the firm', *Journal of Industrial Economics,* July, 1972, pp. 199–219 provides an overview of much of the earlier literature on this view of growth, and Steinmetz, *ibid.,* provides one version.

45 A study of death rates among new small firms in Britain, for example, estimates that 46 per cent of all new firms died in their first four years of existence. See Ganguly, R., 'Facts of life: analysis of the infant years of UK businesses', *British Business,* October 7th, 1983, pp. 306–309.

46 Golby and Johns, *op. cit.,* p. 17.

47 See 'The Bolton Report', *op. cit.,* pp. 8–9. A recent analysis of the owner-managers and the self-employed sub-samples in the large-scale 1980 *General Household Survey,* carried out by one of the present authors, also tends to confirm this. However, certain kinds of small business owners, such as those in high technology small firms, may be expected to be exceptions.

48 For a recent version of this argument see Curran, J., 'The survival of the petite bourgeosie: production and reproduction' in Curran, J. *et al.* (eds.), *op. cit.,* Vol. 2.

49 For a detailed version of this argument see Stanworth, J. and Curran, J., 'Growth and the small firm: an alternative view', *Journal of Management Studies,* **13**, no. 2, 1976, pp. 95–110.

50 Samuels, J. M. and Morrish, P. A., 'An analysis of concentration' in Levicki, C. (ed.), *Small Business Theory and Policy,* Croom Helm/Acton Society Trust, 1984.

51 Kirby, D., 'The small retailer' in Curran, J. *et al., op. cit.,* Vol. 1.

52 Rainnie, A., 'Combined and uneven development in the clothing industry: the effects of competition and accumulation', *Capital and Class,* no. 22, 1984, pp. 141–56.

53 Anthony, D., *op. cit.*

54 An exceptionally clear account of these processes is offered in Rothwell, R., 'The role of small firms in the emergency of new technology', *Omega,* **12**, no. 1, 1984, pp. 19–29.

Author Index

Subject Index